NATURAL THEOLOGY

NATURAL THEOLOGY

FIVE VIEWS

EDITED BY

James K. Dew Jr.
and
Ronnie P. Campbell Jr.

Baker Academic
a division of Baker Publishing Group
Grand Rapids, Michigan

© 2024 by James K. Dew Jr. and Ronnie P. Campbell Jr.

Published by Baker Academic
a division of Baker Publishing Group
Grand Rapids, Michigan
BakerAcademic.com

Printed in the United States of America

Library of Congress Cataloging-in-Publication Data
Names: Dew, James K., Jr., editor. | Campbell, Ronnie P., Jr., editor.
Title: Natural theology : five views / edited by James K. Dew Jr. and Ronnie P. Campbell Jr.
Description: Grand Rapids, Michigan : Baker Academic, a division of Baker Publishing Group,
    [2024] | Includes bibliographical references and index.
Identifiers: LCCN 2023035151 | ISBN 9781540960443 (paperback) | ISBN 9781540967251
    (casebound) | ISBN 9781493444229 (ebook) | ISBN 9781493444236 (pdf)
Subjects: LCSH: Natural theology.
Classification: LCC BL183 .N3895 2024 | DDC 210—dc23/eng/20230929
LC record available at https://lccn.loc.gov/2023035151

Baker Publishing Group publications use paper produced from sustainable forestry practices and postconsumer waste whenever possible.

24   25   26   27   28   29   30   7   6   5   4   3   2   1

From James K. Dew Jr.
To James K. Dew Sr.
A constant source of strength, encouragement, and love

From Ronnie P. Campbell Jr.
To Abbey, Caedmon, Caleb, and Zeke
Remain steadfast in the Lord

Contents

Acknowledgments

J ust as for many of our colleagues, natural theology has been a major
interest for both of us throughout our careers. The questions that fuel
the dialogue are complex, challenging, and important, and the way we
answer those questions has major implications for our theology and apologetic work. As such, the opportunity to work on this volume is in many ways
a chance of a lifetime. With this in mind, we would like to offer our gratitude
to a variety of people.

First, we would like to thank Dave Nelson (now the director at Baylor
Academic) for his interest in the project and allowing us the opportunity. We
would also like to thank our acquisitions editor Brandy Scritchfield, who took
over halfway through the project, for her kind support and encouragement
along the way. As always, the Baker Academic team has been fantastic to work
with, and we are grateful for them.

We also want to thank each of our contributors—Charles Taliaferro, Andrew Pinsent, Alister McGrath, Paul Moser, and John McDowell—for joining
the project. Before we began work on this volume, we knew that showcasing
these individuals in a debate on natural theology would be both exhilarating
and significant to behold, and they did not disappoint! In fact, their work
surpassed our expectations, and we are excited about the result.

We have been assisted along the way by our administrative teams at Liberty
University and New Orleans Baptist Theological Seminary. Special thanks to
Chris Shaffer and Jordan Faison for their work on a few proofreading and
clerical items. And special thanks to Collyn Dixon, a bright young philosopher
who took a heavier load in these matters. We couldn't put all this together
without each of you!

Finally, we would like to thank our families for their constant support and encouragement. Ronnie would like to thank his former teachers and mentors Gary Habermas, John Morrison, Dave Baggett, and Ed Martin, who not only introduced him to the topic but also played a vital role in his understanding on natural theology. He would also like to thank his wife, Debbie, who remains an immutable source of strength, encouragement, and friendship. Jamie would like to thank his trustees and administration at New Orleans Baptist Theological Seminary for their constant support and encouragement. And thanks especially to the DewKrewe (Tara, Natalie, Nathan, Samantha, and Samuel). You all give me deep joy, and I love you!

Introduction

JAMES K. DEW JR. AND RONNIE P. CAMPBELL JR.

Virtually every topic in theology is filled with debate, but this is especially true for natural theology. From the patristics to the present, believers have disagreed (and still disagree) on what it is and its place within our broader theological and apologetic work. For some, natural theology is an enterprise that provides wonderful apologetic resources for those defending the faith. But for others, natural theology is a failed experiment that is filled with theological compromise, weak philosophical arguments, and poor scientific data. Suffice it to say, anyone looking for a robust theological, philosophical, and scientific debate will find plenty of it in the topic of natural theology. A small example of such is found in the essays and responses that follow in this volume.

Several factors make the debates surrounding natural theology so rich and important. Throughout its history, natural theology has given rise to some of the most significant discussions and developments in science, theology, and philosophy. Scientifically speaking, for example, insights from the natural world have been one of the major feeders for the debates in natural theology. For instance, natural theology seems somewhat inevitable in light of the metaphysical implications of scientific discoveries in the past century. From cosmological discoveries about the universe's beginning to the complexities entailed in atomic structures, recent discoveries have provided fresh and new reasons to think that divine causation is at play in the origins of the physical universe. But on the other hand, many scientists remain agnostic about God, if not atheistic, suggesting that science either eliminates the need for God or simply does not support theistic conclusions.

The same complexities are also found in philosophy. The existence of God (as well as the divine nature) is of great importance, and philosophers throughout the ages have given great attention to the question. For some philosophers, God is the necessary first cause of all that exists, and his existence can be demonstrated in any number of rational or evidential ways. As such, the history of Western philosophy is rich with cosmological arguments, teleological arguments, moral arguments, ontological arguments, and much more. But, of course, not all philosophers are convinced that these arguments are of any value. Because of this, the debates in philosophy add a rich layer of consideration to the explorations of natural theology. Theologically speaking, the debates surrounding natural theology are also vitally important. For some, natural theology is a valuable resource for demonstrating the truth claims of Christianity, while others, like Karl Barth, reject natural theology emphatically as a compromise that inevitably leads to theological destruction.

Some of these debates will unfold in this volume. But before we get to those, a quick historical overview will be helpful as we set the stage for the dialogues that follow.

Historical Framework

Theological discussions and considerations that arise from our reflections on the natural order are as old as philosophy itself. As such, natural theology predates the Christian tradition itself. Plato and Aristotle, for example, gave significant attention to the question of God, developing several arguments for a divine being that might be categorized as cosmological or moral arguments.[1] Yet, most of the history of natural theology is located within the Christian era, and it received its most significant contributions from Christian theologians and philosophers devoted to the work of apologetics.

Countless examples could be offered to show how believers developed and deployed natural theology in the patristic and medieval eras, but several Christians are particularly noteworthy. Saint Augustine, for example, is often noted for the way he utilized natural philosophy as a means of confirming the Christian view of the world. Like others throughout history, Augustine

---

1. To be clear, neither Plato nor Aristotle argues for the theistic God of Christianity. In Plato's case, he is arguing for a soul that is prior to and the cause of all other things. Yet, their understanding of a first cause of all things and the arguments they use to make the point are indications of pre-Christian philosophers making natural theological arguments. See Plato, *Timaeus* 25–35b; *Laws* 10.896–910d. See Aristotle's treatment of physics in Aristotle, *Physics*, books 1–4; as well as *Metaphysics* 2.994a.

offered various proofs and arguments for the existence of God.[2] But what is particularly interesting about him are his reflections on the nature of creation and what they allow us to say about God.

Importantly, drawing on the insights from the New Testament, it was Augustine who articulated and championed the idea of *creatio ex nihilo*,[3] which came to be the standard of viewing creation in Christian theology. In this view, creation is ontologically dependent on the Creator and yet distinct from the Creator. Because it is created by a divine being who is rational, creation bears a rationality and orderliness that reflects a divine rationality itself. As a result, Christianity's distinct view of creation makes scientific inquiry and investigation possible and suggests something to us about the divinity that brought it forth. The implications of this for natural theology are enormous. As Alister McGrath notes, it was Augustine's view that "laid the foundation for the assertion that whatever was good, true or beautiful could be used in the service of the gospel. It was this approach which would prove dominant in the western church, providing a theological foundation for the critical appropriation by Christian writers of philosophical ideas and literary genres whose origins lay outside the church."[4]

But for Augustine, Christians were not the only ones who could see the divine implications of the natural realm. In a reflection on Plato's works, Augustine offers his praise for Plato's ability to see the theological implications of our world, noting that "none of the other philosophers have come so close to us as the Platonists have."[5] In fact, Augustine is so intrigued by how close Plato's theological inferences are to Christian theology that he openly wonders whether or not Plato could have had access to the prophet Jeremiah while journeying through Egypt. Realizing, however, that this was impossible, Augustine concludes that Plato was able to glean the theological insights from nature itself. He says, "Plato got his ideas from the works of earlier writers or, as seems more likely, in the way described in the words of the apostle: 'because that which is known of God is manifest in them. For God hath manifest it unto them. For the invisible things of him, from the creation of the world, are clearly seen, being understood by the things that are made: his eternal power also and divinity.'"[6]

---

2. See, e.g., Augustine, *Confessions* 1.1.1; 7.10.15–16; Augustine, *Lectures or Tractates on the Gospel according to St. John* (in *Augustine: Homilies on the Gospel of John*, 400); Augustine, *First Catechetical Instruction* 12.41–42.

3. See Augustine, *Confessions* 11.5.7.

4. McGrath, *Scientific Theology*, 1:15.

5. Augustine, *City of God* 2.8.5.

6. Augustine, *City of God* 2.8.12. Augustine's reference to the apostle is Paul, in Rom. 1:19–20.

In the medieval era, St. Anselm's and Thomas Aquinas's use of natural theology is significant. In Anselm's case, he offers an approach to the divine arguments that starts from faith and utilizes the arguments as ways of demonstrating the truth of theism. His arguments are for both the believer seeking confirmation and the nonbeliever who is unconvinced. Most known for his ontological argument in the *Proslogion*, Anselm argues that God's existence can be proven from the very concept itself. But what is often overlooked about Anselm is that he also makes a variety of other arguments for God in the *Monologion*. There he makes arguments for God from goodness, existence, and dignity, suggesting that each of these must arise from one supreme being that is the first cause of all that is. Anselm concludes these arguments by saying, "Therefore, there is a certain nature or substance or essence who through himself is good and great and through himself is what he is; through whom exists whatever truly is good or great or anything at all; and who is the supreme good, the supreme great thing, the supreme being or subsistent, that is, supreme among all existing things."[7]

But there is an important note to make here about Anselm. While some versions of natural theology are committed to starting from premises that are "neutral" or that do not already presuppose Christian faith, Anselm is decidedly not doing this. Rather, starting with belief in God already in hand, Anselm simply uses the arguments he makes as an attempt to better understand God. He says, "I do not try, Lord, to attain Your lofty heights, because my understanding is in no way equal to it. But I do desire to understand Your truth a little, that truth that my heart believes and loves. For I do not seek to understand so that I may believe; but I believe so that I may understand. For I believe this also, that unless I believe, I shall not understand."[8] For Anselm, the work of natural theology is an exercise in "faith seeking understanding."

Like Augustine before him, Aquinas believed that nature, created by the God of Christianity, bore particular marks and features that allow us to use it as a way of supporting our theological beliefs. He says: "Every effect in some degree represents its cause, but diversely. For some effects represent only the causality of the cause, but not its form; as smoke represents fire. . . . Other effects represent the cause as regards the similitude of its form, as fire generated represents fire generating. . . . Therefore in rational creatures, possessing intellectual act and will, there is found the representation of the Trinity by way of image, inasmuch as there is found in them the word conceived, and

---

7. Anselm, *Monologion* 4, in *Anselm of Canterbury*, 15–16.
8. Anselm, *Proslogion* 1, in *Anselm of Canterbury*, 87.

the love proceeding."[9] From this, Aquinas argues for God's existence in five distinct ways: (1) the argument from motion, (2) the argument from causation, (3) the argument from possibility and necessity, (4) the argument from gradation, and (5) the argument from purpose.[10]

Because of this, Aquinas is often argued to place reason above revelation, or to make theology dependent on philosophy and science. But this is likely a misunderstanding of his view. Like Anselm, Aquinas holds that creation points us to the Creator without any implication that theology needs science and philosophy to undergird our doctrine. Aquinas says,

> [Theology] can in a sense depend upon the philosophical sciences, not as though it stood in need of them, but only in order to make its teaching clearer. . . . Therefore it does not depend upon other sciences as upon the higher, but makes use of them as of the lesser, and as handmaidens. . . . That it thus uses them is not due to its own defect or insufficiency, but to the defect of our intelligence, which is more easily led by what is known through natural reason.[11]

There are plenty of other thinkers and developments from the medieval era that are worth our consideration, but space does not allow for it here. Before moving forward, we must say a quick word about how natural theology shifted, evolved, and eventually declined in modernity and the Enlightenment.

In the early seventeenth century, René Descartes initiated a major shift in Western philosophy with his quest to establish new epistemic foundations for our knowledge. In the process of his work, however, he also makes an argument for God's existence that is often thought of as an ontological argument but might also be described as an argument from perfection.[12] The late seventeenth-century philosopher and scientist Robert Boyle also made considerable use of natural theology. Believing that the work of science was a religious act, he suggested that the natural order offered opportunities to gain insights and understanding about the Creator.[13] And in the following century, Joseph Butler used the moral features of our world to argue in favor of Christian theism. In the *Analogy of Religion*, for example, he offers an early version of the watchmaker argument that would later be popularized by Voltaire and William Paley and defends divine truths that arise from both natural and special revelation.

There are plenty of other examples of natural theology during this period, but none more important than Paley and his 1802 work *Natural Theology*.

---

9. Aquinas, *Summa Theologiae* I.45.7.
10. Aquinas, *Summa Theologiae* I.2.3.
11. Aquinas, *Summa Theologiae* I.1.5.
12. Descartes, *Discourse on Method*, part 4.
13. Boyle, "Of the Study of the Book of Nature."

As others before him, Paley seeks to argue for the existence of God from the evidence of design in nature. By carefully considering the function of dozens of objects in nature, Paley concludes that nature displays numerous cases of design and contrivance. That being the case, he argues by way of analogy that these examples of contrivance require a designer. Paley's argument from design in nature is considered to be a classical expression of the teleological argument. In the opening chapter of *Natural Theology*, Paley introduces his argument with an analogy:

> In crossing a heath, suppose I pitched my foot against a stone, and were asked how the stone came to be there, I might possibly answer, that, for anything I knew to the contrary, it had lain there for ever: nor would it perhaps be very easy to shew the absurdity of this answer. But suppose I had found a watch upon the ground, and it should be enquired how the watch happened to be in that place, I should hardly think of the answer which I had before given, that, for anything I knew, the watch might have always been there. Yet why should not this answer serve for the watch, as well as for the stone? Why is it not as admissible in the second case, as in the first? For this reason, and for no other, viz. that, when we come to inspect the watch, we perceive (what we could not discover in the stone) that its several parts are framed and put together for a purpose, e.g. that they are so formed and adjusted as to produce motion, and that motion so regulated as to point out the hour of the day; that, if the several parts had been differently shaped from what they are, of a different size from what they are, or placed after any other manner, or in any other order, than that in which they are placed, either no motion at all would have been carried on in the machine, or none which would have answered the use that is now served by it.[14]

For Paley, this framing, adjusting, regulating, and shaping of parts could only be taken as evidence that the discovered watch was a product of design. He says, "The inference, we think, is inevitable; that the watch must have had a maker; that there must have existed, at some time and at some place or other, an artificer or artificers who formed it for the purpose which we find it actually to answer; who comprehended its construction, and designed its use."[15]

As you can see, natural theology has a long, rich history in the Christian tradition. It has been adopted and developed by a wide variety of philosophers and theologians. But as the next section will show, it has also had major critics and was largely rejected and abandoned for extended periods of time.

14. Paley, *Natural Theology*, 7.
15. Paley, *Natural Theology*, 8.

The Demise (and Revival) of Natural Theology

In addition to the new interest and development in natural theology, the Enlightenment brought significant criticisms for it as well. In a multifaceted attack, criticisms from philosophy, science, and theology eventually converged to render natural theology as obsolete and unattractive in Western thought. In fact, once these criticisms were leveled against it, natural theology was largely rejected by Christian philosophers and theologians for the next few centuries. One classic example of the philosophical criticisms of natural theology comes from David Hume's *Dialogues concerning Natural Religion*. Set as a dialogue between three friends named Cleanthes, Demea, and Philo about the existence of God, and our ability to prove his existence from design features in the physical world, Hume offers several objections to the design argument: (1) who designed God objection, (2) coherent universe objection, (3) insufficient evidence objection, (4) problem of evil objection, and (5) weak analogy objection.[16] There were plenty of other philosophical critics during this period, but Hume's objections had the greatest, and most lasting, impact for sure.

Scientifically, Charles Darwin's *Origin of Species* significantly changed the perception of natural theology in Western thought. From 1802, when Paley wrote *Natural Theology*, until 1859, when Darwin published *On the Origin of Species*, Paley's work was read and highly regarded by theologians, scientists, and philosophers. Yet, with Darwin's work, Paley's design argument was rejected, and the perceived plausibility of all such arguments was greatly diminished. Specifically, Darwin's theory of natural selection provided scientists with a plausible explanation for how wide diversity could have originated without any need for divine causation. This gave those already inclined toward theological skepticism an explanatory mechanism that they had not had until Darwin's work. Neal Gillespie notes that it "has been generally agreed (then and since) that Darwin's doctrine of natural selection effectively demolished William Paley's classical design argument for the existence of God. By showing how blind and gradual adaptation could counterfeit the apparently purposeful design, . . . Darwin deprived their argument of the analogical inference that the evident purpose to be seen in the contrivances by which means and ends were related in nature was necessarily a function of mind."[17]

Theologically, no criticisms were as important as those offered by Karl Barth, who suggested that such arguments for God "obviously have no

---

16. Hume, *Dialogues concerning Natural Religion*, 53. For the summary of Hume's critics, we are indebted here to Stephen T. Davis's categorizations. See S. Davis, *God, Reason and Theistic Proofs*, 101–6.

17. Gillespie, *Charles Darwin and the Problem of Creation*, 83–84.

value."[18] And in his written debates with Emil Brunner (who offered a defense and vision for natural theology) on natural theology, Barth famously replies with a simple one-word German title to his essay: *Nein!*[19] McGrath offers a helpful synopsis of Barth's primary critiques: "Barth's hostility towards natural theology thus rests on his fundamental belief that it undermines the necessity and uniqueness of God's self-revelation. If knowledge of God can be achieved independently of God's self-revelation in Christ, then it follows that humanity can dictate the place, time and means of its knowledge of God. Natural theology, for Barth, represents an attempt on the part of humanity to understand itself apart from and in isolation from revelation, representing a deliberate refusal to accept the necessity and consequences of revelation."[20] With powerful philosophical and scientific criticisms already in place, Barth's stinging theological criticisms of natural theology had a huge impact in Christian theology. Reflecting on how devastating these criticisms were for natural theology, McGrath says, "If my personal conversations with theologians, philosophers, and natural scientists over the last decade are in any way representative, natural theology is generally seen as being like a dead whale, left stranded on a beach by a receding tide, gracelessly rotting under the heat of a philosophical and scientific sun."[21]

As such, natural theology was mostly dormant from the mid-nineteenth century until the later twentieth century. During this time, the disdain for natural theology was so universal that most would have never expected the vibrant revival in natural theology that we have seen over the past few decades. To the surprise of many, natural theology is back, more robust than ever before, reigniting debates and dialogues of old. James Sennett and Douglas Groothuis suggest that this is because proponents of natural theology are "using many new developments in science, theology and philosophy to make new and intriguing cases for the justification of theistic and Christian concepts and beliefs."[22]

Indeed, the discoveries in physics, chemistry, biology, and cosmology over the past few decades—along with major revisions to the versions of the arguments from philosophers—have given new life to what was once considered a dead enterprise. In short, the metaphysical and theological implications of many recent scientific discoveries are clear and, for many, overwhelming. As the late Fred Hoyle has said, "A common sense interpretation of the facts suggests that a superintellect has monkeyed with physics, as well as with

---

18. Barth, *Church Dogmatics* II/1, 76.
19. See Baillie, *Natural Theology*.
20. McGrath, *Scientific Theology*, 1:269.
21. McGrath, *Fine-Tuned Universe*, 5.
22. Sennett and Groothuis, "Introduction," 11.

chemistry and biology, and that there are no blind forces worth speaking about in nature. The numbers one calculates from the facts seem to me so overwhelming as to put this conclusion almost beyond question."[23] And with the revival in natural theology, the debates once again take a significant place within our work in theology and apologetics. As our volume will now show, some will embrace it, while others will rail against it.

The Questions of This Volume

Question One: What is natural theology? This may seem like a ridiculous question. But as we will see in this volume, scholars are divided over just how we should think about natural theology. For example, Ronald Nash says, "Natural theology is an attempt to discover arguments that will prove or otherwise provide warrant for belief in God without appealing to special revelation, e.g., the Bible."[24] Similarly, William Alston defines it as "the enterprise of providing support for religious beliefs by starting from premises that neither are nor presuppose any religious beliefs."[25]

Yet, this understanding of natural theology is at odds with the actual practice of some historical Christian philosophers like Augustine, Anselm, and Aquinas. Given that these philosophers and theologians, and many others, reject the notion that natural theology starts from neutral premises but argue that it more properly starts from within the faith itself, scholars like McGrath define natural theology as "the enterprise of seeing nature as creation, which both presupposes and reinforces fundamental Christian theological affirmations."[26] So then, we are left to wonder just what natural theology is in the first place. This will be one of the major questions that our contributors take up in this volume.

Question Two: Should we do natural theology? A second major question for our inquiry into natural theology is whether or not it should be done at all. As we will see, some Christian intellectuals are highly convinced of its place and value within our work, while others are much more pessimistic. Perhaps there is apologetic value in this kind of work, or maybe it creates more trouble than it is worth or is misguided from the start. Our contributors come to very different conclusions about this matter. The design of the volume is to help you see the merits and potential problems and then decide for yourself. But either way, venturing through this debate with our contributors will be helpful.

23. Hoyle, "The Universe," 16.
24. Nash, *Faith and Reason*, 93.
25. Alston, *Perceiving God*, 289.
26. McGrath, *Science of God*, 113.

Question Three: How should we do natural theology? And finally, if natural theology is to be done, how should we go about doing it? Should we, as some suggest, start from purely objective premises that are accepted by everyone? Or like McGrath suggests, should we start from within our faith? Should our natural theology, assuming it should be done, take the form of arguments? Or should it be more of a lens through which we look at creation? Once again, our contributors take different views, and their dialogues will be instructive for anyone working through these big questions.

What's to Come

Considering the rich background of natural theology, we are excited to showcase the contributors of this volume, who represent the contemporary debates on the subject. Each contributor is a thoughtful advocate or critic of natural theology who interacts with the major questions mentioned above. (What is natural theology? Should we do natural theology? If so, How should we go about it?) Representing a perspective with deep historical roots and passionate opinions, each contributor offers an essay advocating for their view on natural theology and is then followed by responses from each of their fellow contributors. After this, each offers one final response to the criticisms of their view.

In chapter 1, we explore Charles Taliaferro's contemporary view. Dr. Taliaferro is professor emeritus of philosophy and emeritus Oscar and Gertrude Boe Overby Distinguished Professor at St. Olaf College. As you will see, Taliaferro understands natural theology as "philosophical reflection on God based on reasoning that does not rely on revelation (or revealed theology)." As an advocate of natural theology, Taliaferro suggests that it is best to approach natural theology abductively, using it to show that Christian theism has greater explanatory power than other worldviews. To make that case, Taliaferro offers a cosmological argument, a teleological argument, and an argument from consciousness.

Chapter 2 offers dialogue surrounding Fr. Andrew Pinsent's Catholic view. Dr. Pinsent is research director for the Ian Ramsey Centre for Science and Religion at the Harris Manchester College at Oxford University. Drawing on the theological insights of Thomas Aquinas, Pinsent illustrates the rich Catholic perspectives on natural (known from nature and reason) and supernatural (known through God's special revelation) theology. He offers a range of possibilities related to natural theology, including (a) a natural understanding of natural matters; (b) a natural understanding of supernatural matters; (c) a supernatural understanding of natural matters; and (d) a supernatural understanding of supernatural matters.

In chapter 3, Alister McGrath defends what he understands to be a classical view of natural theology. Dr. McGrath serves at Oxford University, where he holds the Andreas Idreos Professorship in Science and Religion in the faculty of theology and religion, is a fellow of Harris Manchester College, and is professor of divinity at Gresham College. Situated somewhere between the perspectives of the other contributors, McGrath defends natural theology while also taking seriously the major criticisms from Barth and many others. He shows that, properly understood and practiced, natural theology always assumes a distinct theology of nature and humanity, such that it never actually arises from "neutral" premises or perspectives about nature. As such, on his view—an approach he understands to be in keeping with the actual practice of natural theology prior to the Enlightenment—Christian theology provides a basis for natural theology, allowing it to start from within the faith, not outside of it. While, like Taliaferro, McGrath defends natural theology, his approach has considerable differences with Taliaferro's contemporary account.

In chapter 4, we showcase Paul Moser's deflationary view, which seeks to "deflate the pretensions of natural theology." Dr. Moser is a professor of philosophy at Loyola University in Chicago and has written extensively on his concerns with natural theology. As one of the most vocal and thoughtful contemporary critics of natural theology, Moser raises substantial concerns about the revival of natural theology. Specifically, as you will see, he asserts that the arguments from natural theology—past and present—fail to point us to the actual God of Christianity, a God who is good and worthy of worship. Because of this, natural theology yields nothing "conclusive or even confirmatory" about the God of Abraham, Isaac, Jacob, and Jesus Christ.

Finally, in chapter 5, we have John McDowell's Barthian view of natural theology. Dr. McDowell is professor of theology, philosophy, and moral theology and currently associate dean at Yarra Theological College in the University of Divinity in Australia. As noted above, Barth's criticisms of natural theology have been some of the most important criticisms of the apologetic enterprise. Specifically, Barth rejected the attempt to reason about God from the natural order, seeing it as an attempt to be autonomous and independent of God. McDowell unpacks the theological nuance of Barth's theological perspective and the concerns with natural theology that come along with it.

Debate is a necessary and important element of theological discourse, and the contributions to this volume on natural theology by Taliaferro, Pinsent, McGrath, Moser, and McDowell are a gift to everyone interested in this important subject matter. We trust that it will be a helpful tour of the important issues for everyone concerned with the topic.

1

A Contemporary View

CHARLES TALIAFERRO

At the outset of my essay on natural theology, it is important to be clear about what natural theology is and how it might be done. As I understand it, natural theology is the philosophical reflection on God based on reasoning that does not rely on revelation (or revealed theology). Unlike revealed theology, which may presuppose the truth or reliability of the Christian Bible, natural theology develops a philosophy of God based on observations about the cosmos, pursuing questions about the nature of the cosmos, its origin, and its continuation. Natural theology was robustly pursued in late medieval and early modern philosophy in Europe by Jewish and Christian philosophers and in the Near and Middle East by Islamic philosophers. Many of the great early modern thinkers—Descartes, Leibniz, Cudworth, More, Clarke, Locke, and a host of others—developed proofs for the existence of God in their natural theology.

In standard histories of philosophy, it is claimed that natural theology was eviscerated by David Hume and Immanuel Kant, but this seems false, not just due to flaws in Humean and Kantian philosophical methodologies, but due to the ingenuity and resilience of theistic philosophers. Today there are abundant anthologies, companions, and handbooks promoting natural theology. Two things have changed in natural theology since the eighteenth century. First, philosophers rarely advance what they describe as a proof or disproof of the existence of God; in fact, philosophers rarely use the language of "proof" in almost any domain of philosophy outside of formal logic. Instead, chastened by centuries of criticism, philosophers now are more ready to refer to good (or cogent or persuasive or sound) arguments or arguments that are poor or weak. Second, while natural theology today is still practiced without relying on the authority of sacred texts, many proponents of natural theology include an appeal to the evidential role of religious experience.

Some critics throughout history have thought that we simply should not do natural theology. But from my vantage point, we certainly should. As the greatest contemporary contributor to natural theology, Richard Swinburne, has argued, if one may philosophically establish theism independent of appeal to the Bible, one has contributed reason for taking seriously the Bible as a divine revelation. Without natural theology, inquiry into the Bible's credibility is hampered. Natural theology has a long and distinguished history, arguably going back to Plato. The practice deserves our attention as a prospective conduit for encountering God.

But if we do natural theology, how should we go about doing it? I propose that the best way to practice natural theology is through what is commonly called "abduction." One should compare what one has some reason to believe are promising worldviews (theism, naturalism, British Idealism, etc.) and then evaluate their internal coherence and their explanatory power. As you will see below, I think the two most promising worldviews are classical theism (in the perfect-being theological tradition) and a form of naturalism. The burden of my approach is to provide reasons for thinking that classical theism is more reasonable because it has greater explanatory power than naturalism.

As I began thinking about structuring this chapter, I was on an airplane. A child in back of me kept repeating the question "Why?" I was not sure what the child was focused on, nor could I make out what an adult said in response, but it set the mood for this chapter. I propose that it is not just extraordinary that we have air travel, but it is extraordinary that our cosmos and we ourselves exist and continue to exist over time. While some philosophers seek to dismiss asking the question *why* about our cosmos as a whole, as one might seek to silence a petulant child, I think the question of why our cosmos and we ourselves exist begs for us to raise further big questions. And I propose that theism provides a successful answer to such big questions.

Let us first address the concept of God in Christian theistic tradition, and then consider what we know about the cosmos and ourselves. I then argue that the existence of our cosmos and ourselves (and other conscious beings) is more reasonably explained by theism than by (what I believe to be) its closest competition, some form of naturalism, to be explained below.

The Concept of God in Christian Theism

Christian tradition has involved more than one concept of God. Yet the concept of God that I sketch here is widely embraced and is not at all a minority viewpoint. In mainline Christian philosophy, God is believed to be unsurpassable in excellence. In the spirit of St. Anselm (1033–1109), God is said to be a being greater than which cannot be conceived. It would be a virtual contradiction to think that while God is good, there could be a greater divine reality. God's greatness is understood to involve the greatest attributes it is possible for a being to possess. The divine attributes include omniscience, omnipotence, essential goodness, existing necessarily (rather than contingently), and being eternal or everlasting. It is in virtue of these attributes that Christians believe God is purposive (intentional), omnipresent (there is no place where God is not), worthy of obedience and worship. Of course, Christians believe many more things about God involving the Trinity, the incarnation, the atonement, the afterlife, and so on. Moreover, Christians (especially Christian philosophers) have differed in their analyses of these attributes: some understand the scope of omniscience as including all future events; others contend that God's being omniscient means that at any time God *knows all that is possible to know at that time* (no being can have more knowledge). The latter position is often taken by philosophers who contend it is not possible for any being to know with certainty future events involving freedom. Another point of order is whether God is in time or outside of time, though Christian philosophers agree that there was never a time when God did not exist or would not exist.

In this chapter, the divine attributes involving goodness, power, knowledge, and God's necessary existence are the most important. God's existing necessarily (God cannot fail to exist) is sometimes put as the claim that God's very nature is existence. The necessity of God's existence flows from God's maximal greatness; a being that had all the other divine attributes but not necessity to exist would not be as great as a being who has the divine attributes, including necessary existence. You and I, the planet, our solar system, and the billions of galaxies in our universe do not exist necessarily. We can (and should) ask why our cosmos exists rather than a different cosmos or why there is any cosmos at all that endures over time.

Let's now consider the comparative explanatory power of theism and broad naturalism.

Three Theistic Arguments

I defend a theistic argument, going back to Anselm and called the *ontological argument*, but because that argument would take too long to defend here, I present instead three other arguments: one is from contingency (commonly called a *cosmological argument*), the second appeals to the apparent purposive nature of the cosmos (or the *teleological argument*), and the third is *an argument from consciousness*. Before I outline these arguments, let us consider some of the data that these arguments will draw on: our understanding of causation and of contingency and necessity, and the evident reality of our conscious, self-aware, purposive life.

On the matter of *causation*, we know in our first-person experience and in our observation of the world that events have causes, understood broadly to include reasons and explanations. Ordinarily, we know when physical injury causes us pain, that we move our arms and bodies, that we engage in reasoning (we answer 2 when asked what is the sum of 1 + 1), that a baseball may break a glass window, that fire causes smoke, and so on. Philosophers have developed multiple theories of causation, sometimes referring to laws of nature, the causal powers and liabilities of objects, psychological associations, and so on. But whichever account one adopts, we seem to have a foundational awareness of when we ourselves bring about events (I am certain that I am typing the keys of my computer intentionally), and we would be baffled by the claim that some event or thing had no cause, reason, or explanation of any kind. Philosophers have sometimes formulated this in terms of the maxim "Nothing comes from nothing." None of us actually believes that a massive whale might come out of nothing and into being inside our bus, crushing us and our fellow passengers, without any cause or reason.

On *contingency and necessity*, each of us has some commonsense grasp of different modalities (ways of being), including necessity, contingency, possibility, and impossibility. Something (an event or proposition or object) is necessary when it cannot but be the case. For example, 1 + 1 is 2, and its denial is necessarily false or impossible. (We know 1 + 1 = 2 because it is an identity statement; 2 simply is 1 + 1, so the proposition is essentially that 1 + 1 is the same as or equivalent to 1 + 1.) Something is contingent (like "The cat is on the mat") when it is not necessary and its denial and its affirmation are possible (it is possible the cat is on the mat and possible that the cat is not on the mat). These categories are relevant in what follows when it is affirmed that the cosmos is contingent and God (if there is a God) exists necessarily.

Regarding *consciousness*, I propose that the most certain thing we know about reality (or the cosmos) is that we are conscious, thinking beings who can move, act, feel, reason, observe, and perceive the world around us. This knowledge is virtually unshakable in the sense that it is foundational to any of our other knowledge claims. It is far more certain than the knowledge we can gain through science, because science itself cannot take place without there being scientists, and scientists are persons who are conscious, thinking beings who move, act, feel, reason, observe, and perceive the world around us. Science is (I suggest) inconceivable without observation, reason, and so on. In fact, our grasp of the methods and content of science cannot be any clearer than our grasp of the relevant concepts or ideas involved. One cannot have a greater grasp of what helium is without having a reliable concept of helium. We have a great deal of knowledge through the natural sciences, but we would have no science at all without a prior or confident antecedent awareness of ourselves as conscious beings.

The certainty of our conscious thinking and our acting purposively may be strengthened by considering the absurdity of denying this certitude. Consider the following claims by Alex Rosenberg:

> Our conscious thoughts are very crude indicators of what is going on in our brain. We fool ourselves into treating these conscious markers as thoughts about what we want and how to achieve it, about plans and purposes. We are even tricked into thinking they somehow bring about behavior. We are mistaken about all of these things.[1]

> You cannot treat the interpretations of behavior in terms of purposes and meaning as conveying real understanding.[2]

> The individual acts of human beings [are] unguided by purpose.[3]

> What individuals do, alone or together, over a moment or a month or a lifetime, is really just the product of the process of blind variation and environmental filtration operating on neural circuits in their heads.[4]

I suggest that Rosenberg's claims are in preposterous conflict with what everyone knows. When Rosenberg wrote the above claims, it is wild to claim that he did that writing without consciously intending to do so. He had a plan or purpose to claim there are no such things as acting (bringing about events) on the basis of plans and purposes. Moreover, unless we (his readers) and he know how to reason and have understandings of arguments and causation, there would be no possibility of us reasoning with each other about anything. I just intentionally wrote this nonsensical sentence: *Thrustitus eats turnips backwards while marching on a cloud.* We can know, praise, or blame each other in our writing and speaking nonsense only because we realize that we are writing or speaking things with full awareness of our responsibility as opposed to being passive, tricked, mistaken entities controlled by "blind variation." Rosenberg's mention of time ("over a moment or . . .") brings up an important counterpoint: unless you were aware of yourself as a conscious subject, existing over time, who was reading this paragraph and could reason, you would not understand any of Rosenberg's or my claims.

Consider any case of successful communication between two persons. Imagine that I warn you of a dangerous, oncoming snowplow. I shout, "Look

1. Rosenberg, *Atheist's Guide*, 210.
2. Rosenberg, *Atheist's Guide*, 213.
3. Rosenberg, *Atheist's Guide*, 244.
4. Rosenberg, *Atheist's Guide*, 255.

out for that plow!" and you step to one side, avoiding injury. For us to interact and bring about events, *we must be confident, conscious, self-aware subjects who are acting purposively and be aware that we are taking responsibility for what we say and do.*[5]

Why would anyone be driven to deny that we bring about events on purpose? We can reason, think, converse; we can decide to go on diets; we can make love, fly airplanes, write and read book chapters, ad infinitum. I suggest that such denial is because of a commitment to some form of naturalism. The most extreme form of naturalism, sometimes called *scientism* or *strict naturalism*, denies that there are any things (broadly speaking) or causal factors that would not be described and explained in the physical sciences (physics, chemistry, biology; we might add that this refers to ideal or complete sciences, acknowledging that, at present, the physical sciences are quite incomplete). Many strict naturalists (like Rosenberg, Daniel Dennett, Paul and Patricia Churchland) are in the awkward position of denying the reality of subjective, conscious experience or awareness. They seem compelled to adopt this extreme position since they have no explanation of the emergence and continued existence of subjective, conscious experience. Their background assumption is that the cosmos is without any purposive structure, that there is no God, and that the cosmos is fundamentally driven by "blind variations."

For many of us, whether we are atheists or agnostics or theists, strict naturalism requires us to pay too high a price. Hence in the field of philosophy more capacious forms of naturalism have emerged, sometimes called *broad* or *liberal naturalism*. These more liberal forms of naturalism recognize the reality of consciousness, reason, thinking, and so on, while still denying the reality of God. I suggest that liberal naturalism is far more reasonable than strict naturalism.

Let us now move to three arguments in natural theology.

A Cosmological Argument

You and I, and the cosmos as a whole, seem contingent. We can imagine there being no cosmos at all or a different cosmos. Why does our cosmos exist?

---

5. Because I am claiming that we all know ourselves as self-aware, conscious beings, am I committed to believing that Rosenberg is self-deceived or lying? No. I do believe that any mature, responsible, deliberate action must presuppose some conscious awareness of one's own thinking and motives; but, I suggest, persons may (at the same time) have an honest but mistaken philosophical belief that their perception of themselves and the world is illusory (e.g., they think they are brains in vats). In my view, Rosenberg must be aware of his powers to intentionally bring about events, even though he thinks this awareness is not authenticated by his philosophical commitments.

Unlike a philosopher such as Spinoza, who maintained that the cosmos and every event in it is necessary (and could not be otherwise; on his view, your existence and action right now could not have failed to occur), most naturalists (narrow or broad) accept *this* position: *it just is*.[6] They take the cosmos to be a brute, not further explainable, fact. In contrast, Christian theism has an account of the cosmos: it exists and is sustained in existence by the purposive, good creativity of God as a necessarily existing being.

Let us straightaway note that the cosmological argument (in most versions) does not give us reason to believe that the necessarily existing being responsible for the existence and continuation of the cosmos has all the divine attributes (this being might or might not be omniscient). Most forms of the cosmological argument do not compete with science as an explanation of the cosmos. That is because of the scale and scope of theism. So, theism is not employed here to explain the properties of water or volcanoes or why Jupiter has four main moons. Theism, rather, is employed to explain why there is a contingent cosmos at all and why it continues to exist. There is a sense in which a theistic account of the cosmos may be seen as complementing and even supporting the practice of science. In the sciences we search for explanations for what occurs in the cosmos; if that seems reasonable, isn't it reasonable to ask why there is a cosmos at all?

Consider the cosmological argument further in light of four challenging questions.

First challenge. The argument relies on the thesis that the cosmos is contingent. But if its existence is explained by the power of a necessarily existing being, wouldn't the cosmos turn out to be necessary and thus not contingent?

Most Christian theists claim that God creates and sustains the cosmos freely; that is, it was not necessary that God create. However, given that God necessarily exists and is essentially good, one has reason for thinking that creation is a good, fitting, natural act. So the cosmos remains contingent on this account.

Second challenge. Isn't there something unfair about claiming that God necessarily exists, while denying that the cosmos necessarily exists? If theists can say, "God just is," why can't naturalists say, "The cosmos just is"?

Here we do well to recall that the cosmological argument (as customarily developed) does not offer a full vindication of Christian theism. If successful, it provides some reason to believe that the cosmos has a cause that exists necessarily. A defender of the argument can develop it simply as making a case for the cosmos having a necessarily existing cause while conceding (if only

6. For example, see Mackie, *Miracle of Theism.*

for the sake of argument) that it could be that God (if there is a God) does not necessarily exist. The defense could take the shape of asking us to put off claims about God versus the cosmos and focus on whether it is reasonable to believe that a contingent cosmos just exists without some transcendent, necessarily existing reality. After reaching the conclusion that there is some necessarily existing reality sustaining the cosmos, one might only then take up the question of whether such a necessarily existing reality might be God.

Third challenge. The next question is important: Does the cosmological argument take us well beyond what we have a right to consider? In ordinary experience and in the sciences, we come up with accounts of why events occur within our cosmos, whereas the cosmological argument asks us a question about the cosmos as a whole. Doesn't that go to a realm well beyond our cognitive limits?

Maybe so, but one can press on with the thesis (cited earlier) that if we can reasonably raise questions about why events in the cosmos make sense, then it seems unreasonable to deny that it makes sense to reasonably ask why the cosmos as a whole exists. Some have claimed that the cosmological argument involves a logical fallacy. For example, just as it would be a fallacy to argue that because each person's coming into being involves a mother, that is a reason to believe there is a big mother accountable for all of us; so also it is a fallacy to argue that because events in the cosmos have causes, there must be a cause of the cosmos as a whole. But that does not seem right. The cosmological argument appeals not to some big contingent cause explaining other contingent causes and things, but to a noncontingent, necessary reality. The "mother argument" (for lack of a better term) is a fallacy because it falsely appeals to an explanation of a set of things by simply expanding the set, rather than transcending the set to explain why there are any persons (and their mothers) at all.

Fourth challenge. Why only one necessarily existing being? Why not dozens? A defender of the argument need not quibble over numbers. She can use the argument to provide a reason for thinking that there is at least one necessarily existing being. This conclusion alone, along with the conviction that the cosmos itself is (as it appears to be) contingent would yield one reason for thinking that strict and broad naturalism is wanting or, comparatively, not as robust in its account of the cosmos.

A Teleological Argument

Before we turn to a teleological argument, it should be appreciated that in philosophy some positions are defended in light of not just one argument but several. For example, one may argue for some form of political liberalism on the basis of utilitarianism, contract theory, natural law, a theory of human rights, a divine command theory, history, and so on. In the present context, the three arguments presented can also be mutually supportive or cumulative. At the base of the teleological argument presented here is the thesis that the cosmos is, overall, good: stable laws of nature have allowed there to be galaxies, stars, and planets—including our own, which has been the site for the emergence of life, including the conscious lives of self-aware persons capable of moral life and practice. As with the earlier cosmological argument, the thesis is that such a good cosmos is explained better on the grounds of theism than on the grounds of (strict or broad) naturalism. I defend the argument in response to three challenging questions or objections below, but note here how the cosmological and teleological arguments can be mutually reinforcing. Imagine that the cosmological argument gave you some reason to believe a necessarily existing being exists, and that the teleological argument gave you some reason to believe that the cosmos itself is caused and sustained by a purposive, good reality. Combining these two lines of reasoning would count as providing two reasons for favoring theism over naturalism.

First challenge. The teleological argument rests on the claim that the cosmos is, overall, good. But is it? Everything living dies. Suffering pervades our planet. Perhaps other living, conscious beings exist on other planets that are good overall, but we do not know this. What we know about our own world is that it is replete with hideous suffering and death.

I briefly address the problem of evil for theism later on, but for now I propose a counterclaim: Despite all the evident suffering, pain, and death, isn't it still (overall) good that the cosmos exists? Or, putting things a bit differently, isn't it better that the cosmos exists rather than not exist? There is no way to plausibly measure out units of goodness and evil to mathematically calculate good versus evil in our cosmos. (Imagine trying to build a case that our cosmos has 75 percent units of goodness versus 22 percent evil, and 3 percent neither good nor evil!)

Here are four reasons for thinking that most of us consider the cosmos to be good overall (or that it is better for the cosmos to exist than not to exist). First, most of us believe it would be a horrific tragedy if all life on earth were destroyed (either by human causes such as nuclear war or by natural causes such as a giant meteor). Second, most of us think it is good or better overall to live longer (assuming basic health) rather than to die prematurely. Third, most of us think it is good to reproduce and raise children. It would be a dubious "virtue" to have and raise children if we thought we were bringing them into a place where it would be better for everyone if it ceased to be rather than continuing to exist. Fourth, the idea (promoted by some Darwinians) that nature is thoroughly vicious (according to Tennyson "red in tooth and claw") has been superseded by an ecology that sees life as more integrated and mutually beneficial.[7] Yes, any substantial ecological system will include biological death as well as life, but it is not obvious that the death of organisms is always bad.

Second challenge. The teleological argument supposes that a purposive account of our cosmos is better than a naturalist account in which the natural world is not purposive and is driven by impersonal, nonconscious forces. Isn't such a stand a bit anthropocentric (human centered)? We humans make up such a tiny fraction of all living animals. Actually, all vertebrates (including all mammals, birds, fish, and reptiles) make up only 3 percent of living animals. Why think the cause and sustainer of the cosmos is like us (intentional or conscious) rather than like some of the nonthinking living things (like a giant, cosmic plant)?

In reply, it should be recognized that the concept of a purposive, intentional being is not narrowly human. In fact, it seems anthropocentric to think that only humans are or can be persons. Perhaps a variety of nonhuman animals on our planet are persons (great apes, dolphins); I suggest we should not rule out there being indefinitely many nonhuman persons (or purposive, intentional agents) on other life-sustaining planets. The teleological argument is not driven by privileging human beings per se but relies on comparing two types of explanation: teleological (or purposive) explanations and nonteleological ones. In the case of the former, explanations are cast in terms of forces shaped by concepts of goodness (an agent does X in virtue of judging X to be good) in which a purposive being or force has a prevision of the good it is bringing about. On a cosmic scale, theism supplies an account of why there is an (overall) good cosmos rather than not. The goodness of the cosmos is one reason why it exists rather than not exist, because it is created and sustained by a good Creator. Naturalism (as we have seen in the cosmological argument) does not offer such an account.

Third challenge. What if there are infinitely many universes? Wouldn't it be inevitable that at least one universe would be good and appear to be brought into existence and sustained by a purposive being, even if there were no such being?

There are several replies to consider. One might question the possibility of there being an actual infinity of universes, but even if this is entertained as a possible cosmology, the existence of the infinity of universes may itself call for

---

7. See, e.g., Linzy, *Animal Theology.*

an explanation. Why do they exist rather than not exist? I suggest that theism would have an advantage here that naturalism does not. A second response would question the motivation behind the infinity-of-universes hypothesis. If its chief motivation is to avoid theism, then that seems to be a fairly high price to pay, especially in the absence of empirical evidence that there are infinitely many universes. Theism would seem a simpler explanation of our cosmos than naturalism. A third response may involve noting how the infinity hypothesis might lead to some very counterintuitive results. Consider, for example, radical skeptics who suppose that we do not really perceive the world as it is, but we are all subject to the cruel manipulation of superscientists. If the skeptic's concept of reality is possible, who is to say that our world isn't such as imagined by skeptics? Arguably, we have good reason to trust our perception in our cosmos, but the infinity hypothesis can undermine this confidence because perhaps we unluckily are living in the skeptic's possible world.

There are dozens, if not hundreds, of further objections we could entertain and just as many replies. I will count this chapter a success if readers simply conclude "maybe so . . ." rather than be fully convinced.

An Argument from Consciousness

I more briefly address the argument from consciousness, as the basic strategy of this chapter is probably clear. The basic claim is that theism is in a better position to account for consciousness rather than naturalism. The reason for this is that theism contends that God is a conscious reality (a divine mind, as it were), and so it accounts for the existence of contingent, conscious, minded beings in light of a greater conscious mind. I have noted earlier that some naturalists (like Rosenberg) despair of accounting for conscious, purposive beings and so, often, resort to denying the existence (and causal efficacy) of conscious, mindful, purposive agents. I believe this strategy is desperate and unreasonable, for reasons offered earlier.

There are abundant other arguments in natural theology that could be considered: an argument from objective morality, an epistemic argument (to the effect that theism offers a better account of our reasoning than naturalism), ontological arguments, an argument from religious experience, and so on.

Conclusion

In closing this chapter's positive case for natural theology, let me reply to two general concerns, one religious and one secular, and then discuss further the role of natural theology in addressing objections to theism, including the problem of evil.

A Religious Objection

Some Christian philosophers, from Blaise Pascal and Søren Kierkegaard to Paul Moser, object to natural theology on the grounds that, at best, it can make plausible the God of the philosophers but not the God of faith. Recognizing the God of the philosophers might be a purely intellectual matter, and even a source of human vanity. It is more fitting that God would be manifest to us when we passionately seek God, perhaps especially when we seek God through Jesus as revealed in Scripture.

In response I am inclined to think that almost *anything* can be a source of human vanity. Pascal and Kierkegaard might have (based on egotism and a desire for preeminence) claimed to have a superior understanding of God. I do not think this is true at all! I am merely making the modest claim that it is possible. But I will make the claim that, in my view, if natural theology can provide some reason for thinking there is a God, this would provide an important reason to reflect on how this God may be revealed in human history. Natural theology can motivate persons to pursue revealed theology.

A Secular Objection

From a secular point of view, the question might arise: If arguments from contingency, teleology, and consciousness (and the other arguments that make up the long tradition of natural theology) are so good, why aren't more philosophers today theists?

I believe the answer to this is that philosophy as a discipline is complex. It contains multiple (officially) acceptable methodologies and topics. A professional philosopher may be focused on sociopolitical philosophy and never really consider theism one way or the other. I have peers who describe themselves as "atheists," but in some cases I think a more accurate self-description would be "nontheists," because they have never engaged in serious reflection on theism and its alternatives. By analogy, someone who has never seriously considered being a Hegelian would, I think, be better described as a "non-Hegelian" than as an "anti-Hegelian"—someone who actively and intentionally has considered Hegel's work and sought to undermine it. It should also be noted that in philosophy today, there is very little consensus on almost any topic. The fact that a majority of professional philosophers today have not considered the best of natural theology is (from my point of view) regrettable. Standard introductions to philosophy often do not include contemporary, cogent versions of the arguments developed here. One more often sees Aquinas's five "proofs," without any sympathetic commentary, rather than (for example) plausible versions of the cosmological argument developed by Richard Taylor, William Lane Craig, Timothy O'Conner, Alexander Pruss, or Bruce Reichenbach.[8]

Thoughts on the Role of Natural Theology

Traditionally, natural theology as developed by Christian philosophers provides a case for theism that does not rely on revelation. Increasingly, however, natural theology has included appeal to religious experience. This expansion to include religious experience has provided an additional line of reasoning in support of theism. Some Christian philosophers, most notably Eleonore Stump and Marilyn Adams, have appealed to the experience of God's presence in the midst of suffering in addressing the problem of evil for theism.[9]

From my perspective, I think that the best case for Christian theism needs to draw on *both* natural and revealed theology, just as it needs to draw on both reflection on contingency and religious experience. Weighing the case for atheism based on the problem of evil needs, ultimately, to take into account what we reflect on about the natural world as well as to consider the possible resources of theism in the context of revelation (the possibilities of an afterlife, incarnation, atonement, and redemption).

I have set out a positive case for natural theology in providing good grounds for theism over against its closest rival, naturalism. I believe that should be enough for a single chapter, but I readily grant that a fuller project would involve taking into account still other alternatives.

---

8. Reichenbach offers a terrific defense of the cosmological argument in the entry of the same title in the free and online *Stanford Encyclopedia of Philosophy*; see Reichenbach, "Cosmological Argument."

9. Stump has devoted three volumes to the topic of evil and suffering, culminating in *The Image of God: The Problem of Evil and the Problem of Mourning*, which gives a narrative account of how God can bring transformative healing, even glory, in the wake of horrific evil. M. Adams develops her understanding of how God may engulf or defeat evil in a classic book, *Horrendous Evils and the Goodness of God*. For my own treatment of the problem of evil, see Taliaferro, *Cascade Companion to Evil*.

Catholic Response

FATHER ANDREW PINSENT

While reviewing many of the arguments of this volume, I have had occasion to remark that natural theology can and probably should be treated in a broad sense. On this account, natural theology encompasses not only the existence of God and other theological matters independent of revelation but also the natural fruits of revelation. Alister McGrath refers to the latter as the "theology of nature."

Charles Taliaferro's approach, by contrast, takes a broad view of a narrower framing of natural theology. His focus is on the existence of God and, specifically, God in the Christian theistic tradition. His approach to this issue, however, presents a relatively contemporary view by considering competing worldviews, specifically the explanatory power of Christian theism versus naturalism. On this account, one needs to fill out the principle of God beyond bare existence, but one also needs to fill out the principles of any alternative worldview. From the serious perspective of game theory, this move is a good one for two reasons. First, it addresses a common challenge to natural theology that any proofs for God's existence cannot attain to a specific understanding of God, such as the God of Christian theism. Second, it levels the playing field between advocates and deniers of God, given that deniers cannot simply retreat into the generally easier task of finding fault with the arguments of others.

Nevertheless, I have a couple of minor concerns with the implementation of Taliaferro's approach, mainly because they irritate my contrarian nature rather than impacting on the core of his arguments. The first is his offering of an example, that $1 + 1$ makes 2, which, I agree, seems self-evident but is not quite as simple as it might seem. One reason is that the *Principia Mathematica* of Alfred North Whitehead and Bertrand Russell notoriously took several hundred pages to prove that 1 + 1 makes 2, based on rigorous logic, but the *Principia* was later judged to be a kind of magnificent failure. Another reason is that we are surprisingly familiar with nonstandard mathematics. An example is shopping, an experience in which it is common for retailers to offer discounts for buying multiple instances of a product.[1] In such circumstances, we are entirely comfortable with 1 + 1 making less than 2. The second is Taliaferro's claim that none of us believes that a massive whale might come into being inside some inhabited space and crush us. In the quantum world, however, such counterintuitive events do happen, such as particles appearing out of nothing or on the far side of otherwise impassable energy barriers. Admittedly, the appearance of an entire whale without cause or reason is astronomically less likely than a subatomic particle, but not entirely excluded by quantum mechanics.

My pedantry in these examples may be annoying but does illustrate something important, namely, that persons can be prepared to find fault with the most evident, if not quite self-evident, truths, such as 1 + 1 making 2 and the nonspontaneous appearance of whales. Such considerations ought to sound the death knell for any attempt to prove the existence of God rigorously, if by "rigorous" is meant incapable of contradiction. Proofs for the existence of God that meet this standard are impossible, like almost any argument for anything. Indeed, as Taliaferro mentions in his chapter opening, "philosophers rarely use the language of 'proof' in almost any domain of philosophy outside of formal logic." Nevertheless, one can offer arguments that are or may be broadly acceptable on more heuristic grounds. Hence, I endorse Taliaferro's approach to showing the acceptability of Christian theism by comparing this worldview against others, an approach that rests on reasonable judgments.

I would, however, like to expand one of his comments as it touches on another way of showing the plausibility of belief in God by using heuristics. I think he is completely correct that children ask the question *why* to the point, I would add, that they can drive their parents or caregivers almost out of their minds. At about the age of ten, staying in a campsite on the way to a Catholic shrine in France, I encountered a young French boy, also about ten, pestering his mother with the words, "Pourquoi, maman?" Upon reflecting on this experience in later years, I realized that children also ask the why question in other languages, a fact that is consistent with the claim that human beings

---

1. I am grateful to the following book for highlighting the issue of nonstandard mathematics: P. Davis and Hersh, *Mathematical Experience*.

have a universal desire to know.[2] In English, the first word that is typically used in response to a why question—namely, "because"—is a word that throws further light on the nature of the question. The word "because" has two parts: "be" and "cause." Hence, when children or genuine philosophers ask why, the question that is really being asked is, "What is the cause of some being?"

This question leads to all kinds of other questions, such as about the variety of distinct causes, the causes of causes, and whether the chain of causes terminates in a first cause. There is, however, a characteristic of the known causes that tends to attract relatively little attention. As one passes from the consideration of causes to causes of causes, and then causes of those causes, their number tends to decrease. On the question of matter, for example, thirty million chemical compounds are built from a very much smaller number of elements, of which ninety-four occur naturally and an additional twenty-four or so artificially. These elements are in turn built up from a much smaller number of elementary particles, the most basic of which are four in number plus eight more with transitory existences and a few peculiar bits. The pattern of causation is therefore that of an ever-smaller number of ever more powerful causes, and a similar pattern can be found in many other instances of causation, such as motivations for human actions.[3] In other words, causes cluster into a funnel rather than a chain. The exploration of the causes toward the narrow end of the funnel is often challenging, but the heuristic is clear enough in science, philosophy, and everyday life. The funnel narrows, and that narrowing suggests, without proving it formally, that it is pointing toward some ultimate or first cause, the defining characteristic of which is to cause everything else without itself being caused.

Obviously, this pattern of causation, as a funnel rather than a chain, is not a rule or the basis of a formal proof, but it may help to highlight why belief in a first cause of some kind is so widespread. The narrowing of the funnel makes the existence of a first cause plausible, without revealing much, in a positive sense, about what it means for the first cause to be. As has been noted elsewhere in this volume, this consideration draws attention to both the strength and the weakness of natural theology, as traditionally conceived. This consideration also underlines the value of Taliaferro's approach to natural theology, which seeks to evaluate the existence of not merely God but also the God of revealed theology.

2. Aristotle, *Metaphysics* 1.1.980a21.
3. Aristotle, *Metaphysics* 1.1.982a23–30.

Classical Response

ALISTER E. McGRATH

enjoyed reading Charles Taliaferro's chapter. While I appreciate that his specific (and restrictive) understanding of natural theology as "philosophical reflection on God based on reasoning that does not rely on revelation" is widespread within the philosophical community, it is important to appreciate that this is only one such understanding and that others have been developed and deployed within the long tradition of reflecting on the transcendent implications of the natural order. I do not have any problems with guild-specific understandings of natural theology, so long as they are not proposed as normative for other disciplines.

My interest was piqued by Taliaferro's opening statement about how we are to go about doing natural theology: "I propose that the best way to practice natural theology is through what is commonly called 'abduction.'" It would have been interesting to know which particular form of abductive inference Taliaferro favors, so that this interesting discussion could be extended. As is well known, Charles S. Peirce developed his distinctive "abductive" approach partly on account of his dissatisfaction with Aristotle's account of inductive modes of thought (*epagōgē*) in making sense of the natural world.[1] As a former natural scientist, I have long taken the view that natural theology works best when it deploys abductive forms of argument, in that an Aristotelian account of induction is inadequate as an explanation of how we proceed from an array of observations to a generalized theory. Both William Whewell's notion of "consilience"—so significantly misrepresented in Edward O. Wilson's 1998

1. Anderson, "Evolution of Peirce's Concept of Abduction."

scientistic manifesto for the unification of knowledge—and Peirce's idea of "abduction" get round the problems with Aristotle at this point.[2]

Abduction, as Peirce develops this idea, can be seen as the "creative act of making up explanatory hypotheses."[3] Standing on the far side of an array of observations, we generate potential explanatory hypotheses as the first step in proceeding from a logic of discovery to a logic of verification. Having identified a suitable theory—irrespective of whether this is arrived at imaginatively or inductively—we can then test it by considering its capacity to make sense of what we observe. Taliaferro himself provides some excellent examples of this, such as his entirely plausible suggestion that the existence of our world itself requires an explanatory framework. "If we can reasonably raise questions about why events in the cosmos make sense, then it seems unreasonable to deny that it makes sense to reasonably ask why the cosmos as a whole exists."

I find a similar approach in the writings of John Polkinghorne, who championed a new style of natural theology that did not see itself as in explanatory competition with the natural sciences but rather saw itself as focusing particularly on significant questions that the natural sciences recognized and raised, yet were unable to answer using their own methods. Polkinghorne's argument is that such metaquestions are answered by a theistic framework. Three examples of these metaquestions may be noted, each reflecting Polkinghorne's background in the natural sciences. Why is science, in its modern developed form, possible in the first place?[4] Why is the physical universe so rationally transparent to us that we can discern its pattern and structure, even in the quantum world, which bears little relation to our everyday experience? Why is it that some of the most beautiful patterns proposed by pure mathematicians are actually found to occur in the structure of the physical world? Natural theology offers an explanatory framework that supplements—rather than displaces—that of the natural sciences, allowing a fuller and deeper grasp of their potential and limits. Taliaferro's approach, and the perceptive examples that he offers of aspects of the cosmos that are susceptible to theistic explanation, points in a helpful direction, comparable in some ways to the approach mapped out by Polkinghorne.

Taliaferro rightly notes that a natural theology must engage aspects of our world that, at least on the face of it, are problematic for theism—such as the existence of evil. "What we know about our own world is that it is replete

2. See Flórez, "Peirce's Theory"; Wilson, *Consilience*; Niiniluoto, "Hintikka and Whewell on Aristotelian Induction."

3. W. Davis, *Peirce's Epistemology*, 22.

4. For this approach, see Polkinghorne, "New Natural Theology." For a good study of Polkinghorne's approach, see Irlenborn, "Konsonanz von Theologie und Naturwissenschaft?"

with hideous suffering and death." His analysis of this point is important: he indicates the problems in trying to quantify the goodness of our cosmos. Yet what I find especially interesting about Taliaferro's approach is that its logic parallels that of "inference to the best explanation," now generally regarded as the dominant philosophical account of scientific explanation. This approach recognizes that observations are susceptible to multiple explanations, requiring us to develop criteria that allow us to decide which of those explanatory theories might be the "best," yet not requiring us to *prove* that it is right.

Taliaferro uses such a strategy in determining which competing explanation—such as theism or naturalism—offers the best account of what we experience and observe. "A good cosmos is explained *better* on the grounds of theism than on the grounds of (strict or broad) naturalism" (my emphasis). This approach is productive and moves us away from some of the more problematic aspects of older forms of natural theology, which rested on criteria of provability that could not be met in practice. As Taliaferro points out, philosophers nowadays "rarely use the language of 'proof' in almost any domain of philosophy outside of formal logic."

I also appreciated Taliaferro's recognition that more rational approaches to natural theology need to be supplemented by an appeal to religious experience. He rightly notes the ways in which both Eleonore Stump and Marilyn McCord Adams have appealed to the experience of God's presence amid suffering in addressing the problem of evil for theism. This welcome point is made briefly and needs amplification. For example, we might think of C. S. Lewis's celebrated—if often misrepresented—"argument from desire," which begins from the natural human experience of yearning for something that appears to be unattainable, and proceeds to offer three "explanations" of this experience. On the basis of his analysis, Lewis concludes that the best of these explanations is the theistic framework offered by Christianity.[5]

My own view is that this approach is a legitimate form of natural theology and that it has considerable apologetic potential. It can certainly be seen as located within the broad spectrum of possible approaches to natural theology, in that it represents a natural human reflection on a natural experience, which points toward—though in itself does not prove—that this experience *originates from* God and *leads to* God. The approach is productive apologetically, in that it engages a common human experience and argues that it is explained by a Christian theological framework, the benefits of which are not limited

---

5. See Lewis, *Mere Christianity*, 135–37. Lewis's theological framework includes a teleological account of human nature. See also McGrath, "Arrows of Joy."

to the kind of rational explanations developed by William Paley in the early nineteenth century but include a transformation of human experience.

Taliaferro's frustration arising from the limits imposed on him by the stipulated length of his article is clear and entirely understandable. Yet he was able to sketch some promissory notes of how his approach might be developed further, all of which clearly illuminate the potential of his approach to natural theology. A purely rational natural theology is imaginatively barren, aesthetically sterile, and experientially deficient. The approach that Taliaferro develops has rich potential. Yet I end with a question: Does not Taliaferro's project of natural theology, as he develops this in the later stages of this paper, implicitly subvert his own opening declaration that natural theology is "philosophical reflection on God based on reasoning that does not rely on revelation"? This, I must make clear, would not be a problem.

As I appreciatively followed Taliaferro's unfolding exposition of the nature and scope of natural theology, I sensed it was leading us into an expanded vision of this enterprise with the potential for further development. The "reasoning" in question does not require being limited to cool rationalism but can enfold more imaginative and aesthetic approaches, capable of connecting with human beings at multiple levels. Natural theology can be rational; yet it can also transcend the limits of reason, opening up a richer vision of our world, which challenges the reductive distortions of materialism and scientism.

Deflationary Response

PAUL K. MOSER

C harles Taliaferro outlines a case for natural theology in support of God's existence on the basis of abduction, or inference to a best available explanation. His case is straightforward, but I contend that it does not take us to a God worthy of worship of the kind found in traditional monotheism.

Taliaferro's Natural Theology

According to Taliaferro, "natural theology is the philosophical reflection on God based on reasoning that does not rely on revelation (or revealed theology). Unlike revealed theology, which may presuppose the truth or reliability of the Christian Bible, natural theology develops a philosophy of God based on observations about the cosmos, pursuing questions about the nature of the cosmos, its origin, and its continuation." We should add that typically natural theology goes on to claim that its case for God is *recommended by natural evidence and reason.* The latter claim, however, invites considerable controversy about what our natural evidence and reason actually support regarding God. I contend that the alleged support from natural theology is less compelling than many advocates of natural theology claim.

Taliaferro finds two improvements in natural theology since the eighteenth century:

> First, philosophers rarely advance what they describe as a proof or disproof of the existence of God; in fact, philosophers rarely use the language of "proof" in almost any domain of philosophy outside of formal logic. Instead, chastened

by centuries of criticism, philosophers now are more ready to refer to good (or cogent or persuasive or sound) arguments or arguments that are poor or weak. Second, while natural theology today is still practiced without relying on the authority of sacred texts, many proponents of natural theology include an appeal to the evidential role of religious experience. . . . Without natural theology, inquiry into the Bible's credibility is hampered.

These two developments are indeed important because they promise to add plausibility to natural theology. Even so, it is an open question whether they are adequate to make natural theology successful in its case for God. We shall see that the result is far from compelling in favor of natural theology.

Taliaferro recommends that natural theology proceed on the basis of explanatory considerations. He claims: "The best way to practice natural theology is through what is commonly called 'abduction.' One should compare what one has some reason to believe are promising worldviews (theism, naturalism, British Idealism, etc.) and then evaluate their internal coherence and their explanatory power." In addition, he narrows the field of competitors as follows: "I think the two most promising worldviews are classical theism (in the perfect-being theological tradition) and a form of naturalism. The burden of my approach is to provide reasons for thinking that classical theism is more reasonable because it has greater explanatory power than naturalism." He claims that "theism provides a successful answer to . . . big questions" about the origin of the cosmos.

Taliaferro defends a cosmological argument and a teleological argument to make his case for theism. He begins with a large concession about his cosmological argument: "Let us straightaway note that the cosmological argument (in most versions) does not give us reason to believe that the necessarily existing being responsible for the existence and continuation of the cosmos has all the divine attributes (this being might or might not be omniscient). . . . Theism, rather, is employed to explain why there is a contingent cosmos at all and why it continues to exist." It seems right that a typical cosmological argument does not yield omniscience in its first cause. Omniscience in the cause is not needed to explain the empirical phenomena of the natural world we experience. Likewise, perfect moral goodness in the cause is not needed. We shall see that the latter consideration raises a serious problem for a cosmological argument.

Taliaferro suggests a further retreat from a cosmological argument for the God of traditional monotheism: "A defender of the argument can develop it simply as making a case for the cosmos having a necessarily existing cause while conceding (if only for the sake of argument) that it could be that God (if there is a God) does not necessarily exist. The defense could take the shape of asking us to put off claims about God versus the cosmos and focus on whether it is reasonable to believe that a contingent cosmos just exists without some transcendent, necessarily existing reality." This is a *logically* available option, of course, but it is unclear why it is emerging in a discussion of natural *theology*. If God drops out of the first cause, that cause will not yield a natural theology even if it figures in a broad metaphysics. The following option likewise falls short of a natural theology: "After reaching the conclusion that there is some necessarily existing reality sustaining the cosmos, one might only then take up the question of whether such a necessarily existing reality might be God." Our best explanatory answer to the latter question may not rely on God at all; at least, we now have no reason to suppose otherwise.

Taliaferro recommends that natural theology focus not just on a first cause of nature but also on the evidence for a "good cosmos." He remarks: "At the base of the teleological argument presented here is the thesis that the cosmos is, overall, good: stable laws of nature have allowed there to be galaxies, stars, and planets—including our own, which has been the site for the emergence of life, including the conscious lives of self-aware persons capable of moral life and practice. As with the earlier cosmological argument, the thesis is that such a good cosmos is explained better on the grounds of theism than on the grounds of (strict or broad) naturalism." An immediate issue concerns what kind of "goodness" figures in this claim about the explanatory power of theism. Goodness comes in different kinds, such as moral, prudential, and aesthetic goodness; inquirers will need to know which kinds are relevant to the alleged explanatory power of theism. Otherwise, they will be unclear about how, if at all, the alleged goodness of the cosmos fits with the goodness of *God*. The argument needs to plug this gap in a compelling way for it to succeed.

Taliaferro asks: "Despite all the evident suffering, pain, and death, isn't it still (overall) good that the cosmos exists? Or, putting things a bit differently, isn't it better that the cosmos exists rather than not exist?" This is a rhetorical question, but it is too quick to gain explanatory traction. Is it concerned with moral "goodness" and "betterness," or instead with some other kind of goodness, such as aesthetic goodness? Perhaps a mixture of kinds of goodness is relevant. In any case, we are at a loss to undertake a stable assessment in the absence of conceptual clarity about the relevant kind of goodness here.

Taliaferro claims: "On a cosmic scale, theism supplies an account of why there is an (overall) good cosmos rather than not. The goodness of the cosmos is one reason why it exists rather than not exist, because it is created and sustained by a good Creator. Naturalism (as we have seen in the cosmological argument) does not offer such an account." The key claim is that "the goodness of the cosmos is one reason why it exists rather than not exist," and the support offered is as follows: "because it is created and sustained by a good Creator." I fail see how one can use the previous support in a teleological argument without begging the key question at hand, namely, the question of whether the cosmos is "created and sustained by a good Creator." Inquirers who are wondering whether the cosmos depends on a good Creator will not be convinced by the claim that the cosmos "is created and sustained by a good Creator." If, however, the latter claim will not serve as evidential support now, the question arises of what claim *does* adequately support Taliaferro's affirmation that "the goodness of the cosmos is one reason why it exists rather than not exist." The answer is not clear at all, and therefore we do not have a compelling teleological argument here.

The key issue now is not whether the cosmos is good in various ways. It includes some moral goodness, prudential goodness, and aesthetic goodness, among other kinds of goodness. At least we can grant this for the sake of argument. The issue is whether the goodness of the cosmos somehow *confirms the reality of a good God*, particularly a God who is worthy of worship and thus perfectly good. Clearly, the cosmos overall is not perfectly good, even if it is good in many ways. The bad features of the cosmos should be obvious to any capable person who observes carefully. It is hard to calculate, however, whether the cosmos is, on balance, good, and I know of no way to provide a convincing calculation here.

If the actual observable features of the cosmos are our basis for an explanatory inference to a source, we should have our inference accommodate the observable mixed features, the good and the bad. It would beg important questions to ignore either side of the mix. If we seek the source of the observable good and ascribe it to the reality of a good God, we will have to consider ascribing the source of the observable bad to the reality of a bad God—perhaps a God who has good *and* bad features as the source of the cosmos. At least, we will need a good reason not to infer a mixed God as reflected in the good and the bad mixed in the cosmos. We show an unconvincing partiality if we favor an inference that attends only to the good features of the cosmos. Such partiality will undermine the cogency of an inference to a good God who is free of bad features. Inquirers can properly ask for evidence that blocks an analogous inference to a God who has bad features.[1]

---

1. A similar line of concern bears on Taliaferro's following inference (above) from consciousness: "The basic claim is that theism is in a better position to account for consciousness rather

Familiar cosmological and teleological arguments fail to confirm the reality of a God who is worthy of worship and thus perfectly morally good. They thus fail to confirm the reality of the perfectly good God acknowledged by Jesus. Some philosophers may not be troubled by this limitation, but it does raise a question for Christian advocates of natural theology: How can one reasonably move from natural theology, given its shortcoming regarding worthiness of worship, to the morally perfect God acknowledged by Jesus? Some additional kind of evidence is needed, but it will not come from the natural theology on offer.

Beyond Natural Theology

Taliaferro seeks a combination of sources to bolster his case for Christian theism. He writes: "From my perspective, I think that the best case for Christian theism needs to draw on *both* natural and revealed theology, just as it needs to draw on both reflection on contingency and religious experience." We have noted that the arguments outlined by Taliaferro do not by themselves confirm the reality of a God worthy of worship. So, we might propose, as does Taliaferro, that those arguments should be supplemented by "revealed theology" and "religious experience." The plot thickens here, however, because we need to know *which* revealed theology will serve *and* how, if at all, that theology can earn its keep from an evidential point of view. Somehow "religious experience" might be factored in, but *which* religious experience? *And* how, if at all, will it supply needed evidence for a God worthy of worship? We lack answers to these pressing questions: in the absence of answers, a case for the Christian God will fail.

I have suggested, in my own chapter and other responses in this book, that the apostle Paul acknowledges a role for religious experience of divine love and its leading power in grounding faith and hope in God and thus in saving them from the "disappointment" of wishful thinking (see Rom. 5:5; 8:14). It is doubtful, however, that Paul's position needs to rely on arguments from natural theology, whether cosmological, teleological, or ontological arguments. I see no reason to suppose that it does. In addition, we find no evidence of Paul using such arguments.

Instead of turning to questionable philosophical arguments, Paul asks: "Do you not realize that God's kindness is meant to lead you to repentance?" (Rom.

---

than naturalism. The reason for this is that theism contends that God is a conscious reality (a divine mind, as it were), and so it accounts for the existence of contingent, conscious, minded beings in light of a greater conscious mind."

2:4 NRSVue). He does not suggest any need for a cosmological, teleological, or ontological argument to support his endorsement of God's kindness on the basis of religious experience. This saves him from relying on a questionable argument that distracts attention from the important religious experience of God's distinctive character. One can use abduction to support a claim that such an experience comes from God (instead of, say, oneself), but this would not return us to a dubious cosmological, teleological, or ontological argument.

My chapter in this book takes exception to a suggestion that Paul relies on an argument of natural theology in Romans 1. According to his remarks in Romans 1, *God* shows (some) people God, if at times through nature as a medium. Contrary to some proponents of natural theology, Paul does not say or suggest that nature by itself, as a *purely natural fact*, shows us God or grounds an argument for God's existence. It would be misleading, then, to assign a cosmological argument or a teleological argument to Paul. It would also be misleading to suggest that he needs to rely on such an argument.

Paul thinks of God as *self-manifesting* to people, perhaps in conscience, with the divine goodness of God's distinctive moral character (cf. Rom. 10:20 and Isa. 65:1). In this perspective, God *self-authenticates* God's reality for receptive humans, owing to God's presentation of God's distinctive good character in human experience, including the moral experience of conscience. So, the controversial arguments of natural theology fall away as unnecessary, and that is a benefit. Humans can suppress or ignore divine presence in their moral experience because God does not function by the divine coercion of human wills. Even so, the evidence of divine goodness can be *available* for people suitably receptive, for those with "eyes . . . to see" and "ears . . . to hear" (Mark 8:18 NRSVue). Such people are willing to cooperate with divine goodness in a way that allows it to come to fruition in their lives, for the sake of extending God's kingdom of righteous love. If we resist such cooperation, God can properly hide from us until we are ready to treat divine evidence as God intends it to be treated.[2]

In conclusion, then, I recommend that we avoid commitment to the troubled, unnecessary, and distracting arguments of traditional natural theology. I also recommend that we return the focus to the apostle Paul's appreciation of religious and moral experience of God's distinctive character of perfect goodness. Philosophy and theology will benefit as a result.

---

2. For elaboration of this approach, see Moser, *God Relationship*; Moser, *Understanding Religious Experience*.

Barthian Response

JOHN C. McDOWELL

Some thinkers might wonder whether letting the genie out of the rational evidentialist bottle results in nothing getting done by an idle "god of the philosophers" (Pascal's term) who cannot feed the hungry or clothe the poor or be worthy of worship. "Argument," Theodor Adorno claims, "is consistently bourgeois."[1] But this can be a somewhat disingenuous response. Considering the nature of a thing's existence, and developing publicly accountable arguments concerning it, is philosophically important. For instance, a historian asking about Jesus's existence does not lead directly to a Jesus worthy of being followed by disciples. In fact, certain ways of worrying about the rational inquiry, or appealing to the rational basicness of belief in "God," can themselves appear to be evasions from taking seriously the integrity of truth claims concerning beliefs and the trustworthiness of those who make them. Such approaches claiming theological rationality make it possible to understand the sense behind Norman Malcolm's comment, albeit he was speaking specifically of those who pursue legitimacy behind arguments for God's existence, that they "make up the rules as they go along, in accordance with their inclinations. Since there are different inclinations, there is no agreed-upon right or wrong in this kind of reasoning."[2]

The reference to a reasoner's "inclinations" here is significant. Charles Taliaferro recognizes that "the debate over the coherence of theism seems to me to be profoundly affected by one's background beliefs."[3] This observation

1. In Adorno and Horkheimer, *Towards a New Manifesto*, 73.
2. Malcolm, "Is It a Religious Belief That 'God Exists'?," 108.
3. Taliaferro, "Possibility of God," 252.

could enable the theist to recognize why theistic arguments, in practice, tend to be uncompelling to those who read the "evidence" differently. Taliaferro's chapter, at least, displays a sensibly chastened sense of the potential success of an explanatory theistic case: consequently he avoids talk of "proofs" in favor of a best-case tactic. Even so, he displays considerable confidence that the theistic case still offers a better explanation than does naturalism. It is, he says, "a successful answer" to the question of the origins of the universe, consciousness, and so on.

Others may press the notion of the successfulness of the apparently "more reasonable" explanation that possesses "greater explanatory power." Taliaferro, Richard Swinburne, and others have spoken of theism as the "simplest explanation," and consequently the most rationally compelling one.[4] First, if it is the most convincing explanation, then an honest explanation, beyond the haste for apologetic advocacy as to why it is that more than a good few philosophers find it distinctly uncompelling, would need to be provided. Taliaferro, however, dispenses with the likes of David Hume and Immanuel Kant far too effortlessly, with a swift set of strokes of the keyboard, even though arguments from their oeuvre reappear among, and are redeveloped by, contemporary philosophers skeptical of the soundness of theist arguments. They are neatly dismissed "due to flaws in . . . [their] philosophical methodologies": end of story! Yet John Bishop, for instance, maintains that, for many philosophers, the "evidence" for theism is simply ambiguous and inconclusive: "Arguably, all the evidence admissible under our widest evidential practice is equally coherently interpretable both under the assumption of theism and under the assumption of atheist-naturalism."[5]

Second, Taliaferro's case is set alongside what he deems to be the unpersuasiveness of "naturalism." Several issues are worth raising here. For instance, there is a distinct lack of textual engagement with, or "disciplined attentiveness" to, those who argue for the competing perspective. Consequently, the presented case takes on something of an air of a "trust me about naturalism: it fails to explain matters as well as theism does."[6] Moreover, the term "naturalism" is used as a grammatical singular and, therefore, the different types of naturalism are subsumed under one instance. Early in his chapter, Taliaferro refers to considering "the comparative explanatory power of theism and broad naturalism"; yet the instance that is paired with theism as its competitor is quite particular: "the most extreme form of naturalism,

4. See Swinburne, *Existence of God*, 23–72; Swinburne, "Philosophical Theism," 10.
5. Bishop, "Evidence," 177.
6. Citation from Lash, *Easter in Ordinary*, 13.

sometimes called *scientism* or *strict naturalism*." The only other mention of naturalism that is composed of more than a singular and dismissive reference to how it is less compelling than theism comes with a citation from a pop philosophy book by Alex Rosenberg, hardly the most rigorous study to tackle; it too is waved away with the rhetorical swipe of terms, regarding it to be "in preposterous conflict with what everyone knows." Presumably if Rosenberg does not know "what everyone knows," then the supposed common sense may be less reasonable than this rhetoric supposes. Yet Evan Gales claims, "An initial difficulty that faces any discussion of naturalism is that there is surprisingly little agreement over just what naturalism is. Many different positions have been characterized as naturalistic, and it would be tendentious to bestow special status to any one of these."[7] Perhaps some family resemblances can be described, but this claim should itself be the fruit of a demonstration in its turn. Unless Taliaferro's account engages in a thicker description, then an unsympathetic critic may be inclined to suggest that, after all, the comparative case is not to be trusted without further substantive work being done.

Third, talk of the "simplest explanation" is arguably rationally fragile. After all, more complicated explanations are not necessarily irrational, and occasionally the simplest explanation is more complicated than it looks. A creationist, with a pop-up version of the original appearance of creatures, may lay claim to offering the simplest explanation, especially in the light of the significant explanatory complications with an evolutionary account, compounded by the variations in, and scientific disagreements between, evolutionary biologies. Galileo Galilei had to counter a seemingly simpler explanation of how things appeared to be to the immediacy of sight, and his ability to do so was largely dependent on a specialist piece of equipment. Is "God" a simple explanation anyway? It is commonly objected, Robin Collins argues, that "theism explains what is puzzling about the world by hypothesizing a reality that is even more puzzling."[8] Given the complications in overusing "God" as an explanatory item, how are the theistic arguments any better off? Considerable intellectual work needs to be done to convince skeptics that the existence-explaining "God" is not a "god of the gaps," a believer's deus ex machina who saves the day when reason gets itself stuck, a vacuous "placeholder for an explanation."[9]

This, however, is not what so-called Barthians would find most intellectually interesting and most contestable. When working carefully with Barth's critique

7. Gales, "Naturalism and Physicalism," 121.
8. R. Collins, "Naturalism," 194.
9. Nagel, *Last Word*, 132–33. Nagel does admit that his verdict may be due to "my inadequate understanding of religious concepts" (76).

of the *theologia naturalis*, in the context of his theology it is fairly clear that it is not theological *argument* as such that bothers him. After all, the expansive *Church Dogmatics* engages in substantive argument, most evident in the richly detailed small-print sections. Likewise, it is not rationality that worries him, as if the theologian's task is to employ skills that bypass rational reflection. To claim, for instance, that Barth's theology is homiletic rather than theo-*logical* is to exhibit a disturbingly unreasonable failure to pay attention to his oeuvre. For instance, in *Church Dogmatics* I/1 he explains at length the *wissenschaftliche* quality of theology, in critical response to the tendency among those like Rudolf Bultmann, who reduce its claims to articulations of "faith." Moreover, it is not even that the theologian might engage in public conversation that is at issue, as if the theologian were directed away from speaking positively about matters that do not have their *Sitz im Leben* in specific church signs and symbols (such as the "natural world," cultural artifacts, and so on). Barth's work is full of examples of philosophers from and against whom he learned to clarify certain issues (for example, the German Idealist tradition on divine mystery). My chapter has drawn attention to his theological setting of all things within a theo-*logical* hermeneutic, referring to them as "parables" or "little lights." Barth's rejection of natural theology is not done in the name of the transcendence of God, if by that is imagined a differentiation from divine immanence that is not sufficiently capacious to speak of God as the ground and grammar of all things. Far too much ink continues to be spilled over a sloppy caricature of Barth, and these really are now of only academic interest among those who care about such things to deal with them with any patience.

Matters become interesting, instead, when the *substance* of Barth's concern is considered. His rejection of natural theology was made, instead, on the grounds of a concern for a well-ordered sense of the God who is immanent to God's elect creatures. This matter can be opened up through a somewhat heavy-handed contrast drawn by Nicholas Lash: "The mood of apologetics is assertive, rather than interrogative. The apologist sets out to teach rather than to learn, to prove or refute rather than to enquire, to give rather than to receive. Academic theology, on the other hand, as I understand it, is—or should be—fundamentally interrogative in character. . . . The theologian's . . . responsibilities are critical, interpretive or clarificatory rather than declaratory."[10]

The implication is that the apologist can make seriously substantive theological mistakes in the sophistic haste to advocate a rhetorically compelling

10. Lash, *Matter of Hope*, 5.

argument. Among those mistakes, D. Z. Phillips argues, is the one of theology proper. He proclaims that "dominant trends in the subject [of philosophy of religion] today distort and confuse the grammar of 'God.'"[11] This critique suggests that even though the philosophers of religion in question continue to use language of "God" and may even inhabit overlapping liturgical contexts for their practice, it is crucial to pay attention to differences in theological grammar, to how "God" functions.[12]

For Barth, and here his own reading is problematic, Thomas Aquinas reduced God to "being." Even if we were to capitalize this as "Being," the issue remains that of what happens to theological grammar when God and creatures are drawn onto a single ontological plane. While Thomas F. Torrance occasionally hints at his sharing Barth's concern with an interpretation of Aquinas post-Cajetan and post-Suárez, he sees the threat as one that permeates the dualistic tendencies of the Greeks.[13] It is this that blossoms in early modernity. Colin Gunton's concern in this regard is predominantly with Ockham and others.[14] The point is that through the disagreements over who may be responsible for modernities' theological reductionisms, there is a shared concern specifying that the theism of modern philosophy of religion inhabits just such an ontological framework. The apprehension is far from limited to so-called Barthians. Catholic philosopher David Burrell, for instance, proclaims, "Without a clear philosophical means of distinguishing God from the world, the tendency of all discourse about divinity is to deliver a God who is the 'biggest thing around.' That such is the upshot of much current philosophy of religion cannot be doubted." Consequently, he continues, "the current surge of interest in philosophy of religion may ill-serve religion."[15]

Among the genealogical accounts in this vein, some more intellectually sophisticated than others, it is worth mentioning Amos Funkenstein's thesis: "Medieval theology in most of its varieties" was so concerned to protect "God" from any traces of projection from finitude that "not only physical predicates, but also general abstract predicates such as goodness, truth, power, and even existence were at times considered an illicit form of speech when predicated of God and his creation univocally."[16] In early modernity, Funkenstein argues,

11. Phillips, "God and Grammar," 1.
12. "You cannot be guaranteed to be doing Christian theology," Denys Turner warns, "just because you quote Scripture and use a lot of Christian theological terms" (*Faith, Reason and the Existence of God*, 46). After all, "there are plenty of Christian idolaters."
13. See Torrance, *Ground and Grammar of Theology*, 79.
14. See Gunton, "The Trinity, Natural Theology, and a Theology of Nature," 96; *Promise of Trinitarian Theology*, 41.
15. Burrell, *Faith and Freedom*, 4–5.
16. Funkenstein, *Theology and the Scientific Imagination*, 25.

the shift into forms of univocal predication took root in the philosophical imagination. "I do not necessarily mean that the seventeenth-century thinkers always claimed to know more about God than medieval theologians. To some of them, God remained a *deus absconditus* about whom little can be known. What I mean to say is that they claimed what they knew about God, be it much or little, to be precise, 'clear and distinct' ideas."[17] As a result, what is meant by "God" begins to shift in its sense, in its terms of reference. Therefore, Funkenstein laments, "How much more deadly to theology were such helpers than its enemies!"[18] It is precisely this kind of criticism that is developed by Michael Buckley in his genealogy of modern atheism, and in William Placher's claim that "some of our current protests, it turns out, should not be directed against the Christian tradition, but against what modernity did to it."[19] The early modern tradition comes to generate its own denials. Lash summarizes Buckley's argument:

> During the seventeenth and eighteenth centuries, the word "god" came to be used to name the ultimate explanation of the system of the world. And, when it was in due time realised that the system of the world was such as not to require any such single, overarching, independent, explanatory principle, the word "god" was dispensed with, and modern "atheism" was born. . . . In a nutshell, my argument will be that "gods" which, before modernity, were understood to be whatever people worshipped, became, instead, beings of a particular kind—a "divine" kind, we might say.[20]

According to Phillips, "It is obvious, or should be, that in any theistic context, everything depends on what is meant by 'God.'"[21] In responding to this, a sophisticated and attentive hermeneutics is required. After all, Phillips rhetorically asks, "How is one to tell the difference between genuine religious or theological differences and confusion if not by drawing out the implications of our words and their surroundings?"[22] It is crucial that theo-discourses understand what kind of claims they are making, and what the setting or language game is for them to take the shape they have. By "language game" is meant, here, not different linguistic performances that are hermetically sealed off against each other, but the linguistic and interpretive contexts and practices

---

17. Funkenstein, *Theology and the Scientific Imagination*, 25.
18. Funkenstein, *Theology and the Scientific Imagination*, 8.
19. Placher, *Domestication of Transcendence*, 2; cf. Buckley, *At the Origins of Modern Atheism*.
20. Lash, *Holiness, Speech and Silence*, 9.
21. Phillips, "God and Grammar," 1.
22. Phillips, "God and Grammar," 7.

whose overlap cannot be assumed in advance of attending to their concrete particularities, and with which hard contextual work is required to ascertain where there may be fitting critical conversational possibility. This entails that when different linguistic contexts use similar terms, such as "God," those terms may *not necessarily be doing the same kind of work*. At the very least, here it is worth asking—in spite of the assumptions of philosophy-of-religion textbooks—are Anselm and Descartes, Aquinas and Swinburne, and so on, engaged in the same intellectual task? Only deep exegetical and contextual attention to their texts can establish and sustain the textbook presumption that simply because they use similar terms, they are deploying similar forms of argument. If it quacks like a duck, waddles like a duck, but lives only in deserts and eats sand, then it may very well not be a duck. Scholars of the medievals certainly encourage serious questions to be asked regarding this lazy textbook method. It is in this critical hermeneutics of theological claims, and only here, that Vladimir Lossky's use of the rhetoric of "the God of the philosophers" and "the God of the Hebrew patriarchs" has its place.[23]

The contrast between this and the theo-grammatical protocols of the tradition is stark. In the fifteenth century, when Nicholas of Cusa argues that God is the "maximal," he denies he means by this that God is the maximum. God is beyond such categories—beyond, in fact, any and every category.[24] Yet, under the broad theological modification that began to occur in the seventeenth century, "God" instead becomes the *maximum* of being: the apex of being in metaphysics functioning from univocal ontological assumptions and differing from everything only "in degree rather than in kind."[25] This, when couched through further descriptions of this "God's" beneficence, sets the terms for rational creatures' sense of well-being. But it could take the kind of imposing existence that diminishes creatures, such as we find in the critical analysis of Ludwig Feuerbach within which creatures, one could say, are minimized by the maximum, the many by the One. Accordingly, Placher argues, "Rather than explaining how all categories break down when applied to God, [certain early modern philosophers] . . . set the stage for talking about transcendence as one of the definable properties god possesses."[26] So when Taliaferro speaks of his "assuming God (*ex hypothesi*) is a substantial reality or subject who would (if God exists) be referred to as one of the 'things' that exists," the pressure from the genealogical account is how the *esse* of "God" is being characterized, and how this envisages itself as in any way continuous with the pronounced

23. Lossky, *Orthodox Theology*, 17–27.
24. Nicholas of Cusa, *On Learned Ignorance*.
25. Placher, *Domestication of Transcendence*, 181.
26. Placher, *Domestication of Transcendence*, 7.

apophaticism of the ancient Christian traditions.[27] Similar pressure needs to be exerted when he speaks of "God" as "a nonphysical reality," or of God as personal, which requires "a more immanent view of God," and so on.[28] Here Swinburne recognizes "the Barthian objection that philosophical theism has too anthropomorphic a view of God," but he entirely misses the substantive *ontological* point being made when he asserts that "the Christian view of God is in crucial respects anthropomorphic: . . . God is like man because man is like God."[29] The issue is not whether anthropomorphic language identifies "God" or not, since *all* language about God is under erasure. Nicholas of Cusa (familiarly known as Cusanus) would be as deeply disturbed by the nonanalogical application of the theistic concepts of omnipotence, and so on, to God, as if these abstract categories theologically fare better than those speaking of God as a sitting, walking, talking, watching, touching, sorrowing, suffering, angering, responding, changeable, commanding, personal being.

Lash explains, "As Christians, we can dispense with theism. . . . I am not suggesting, however, that theism should be contradicted, but rather that we try to avoid falling into the trap of accepting some of the assumptions on which it is constructed."[30] The point of my own critical analysis is not to seclude theological claims from exposure to appropriate critical testing and even to intellectual ridicule, or to subvert the need for the fittingness of rational "order and clarity" in belief.[31] It is not an exercise in closing theological claims to publicly rational accountability and responsibility, or of refusing to keep the question of contingency open for rational enquiry, allowing reason's "resting in a full stop of 'just thereness.'"[32] Instead, it is an effort to open up for theological examination Taliaferro's "successful answer" and to indicate why Barth and a good many others would subject its most banally determinate assumptions with regard to "God" and the statement "God exists" to the most exacting of *theological* interrogations. After all, "part of the theologian's responsibility is to help discipline the propensity of the pious imagination to simplify facts, texts, demands, and requirements that are resistant to any such simplification."[33]

27. Taliaferro, "Project of Natural Theology," 11.
28. Taliaferro, "Personal," 104.
29. Swinburne, "Philosophical Theism," 12; cf. Swinburne, *Coherence of Theism*, 1.
30. Lash, *Easter in Ordinary*, 103.
31. MacIntyre, *Difficulties in Christian Belief*, 82.
32. Turner, *Faith, Reason and the Existence of God*, 258.
33. Lash, *Easter in Ordinary*, 290–91.

A Contemporary Reply

CHARLES TALIAFERRO

I n terms of authors probably best known by most readers of this book, my position is in line with C. S. Lewis, who advocated philosophical arguments for theism (famously an argument from reason in *Miracles* and a moral argument in *Mere Christianity*) that complemented his appeal to experience (especially our longing for joy and the numinous experience of the divine, imaginatively featured in the experience of Aslan in Narnia).[1] Lewis's position has deep roots. There is biblical support for the natural theology he practiced (Ps. 19:1–4; Acts 17:26–27; Rom. 1:19–20, 32; 2:14–15) and strong advocacy of his natural theology among early Christian philosophical theologians (Aristides, Justin Martyr, Tertullian, Athanasius, Gregory of Nazianzus, Gregory of Nyssa) and among many early and contemporary Eastern Orthodox theologians.[2] I have argued elsewhere that the Anglican legacy of advocating natural theology has had an important role in helping people appreciate the goodness of creation—with important implications for environmental stewardship and in fostering a collaborative relationship between religion and science.[3] In light of this last point, I suggest that natural theology has an important role, not just for the practice and history of philosophy or for Christian apologetics but also in terms of how we live and approach the environment.

1. See MacSwain and Ward, *Cambridge Companion to C. S. Lewis*, especially the introduction and chaps. 6–9.
2. See Haines, *Natural Theology*; Bradshaw and Swinburne, *Natural Theology in the Eastern Orthodox Tradition*.
3. See Taliaferro, "Three Elements of Creation Care."

Response to Andrew Pinsent

In addition to his many academic degrees, honors, and publications, Andrew Pinsent is a Roman Catholic priest. So this might be an appropriate place to further acknowledge my debt in terms of a positive view of natural theology to a Roman Catholic clergyman: the great twentieth-century philosopher Frederick Copleston (1907–1994). In my view, Copleston's masterful appeal to natural theology in debate (especially with Bertrand Russell) and his magisterial work on the history of philosophy remain unsurpassed philosophically.

I have learned much from work by Pinsent. In this context, his observation about how some explanations can take the shape of a funnel is illuminating. I love his appreciation for children's curiosity (asking *Pourquoi?*). Maybe he is right about quantum events seeming causeless, but I have yet to find compelling reason to deny *ex nihilo nihil fit* (nothing comes from nothing) or that events occur in our cosmos with no cause or explanation whatever.[4] Perhaps wrongly, I persist in thinking that the existence and endurance of our contingent cosmos calls for an account involving a necessarily existing causally efficacious being (more on the cosmological argument below).

As for what is self-evident, I do think that $1 + 1 = 2$ is self-evident, given that it is an instance of the law of identity: 2 is simply $1 + 1$, so the proposition in question ($1 + 1 = 2$) is that $1 + 1$ is the same as $1 + 1$. I suggest that the logical laws of identity (A is A) and noncontradiction (A is not not-A) are indispensable for thinking and language, and I would go so far as to claim that they cannot be understood without being believed. The reason why it is so horrifying in George Orwell's novel *1984* that the character Winston is subject to forces bent on getting him to assent to $2 + 2 = 5$ is that if he embraces such an evident absurdity (for there is no possible world in which $2 + 2 = 5$), he is utterly broken, a cognitive zombie. Contra Pinsent, stores that offer something more after you purchase one plus one items is not a counterexample to the mathematical proposition $1 + 1 = 2$. One apple and one apple are two apples, whether or not you get an orange after purchasing them.[5] But the philosophy of mathematics and the issue about what is self-evident are not crucial for the topic of this book, or at least not crucial between Pinsent and myself, since I am not claiming that God's existence is self-evident or that it can be proved or known by us with infallible, incorrigible certainty in this life. Let's check

4. John Cottingham observes, "Quantum theory, for all its impressive success, does not remotely undermine the unshakeable logical maxim '*ex nihilo nihil fit*'" ("Transcending Science," 26–27).

5. Examples of evident necessary truths and impossibilities outside of mathematical propositions are limitless: if there is a red ball, there is a ball; if there is a duck, it is false that there is no duck; etc. For a more in-depth discussion, see Hospers, *Introduction to Philosophical Analysis*.

in later in the next life. (To clarify, I actually believe in the individual survival of death, and so I am not being sarcastic.)

Response to Alister McGrath

I have read the majority of McGrath's published work with great profit. In my view, he is one of the best Christian philosophers today in addressing the relationship between religion and science. His contribution to this volume is outstanding, and his comments on my (comparatively) less-than-elegant contribution are charitable.

Being invited to write more on abduction and various topics is almost irresistible. I shall, however, resist outlining my next project that will do so, except to note that I find that a great deal of philosophy involves aesthetic experience. This is something I explore in two books, coauthored with Jil Evans, an American painter.[6] What I go on to develop will undoubtedly be improved by reading McGrath's past and (I hope) future work. I recommend that after finishing this book, readers do a deep dive into the work of this brilliant philosophical theologian.

Response to Paul Moser

There is much to admire in Paul Moser's work on Christian belief in multiple publications; I have learned a great deal from them. Still, we differ, not in being Christian theists, but on the philosophical credibility of natural theology.

Let me first offer a personal note. At a recent conference I was asked whether individual experiences can shape one's philosophy of religion. Maybe different experiences underlie our divergence.[7] I do not dispute Moser's reading and advocacy of a Pauline account of the knowledge of God and salvation, but my own path to Christianity was less akin to Moser's account of the Pauline route, and more along the lines of C. S. Lewis—a blend of natural and revealed theology—and a kind of numinous experience of Christ as revealed in the Johannine literature, sacramental rites (prayer, meditation, the Eucharist), and the testimony (and witness) of Christians about God's love. Again, I do not dispute the legitimacy of Moser's depiction of making a cognitive submission to the God who is worthy of worship and then finding evidence of the reality of this God in one's agape-centered life. Perhaps many Christian readers of this book have had experiences like Moser, but

6. Taliaferro and Evans, *The Image in Mind: Theism, Naturalism, and the Imagination* and *Is God Invisible? An Essay on Aesthetics and Religion.*

7. I address my coming to Christian faith in Taliaferro, *Love, Love, Love, and Other Essays.*

perhaps some are more akin to Lewis, who first became convinced of the
truth of theism and only then became awestruck by Christian claims about
the incarnation.

On philosophical arguments: when I present an overall case for Christian
theism, I bring together the ontological, cosmological, and teleological arguments (taking into account fine-tuning and the emergence of consciousness),
and a theistic argument from religious experience. As an example, see my
Dialogues about God. Making an overall case for Christian theism takes time
and coordination. So, most versions of the cosmological argument I have defended do not purport to establish all (or even most) of the divine attributes.
The cosmological argument can do some positive work, but other arguments
(or reasons) are needed.[8]

As for specifying the goodness of God, I am in the Christian Platonist
tradition that conceives of God as the highest good, encompassing the moral
and the aesthetic. God is the wondrous, abundant, indestructible source of
creation, and we are called to live in relation with this overwhelmingly sacred reality, worthy of worship in the context of an abiding, never-ending,
transforming life.[9]

A minor note on philosophy and apologetics that may (or may not) be
germane. Moser commends avoiding natural theology and focusing on his
Pauline view of God. Even if Christian apologetics is better served by such a
move, the domain of philosophically reflecting on God and the world without
relying on Scripture remains (in my view) an enduring, exciting, welcoming
undertaking.

Response to John McDowell

I appreciate his passionate call for more work—or, in his phrase, "interrogation"—concerning religious terms and philosophical positions. I have written
multiple books on such matters: religious language, theism, realism, atheism,
naturalism, Hume and Kant.[10] Those looking for nuanced critical attention
and replies to McDowell's remarks/requests for further work can easily find
the books and articles by any standard search engine. Over the last fifteen
years, I have been especially keen to expose the interesting parallels between
the defense of white supremacy by Hume and Kant and their critical dismissal
of miracles and revealed religion.

8. For an excellent recent book, see Loke, *Teleological and Kalam Cosmological Arguments*.
9. See Taliaferro, *The Golden Cord*.
10. See Taliaferro, *Consciousness and the Mind of God* and *The Golden Cord*, along with
Contemporary Philosophical Theology, which I coauthored with Chad Meister.

I wholly part company from McDowell when it comes to assessing the work of D. Z. Phillips and Nicholas Lash. I find the kind of Christianity that they countenance post-Christian. Perhaps many readers embrace their atheistic form of Christianity (or it might be called nontheistic or post-theistic Christianity), but I shall assume this is a minority position. I have critically challenged work by Phillips in multiple places.[11] And I assume, too, that if the natural theology espoused by myself and McGrath, Moser's Pauline philosophy of religion, or Pinsent's understanding of theism have credence, we have reason to reject the atheism of Phillips and Lash.

As these last comments may make clear, the stakes are high when it comes to how Christians today approach natural theology and its alternatives.

11. See, e.g., Taliaferro, "Burning Down the House."

2

A Catholic View

FATHER ANDREW PINSENT

S ince the patristic era, the Catholic faith has acknowledged two kinds of theology, today called "natural" and "supernatural," corresponding to the diverse worlds of discourse about God without and within what is particular to Christian revelation. The Catholic Church also formally defends the teaching that the one true God, Creator, and Lord can be known with certitude by those things which have been made, by the natural light of human reason. Drawing from St. Thomas Aquinas, however, I argue that the deeper distinction of natural and supernatural theology is in terms of subjective understanding, especially the understanding associated with the gift of the Holy Spirit in the life of grace. Progress in natural theology today will need to focus on this difficult topic of understanding, while recognizing that natural theology alone can never bridge the gap between God and ourselves.

The Puzzle of Natural Theology

Consider the following passage: "If, then, God is always in that good state in which we sometimes are, this compels our wonder; and if in a better [state] this compels it yet more. And God is in a better state. And life also belongs to God; for the actuality of thought is life, and God is that actuality; and God's essential actuality is life most good and eternal. We say therefore that God is a living being, eternal, most good, so that life and duration continuous and eternal belong to God; for this is God."[1] Whatever else may be said, this text, from a translation of one of the most famous works of Aristotle, is a reasoned discourse purporting to lead to some conclusions about God that can be expressed in propositions, for example, that God is living, eternal, and most good.

The existence of such arguments, in the works of Aristotle, Plato, Cicero, and many others of the pre-Christian Greco-Roman world, shows that theology is not uniquely about special revelation, let alone the special revelation associated with Judeo-Christian history. Indeed, as Cicero observes,

1. Aristotle, *Metaphysics* 12.7.1072b25–30.

This belief of ours [in the gods] is not based on any prescriptions, custom, or law, but it abides as the strong, unanimous conviction of the whole world. We must therefore come to the realization that gods must exist because we have an implanted, or rather an innate, awareness of them. Now when all people naturally agree on something, that belief must be true; so we are to acknowledge that gods exist. Since this is agreed by virtually everyone—not just philosophers, but also the unlearned—we further acknowledge that we possess what I earlier called an "anticipation" or prior notion of gods.[2]

What is striking in this passage is the claim that even the unlearned as well as the philosophers have some notion of gods, implying that acknowledgment of the gods is like a law of nature. In recent times, Justin Barrett has argued that studies with children suggest that human beings have a strong potential, very easily catalyzed, to believe in God, sometimes along with a range of lesser "gods."[3]

Given these widespread references to divinity, sometimes combined with philosophical reflection, it was clear, fairly early in the history of Christianity, that at least two distinct worlds of theological discourse exist: on one hand, there is reasoning about the special revelation associated with Christ, Scripture, and tradition; on the other hand, there is reasoning, as in the texts above, that lacks special sources.

This distinction has been reinforced by centuries of experience interacting with a vast range of non-Christian cultures, from philosophical discussions of God in the ancient Greco-Roman world to contemporary work with tribes that have pertinent religious traditions even if they lack a written language. As a contemporaneous example, more widely known in recent decades, the Turkana people of northwest Kenya believe in the reality of a supreme being named Akuj, who alone created the world and is in control of the blessings of life. Akuj creates only what is good, although he permits some evils.[4] In this and other cases, monotheism exists alongside a complex range of other religious beliefs; yet Catholic philosophers and missionaries have often found many points of consonance to work upon, filtering and adapting elements of the traditional beliefs while introducing specifically Christian revelation.

Aquinas sets out these distinct but interrelated worlds of discourse as follows: "Now in those things which we hold about God there is truth in two

2. Cicero, *The Nature of the Gods* 1.44.
3. J. Barrett, *Born Believers*.
4. I had the privilege of long conversations with a priest, Anthony Barrett, who spent several years living among the Turkana people. He wrote one of the first dictionaries of their language and an account of their traditional religion. See A. Barrett, *Sacrifice and Prophecy in Turkana Cosmology* and *Turkana-English Dictionary*.

ways. For certain things that are true about God wholly surpass the capabil-
ity of human reason, for instance that God is three and one: while there are
certain things to which even natural reason can attain, for instance that God
is, that God is one, and others like these, which even the philosophers proved
demonstratively of God, being guided by the light of natural reason."[5] In other
words, Aquinas holds that some theological truths, including the existence
and unicity of God, can be known through natural reason alone, but the truth
of the existence of the Trinity, and by implication many other teachings of
revelation, surpass unaided reason.

After Aquinas, these two ways of theological reasoning came gradually to
be described, respectively, as *natural theology*, and what is variously called
theology, without qualification, or *revealed theology*, or *supernatural theology*. By the 1950s, one of the most influential of the neo-Scholastic manuals
introduced theology under the species of *natural* and *supernatural*, noting
that these species differ (1) in their principles of cognition: unaided reason
versus reason illuminated by faith; (2) in their means of cognition: the study
of created things versus divine revelation; and (3) in their formal objects: God
as Creator and Lord versus God as one and three.[6]

The distinction of the formal objects seems easiest to grasp and to use as an
objective standard of demarcation of natural theology vis-à-vis supernatural
theology. Although there are differences of opinion regarding the potential and
actual scope of these formal objects, the Catholic Magisterium has defined
the following minimum. One of the canons of the First Vatican Council in
1870 states, "If anyone shall have said that the one true God, our Creator and
our Lord, cannot be known with certitude by those things which have been
made, by the natural light of human reason, let him be anathema (DZ 1806,
cf. 1785)."[7] In other words, according to this canon, one places oneself outside
the Catholic faith if one denies that it is possible to know by natural reason
alone that there is one true God. This definition makes no judgment about
any specific proofs for the existence of God, or whether there are in fact any
adequate proofs. But the canon does define that the existence of God can be
known with certitude from created things and by the light of natural reason,
placing the existence of God firmly within natural theology. Moreover, by
"God" is meant here "our Creator and our Lord," implying some potentially
knowable natural obligations to God, such as worship and obedience, even
beyond the scope of specific revelation.

5. Aquinas, *Summa contra Gentiles* 1.3.
6. Ott, *Fundamentals of Catholic Dogma*, 1.
7. Denzinger, *Sources of Catholic Dogma*. The "DZ" refers to the Denzinger number, which
is still widely used today as a means of classifying dogmatic declarations.

On the other hand, as noted previously in Aquinas's reference to the Trinity, many teachings of the faith are beyond the scope of natural reason, being directly the result of divine revelation or long debate on the content of revelation, culminating sometimes in formal magisterial definitions. To give some of many examples, the formal definition of the canon of Scripture, the articles of the creed, and the sacramental system fall within the scope of supernatural revelation, even though there are a few points within this list, such as articles in the creed about the existence of God and the crucifixion of Jesus under Pontius Pilate, that are accessible to unaided natural reason as well.

A full list of formal supernatural teachings that have developed from revelation is extremely complex and still growing, due to the ongoing unfolding of the implications of revelation and the interaction of revelation with a diversity of cultural interactions and contingent circumstances. As one of the more sublime examples, belief in the Assumption of the Blessed Virgin Mary body and soul into heaven has been widely believed since patristic times and has long been part of the devotional life and culture of Christendom;[8] in 1950, belief in the Assumption was formally declared to be an official part of the content of the Catholic faith.[9] As one of the more bizarre examples, in response to a pastoral situation in Norway, the Catholic Church in 1241 declared formally that it is not permitted to baptize babies in beer.[10]

Setting aside matters of babies and beer, even some of the most directly supernatural beliefs can, however, present some epistemological challenges to the natural-supernatural distinction. Consider, for instance, the central Christian teaching that Jesus is the Son of God, implying also belief in the incarnation and at least two persons of the Trinity. The angel Gabriel (Luke 1:35), St. Martha (John 11:27), and the apostle Peter (Matt. 16:16) all refer to Jesus as the "Son of God," and Jesus affirms the title when questioned by the high priest at his trial (Mark 14:62). In the case of Peter's declaration, "You are the Christ, the Son of the living God" (Matt. 16:16), Jesus responds, "Flesh and blood has not revealed this to you, but my Father who is in heaven" (Matt. 16:17).[11] In other words, Jesus confirms that Peter has received a divine revelation beyond the natural capacities of flesh and blood,

---

8. Martin Luther preached on the Assumption on August 15, 1522, apparently, at least at this time, taking this belief for granted. See O'Meara, *Mary in Protestant and Catholic Theology*, 118–19.

9. Pope Pius XII, "Apostolic Constitution." Cf. DZ 2331–33 (Denzinger, *Sources of Catholic Dogma*, 647–48).

10. DZ 447 (Denzinger, *Sources of Catholic Dogma*, 178).

11. In this and subsequent Scripture quotations, I cite the Revised Standard Version.

and hence of human reason, setting this revelation firmly within the scope of supernatural theology.

The belief that Jesus is the Son of God is one of the core Catholic teachings, defended in the Nicene-Constantinopolitan Creed by the term *homoousious* (consubstantial) to describe the relationship of the Father and the Son, along with several other statements that are a vestige of the long struggle against Arianism in the fourth century. There seems to be no doubt that this teaching is within and only within supernatural theology. But consider the following passage from the Gospel of Matthew: "And when he came to the other side, to the country of the Gadarenes, two demoniacs met him, coming out of the tombs, so fierce that no one could pass that way. And behold, they cried out, 'What have you to do with us, O Son of God? Have you come here to torment us before the time?'" (Matt. 8:28–29). According to this text, the demoniacs, human persons under the control of demons or evil spirits, call Jesus the "Son of God," an expression of a supernatural revelation that is also used, as noted previously and with minor variations, by the angel Gabriel, St. Martha, and St. Peter.

Of course, there are many ways of interpreting these words, including the strong possibility that these demons are testing or mocking Jesus. But whatever else may be said, it can be assumed that demons, by definition, lack a supernaturally inflamed love of God. Such incidents raise the following Gettier-type question. Is it possible to reason through to correct conclusions about supernatural theology by improper means, including, for example, being in a state that is hostile to God?[12] If so, how should such reasoning be classified vis-à-vis the natural-supernatural distinction when the materials and formal object are supernatural but the principles of cognition and reasoning lack the illumination of faith?

This problem is by no means purely theoretical, given the vast range and diversity of materials in the world related to supernatural revelation that can be cognized and reasoned about objectively by almost anyone. These materials include, principally, the narratives and propositions of Scripture, along with creeds, laws, and church teaching. As a practical example, from the Torah of Judaism to the canon law of the Catholic Church—put on a systematic basis in the high Middle Ages by the creative fusion of revelation, Greek philosophy, and Roman law—vast systems of moral and legal law have been inspired by revelation.[13] If one has access to these laws and their

12. Scripture asserts that demons can engage in natural theology, notably in acknowledging the existence of God (James 2:19).

13. This work also helped to form many of the origins of the Western legal tradition. For an influential account of this history, see, e.g., Berman, *Law and Revolution*.

sources, and can reason about the consequences, is that sufficient to establish that one is doing supernatural theology? In the case of the moral law, Jesus seems to cast doubt on this sufficiency: "Woe to you, scribes and Pharisees, hypocrites! for you tithe mint and dill and cummin, and have neglected the weightier matters of the law, justice and mercy and faith; these you ought to have done, without neglecting the others" (Matt. 23:23). Here Jesus directs criticism at those who do know and can reason about the sources of the law, not by claiming that their reasoning or conclusions are wrong as such, but by arguing that they neglect the "weightier matters." Given that they are reasoning about supernatural materials, however, should the reasoning of the scribes and Pharisees be properly described as natural or supernatural?

As another example of the challenge, what about people who appreciate many of the cultural inspirations of revelation, such as J. S. Bach, *St. Matthew Passion*; Mahler, *Symphony No. 2* (*"Resurrection"*); Mozart, *Requiem*; Monteverdi, *Vespers*; Schubert, *Ave Maria*; Handel's *Messiah*; or, in art, Michelangelo's Sistine Chapel ceiling; or Hubert and Jan van Eyck, *Ghent Altarpiece*; or, in literature, Dante's *Divine Comedy*, a poetic account of every state of the soul from the depths of hell to the heights of heaven? Is the appreciation or the study of such works also a matter of engaging in supernatural theology? Where and how, then, should the distinction be made between natural and supernatural theology?

To explore this question further, it is necessary to examine in more detail what is meant by the natural and supernatural categories by which theology today is qualified, and the implications of these categories for cognition and reasoning. If the cognitive implications of the term "supernatural" and its distinction from what is natural are clarified, it will then be easier to address the Gettier-type issue above, along with the questions of whether and how we should do natural theology.

Naturalis and Supernaturalis

The distinction of natural and supernatural is generally understood today in terms of different orders of beings and causal powers. Given the influence of naturalism, a worldview according to which only nondivine causal powers and laws operate in the world, what is "natural" is generally understood today in terms of nondivine beings and causal powers. On this account, anything that is purportedly due to God or divine action is "supernatural," a position, incidentally, that makes much of the content of theology automatically supernatural.

In the Bampton Lectures of 2019 and in a recently published work, Peter Harrison has, however, drawn attention to the fact that the original meanings of the paired Latin adjectives *naturalis* and *supernaturalis* were rather different from their contemporary meanings.[14] Thanks to the availability of massive digital resources for the works of Aquinas, who made the pairing common-place in theology, I have carried out my own analysis of Aquinas's use of the term *supernaturalis* in some detail.[15]

Across Aquinas's largest and most influential systematic work, the *Summa Theologiae (ST)*, there are around one hundred instances of the word *supernaturalis*, excluding those citing other authors that may not be representative of his own thought.[16] A paradigmatic example is the following passage on the rationale of the theological virtues, which I quote in full due to its importance:

> I answer that, man is perfected by virtue, for those actions whereby he is directed to happiness, as was explained above. Now man's happiness is twofold, as was also stated above. One is proportionate to human nature, a happiness, to wit, which man can obtain by means of his natural principles. The other is a happiness surpassing man's nature, and which man can obtain by the power of God alone, by a kind of participation of the Godhead, about which it is written (2 Pt. 1:4) that by Christ we are made "partakers of the Divine nature." And because such happiness surpasses the capacity of human nature, man's natural principles which enable him to act well according to his capacity, do not suffice to direct man to this same happiness. Hence it is necessary for man to receive from God some additional principles, whereby he may be directed to supernatural happiness, even as he is directed to his connatural end, by means of his natural principles, albeit not without Divine assistance. Such like principles are called "theological virtues": first, because their object is God, inasmuch as they direct us aright to God: second, because they are infused in us by God alone: third, because these virtues are not made known to us, save by Divine revelation, contained in Sacred Scripture.[17]

14. Harrison and Roberts, *Science without God?* Cf. Harrison, "Supernatural Belief in a Secular Age."

15. I used the search tools of the Index Thomisticus, a massive digitization project conceived by Robert Busa and funded largely by IBM, which are now available for anyone to use at www.corpusthomisticum.org/it/index.age.

16. Across all his works, a lexicographical analysis reveals around 306 instances of the term *supernaturalis*, excluding instances in which Aquinas is typically quoting from others, such as paraphrases of Peter Lombard, occurrences in the foil arguments of articles and *sed contra* statements, and florilegia.

17. Aquinas, *Summa Theologiae* I-II.62.1c. "Respondeo dicendum quod per virtutem perficitur homo ad actus quibus in beatitudinem ordinatur, ut ex supradictis patet. Est autem duplex hominis beatitudo sive felicitas, ut supra dictum est. Una quidem proportionata humanae naturae, ad quam scilicet homo pervenire potest per principia suae naturae. Alia autem est beatitudo naturam hominis excedens, ad quam homo sola divina virtute pervenire potest, secundum quandam divinitatis participationem; secundum quod dicitur II Petr. I, quod per Christum facti sumus consortes divinae naturae. Et quia huiusmodi beatitudo proportionem humanae

In this passage, Aquinas makes the comment that the theological virtues are known only through revelation, but he reserves the term "supernatural" to explain their rationale, namely, to direct human beings to supernatural beatitude or happiness (*ad beatitudinem supernaturalem*). In other words, the term *supernaturalis*, in this instance, refers not to God or uncreated matters per se but to a certain divinely bestowed change or transfiguration of created human nature. Aquinas refers to a scriptural text, 2 Peter 1:4, in describing this change, that we are made "partakers of the divine nature."

Many other instances of *supernaturalis* follow a similar usage, based on the substantives they qualify, notably an end (11× [times]) or beatitude (9×) or good (7×). The implication is that Aquinas uses the term "supernatural," not to refer to what is distinct and separate from nature, in the modern sense, but principally to refer to a divine gift that is implanted within a nature to transform that nature. Most of the other instances can be easily related to the same understanding, such as cognition (13×), light (5×), truth (14×), gift (6×), principle (3×), virtue (5×), vision (1×), and miscellaneous discourses on knowledge (8×). He also uses *supernaturalis* in discourses on the conception of Christ (5×) and on the Eucharist (3×). In these latter instances, what is at stake, principally, is not what is beyond nature but what is implanted by God into the natural world, a divine act that is not wholly dissimilar to, and is indeed associated with, the transformation of a created personal nature. It is further striking that, unlike in modern sensibilities, Aquinas does not classify angels as supernatural by virtue of their creation, but he underlines how these created personal beings also need a supernatural gift to see the essence of God (*ST* I.62.2).

If one regards what is *supernaturalis* less in terms of separation from nature and more in terms of the divine transformation of a nature that involves a sharing in the divine life, then this theme can easily be seen to extend through a great deal of the *Summa Theologiae*. As I have argued extensively elsewhere, *ST* I-II.55–70 and *ST* II-II.1–170, with a total of 1,004 articles or about one-third of the *Summa Theologiae*, is, in effect, a vast systematic map of the supernatural life, the Christian counterpart to Aristotle's *Nicomachean*

naturae excedit, principia naturalia hominis, ex quibus procedit ad bene agendum secundum suam proportionem, non sufficiunt ad ordinandum hominem in beatitudinem praedictam. Unde oportet quod superaddantur homini divinitus aliqua principia, per quae ita ordinetur ad beatitudinem supernaturalem, sicut per principia naturalia ordinatur ad finem connaturalem, non tamen absque adiutorio divino. Et huiusmodi principia virtutes dicuntur theologicae, tum quia habent Deum pro obiecto, inquantum per eas recte ordinamur in Deum; tum quia a solo Deo nobis infunduntur; tum quia sola divina revelatione, in sacra Scriptura, huiusmodi virtutes traduntur." From https://aquinas.cc/la/en/~ST.I-II.Q62.A1.SC.

Ethics and probably the largest system of virtue ethics ever written.[18] This life, also called the life of grace, is characterized by infused theological and moral virtues, interwoven with gifts, beatitudes, and fruits of the Spirit. As I have argued as well, this state of grace can also be characterized as one of *second-person relatedness*, or *joint attention*, with God, in which one can *know* God, not merely know *about* God. Also on this account, one becomes virtuous in the context of joint attention with the Holy Spirit, in which one can be moved freely to align with God and ultimately become friends with God.

What, then, should theology be like from a specifically supernatural perspective, via a life transformed by sharing in the divine nature? A possible place to begin is to examine how the supernatural life purportedly impacts the intellectual life, starting with the intellectual virtues. But although Aquinas defends the existence and meaning of the intellectual virtues (principally in *ST* I-II.57) and practices them himself to a superlative degree, he does not make them an integral part of his own massive account of the life of grace (*ST* II-II.1–170). In this account of the supernatural life, the key cognitive dispositions are not intellectual virtues but a subset of four of the seven gifts of the Holy Spirit: understanding (*intellectus*) and knowledge (*scientia*), appended to the virtue of faith; wisdom (*sapientia*), appended to the virtue of love (*caritas*); and counsel (*consilium*), appended to the virtue of prudence.

Upon closer examination, however, these intellectual gifts, as Aquinas describes them, are also peculiarly different from the intellectual virtues, even when they share the same names. In particular, the gifts are not about the kind of detailed discursive reasoning associated with the usual practice of theology, especially in academic circles. For example, in his description of the gift of *scientia*, Aquinas writes, "Human knowledge is acquired by means of demonstrative reasoning. On the other hand, in God, there is a sure judgment of truth, without any discursive process, by simple intuition; . . . wherefore God's knowledge is not discursive, or argumentative, but absolute and simple, to which that knowledge is likened which is a gift of the Holy Spirit, since it is a participated likeness thereof."[19] The first part of this passage contrasts human knowledge, which is discursive, with God's knowledge, which is absolute and simple. In the second part of the passage, Aquinas goes on to claim

18. Pinsent, *Second-Person Perspective in Aquinas's Ethics*.

19. Aquinas, *Summa Theologiae* II-II.9.1 ad 1, "Nam homo consequitur certum iudicium de veritate per discursum rationis, et ideo scientia humana ex ratione demonstrativa acquiritur. Sed in Deo est certum iudicium veritatis absque omni discursu per simplicem intuitum, . . . et ideo divina scientia non est discursiva vel ratiocinativa, sed absoluta et simplex. Cui similis est scientia quae ponitur donum spiritus sancti, cum sit quaedam participativa similitudo ipsius."

that the gift of the Holy Spirit, also called *scientia*, is like God's knowledge, that is, absolute and simple, since it is a participated likeness (*participativa similitudo*) of God's knowledge.

Moreover, the way that Aquinas assigns the operations of the gifts of *scientia*, *consilium*, and *sapientia* is also different from how he assigns those of the homonymous intellectual virtues. Specifically, he describes the gifts in terms of a participation in God's right judgment about what to adhere to and what to withdraw from, in relation to created things, possible courses of action, and divine things, respectively. The closest parallel recognized by some contemporary philosophers would probably be moral intuitions, albeit arising from a participation in the stance of a second person rather than self-generated. A possible parallel in everyday life may be the way in which young children often share in the stances of those around them, being attracted naturally to things that other persons are interested in.

The remaining intellectual gift, called the gift of understanding (*intellectus*), is the one most like its homonymous counterpart among the intellectual virtues. Aquinas underlines, however, that the gift of understanding enables an intellectual penetration of what is beyond the natural light of understanding, an enlightenment he describes in terms of a "supernatural light."[20] Aquinas also uses strongly interpersonal examples to illustrate the situations in which the gift of understanding (*intellectus*) fulfills this role. For example, in *ST* II-II.8.4, he illustrates the operation of the gift by reference to John 8:12, "He that follows me, walks not in darkness." In *ST* II-II.8.5 he claims, "Whoever has the gift of understanding, comes to Christ." In *ST* II-II.8.2 he cites an event reported in Luke's Gospel (Luke 24:27, 32) in which the risen Christ is described as walking incognito beside two of his disciples, opening the Scriptures to their understanding.

Given its unique role as the only gift to pertain directly to new intellectual apprehensions, one would therefore expect *intellectus* to play a central role in supernatural theology. But what exactly is the act of *intellectus*? The normal practice, as above, is to translate it as "understanding," but this translation itself raises a problem insofar as understanding remains notoriously difficult to define, analyze, or explain. What can be said, at least, is that understanding has to do with the relation of parts to wholes, and that it is most apparent when it changes. This change may not be related directly to the addition of new facts but may be related to seeing the known facts in new ways, as in the duck-rabbit illusion made famous by Wittgenstein, or the "Eureka!" moment

---

20. Aquinas, *Summa Theologiae* II-II.8.1: "Consequently man needs a supernatural light in order to penetrate further still so as to know what it cannot know by its natural light: and this supernatural light which is bestowed on man is called the gift of understanding."

of Archimedes. These changes of understanding are important enough to have their own name, "insights," and are often associated with metaphors of light and illumination.[21] As an especially influential example in Scripture, the conversion of St. Paul (Acts 9:3–9) was associated with a bright light and a new perspective on all his existing knowledge of theological matters.

In one of his novels, C. S. Lewis, himself a convert to Christianity, offers a description of this kind of transformation from the point of view of the convert: "What awaited her there was serious to the degree of sorrow and beyond. There was no form nor sound. The mould under the bushes, the moss on the path, and the little brick border, were not visibly changed. But they were changed. A boundary had been crossed. She had come into a world, or into a Person, or into the presence of a Person. Something expectant, patient, inexorable, met her with no veil or protection between."[22] In this text, there is nothing factually new in what the woman sees, and there is no reasoning process involved in the change she experiences, and yet the way that she sees the things in front of her is radically transformed and associated with a new sense of a divine, personal presence.

From the points above, it is clear that a distinction must be drawn between a subjective understanding and objective knowledge in regard to theology. For example, there were many people who met and heard Jesus Christ, and there are many people today who can read his words and appreciate the fruits of Christian culture. Typically, however, only a minority of these people, such as Ss. Peter or Martha in Scripture, accept the gift of a supernatural faith and at least some of the associated understanding of these revelations. And while reasoning power can be of service in clarifying and defending revelation, on Aquinas's account, the gift of understanding is more a matter of the harmony of the alignment of one's soul with God, a stance that is ultimately a matter of the response of one's will to grace.

The close connection between the love of God, with its concomitant alignment of the will, and the supernatural understanding of God is a point also highlighted by St. Bonaventure, who, like his contemporary Aquinas, was also declared a Doctor of the Church. Bonaventure observes,

> And you, my friend, in this matter of mystical visions, renew your journey, "abandon the senses, intellectual activities, and all visible and invisible things everything that is not and everything that is—and, oblivious of yourself, let yourself be brought back, in so far as it is possible, to union with Him Who is above all essence and all knowledge. And transcending yourself and all things,

21. See Lonergan, *Insight*.
22. Lewis, *That Hideous Strength*, 395.

ascend to the superessential gleam of the divine darkness by an incommensu-
rable and absolute transport of a pure mind."

If you wish to know how these things may come about, ask grace, not learning; desire, not understanding; the groaning of prayer, not diligence in reading;
the Bridegroom, not the teacher; God, not man; darkness, not clarity; not light,
but the fire that wholly inflames and carries one into God through transporting
unctions and consuming affections.[23]

By phrases like "ask . . . the Bridegroom, not the teacher," and "ask . . . the
fire that wholly inflames and carries one into God," Bonaventure underlines
that the goal of supernatural theology cannot be reduced to generating the
right outcome in a theological discourse. Nor is even a human understanding
sufficient; rather, what he urges his reader to have is a soul that is inflamed
with intense fervor and the glowing love of God.

Whether and How We Should Do Natural Theology

Given the background above, how, then, is it possible to sum up the Catholic
attitude to natural theology, and how should natural theology be done?

From the last section, it should be clear that the range of cognitive theological possibilities must take account of not just the object of knowledge but
also the state of the subject. In particular, one must take account of having
or lacking the supernatural understanding associated with the life of grace,
either because grace has not yet been received or because it has been received
but lost due to mortal sin.

On this basis, one can distinguish the full range of subjective cognitive possibilities as (1) a natural understanding of natural matters; (2) a natural understanding of supernatural matters; (3) a supernatural understanding of natural
matters; and (4) a supernatural understanding of supernatural matters. By the
term "natural," I mean, here, the absence of what is supernatural in regard to
matters or understanding. Unaided natural sources or cognitive powers encompass the first three of these four possibilities and are considered in the following sections as possible situations for some kind of natural theology—that is,
all possibilities except a supernatural understanding of supernatural matters.

A Natural Understanding of Natural Matters

Any theological knowledge arising from a natural understanding of natural
matters is the "purest" kind of natural theology. As noted previously, even

23. Bonaventure, *Journey of the Mind to God*, 39.

if one excludes all knowledge of supernatural matters or the understanding associated with the life of grace, the Catholic Church formally defends the position that it is possible to know of the existence of God, and that God is Creator and Lord, from natural reason alone, hence making possible at least a limited kind of natural theology.

From a Catholic perspective, this kind of theology is not the kind that one can or should properly seek for oneself, insofar as a merely natural understanding implies the exclusion of grace, as well as the exclusion of all knowledge and influences associated with revelation, which is quite a challenging condition to fulfill perfectly even in a post-Christian culture. Nevertheless, the Catholic Church defends the study of natural theological knowledge acquired by others, especially those living in pre-Christian cultures. In practice, for most Catholic clergy and teachers, this purely natural theological knowledge is most frequently encountered in the study of classical philosophy, notably the works of Plato and Aristotle.

Such studies may have considerable value insofar as they often provide training in intellectual virtues that can be, and often have been, fruitfully applied to matters of revelation. Such studies can also reveal points of consonance that can serve to build bridges for communicating the content of revelation, as in the case of St. Paul preaching to the Athenians about finding a pagan altar with the inscription "To an unknown god" (Acts 17:23). But the dissonances can also be useful, especially for providing contrasts when the implications of supernatural revelation are hard to understand. As one example, I often point out that Aristotle describes God as good, eternal, and living, but he never addresses God as "you," let alone in the manner of Augustine's "Late have I loved you."[24] The contrast highlights the covenantal aspect of the relationship with God made possible only by a response to divine grace.

As another of many examples, Aquinas, in commenting on the Beatitudes, states,

> And so Our Lord, in the first place, indicated certain beatitudes as removing the obstacle of sensual happiness. For a life of pleasure consists of two things. First, in the affluence of external goods, whether riches or honors; from which man is withdrawn—by a virtue so that he uses them in moderation—and by a gift, in a more excellent way, so that he despises them altogether. Hence the first beatitude is: "Blessed are the poor in spirit," which may refer either to the contempt of riches, or to the contempt of honors, which results from humility. (*ST* I-II.69.3)

24. Augustine, *Confessions* 10.27.38.

In this text, Aquinas refers, first, to the disposition of a virtue to riches and honor, by which these goods are used in moderation and, second, the disposition of a gift of the Holy Spirit, by which such goods are despised altogether, in the life described by the first beatitude, "Blessed are the poor in spirit." Implicitly, however, he is also employing the Aristotelian account of virtue, in which goods are used in moderation, as a foil for the more radical life of the Spirit. In other words, an account from natural moral philosophy, in which God is an inferred first cause, is used as a contrast to help describe supernatural moral theology, in which one relates to God as "I" to "you."

Even apart from valuable intellectual training, the study of purely natural theological matters from a natural understanding is therefore important for communication of the gospel, both to facilitate the discovery of points of consonance to establish some common ground, and also to highlight differences that can assist by means of a foil or contrast in communicating the newness of the gospel.

A Natural Understanding of Supernatural Matters

As noted previously, there are already many supernatural matters in the world that are, in principle, accessible to anyone, notably the propositions and narratives of Scripture, but also, more indirectly, anything in the world that has been engendered or transformed as a result of revelation.

From a Catholic perspective, such matters properly require the supernatural understanding associated with the life of grace. Dante, for example, concludes his account of hell by proclaiming, "*Let the dead poetry rise to life again*,"[25] implying that poetry itself, as he understands it, is not really alive unless redeemed by Christ. Yet these matters can also be received and studied by persons who lack grace, and the experience and study of the natural reception of such matters is itself important for a number of reasons. First, as Jesus Christ testifies in John 10:37–38, at least some of the works of revelation can be appreciated even by those who lack belief or understanding: "If I am not doing the works of my Father, then do not believe me; but if I do them, even though you do not believe me, believe the works, that you may know and understand that the Father is in me and I am in the Father." According to this text, a natural appreciation of the works of Christ, and by implication of his followers, can be a step toward supernatural knowing and understanding.

Second, the natural reception of supernatural matters can also be an occasion of challenges for both believers and unbelievers. For example, supernatural matters can seem strange to the uninitiated, and it can be important

25. Dante, *Divine Comedy*, part 2, *Purgatorio* 1.7: "Ma qui la morta poesì resurga."

to show that what is beyond the natural powers of reason does not necessarily imply a denial of reason. In addition, challenges raised by unbelievers can also be, and often have been, a spur to deepen theological study and seek deeper understanding.

Mention should also be made of the special role of narrative in regard to the natural reception of supernatural matters. Mark 4:34 reports that Jesus did not speak to people in general without parables, and Matthew 13:13 reports Jesus's reason for speaking in parables as follows: "This is why I speak to them in parables, because seeing they do not see, and hearing they do not hear, nor do they understand." In other words, because most of his listeners lack understanding, Jesus speaks in parables, consistent with the role of narrative in general as a privileged genre for communicating understanding. In the case of the parables and the many other narratives of Scripture, they are very broadly accessible, but they also prepare the way for the transition to a supernatural understanding of revelation.

To what extent, then, do these activities fall under the scope of natural theology? The answer, I think, is that they share some commonalities but more properly fall under the categories of evangelization and apologetics, insofar as it is the principal task of work in these fields to offer reasons to minds that are engaging with supernatural knowledge but lack the corresponding understanding.

A Supernatural Understanding of Natural Matters

Another possibility for the extension of natural theology is to consider whether or not there is something distinctive about a supernatural understanding of nonrevealed matters, such as the natural world. After all, Christianity claims to be a comprehensive faith, encompassing matters of creation as well as salvation. What, then, is the possible impact of the faith on understanding the world?

Once again, this topic is vast, but some indication of an answer can be found in the following passage taken from the writings of an early Christian bishop, Pope Clement I of Rome, in a letter that is one of the earliest Christian documents outside the New Testament. At a time when Christians had many immediate and urgent practical concerns, it is notable that he reflects briefly on cosmology.

> The heavens, revolving under his government, are subject to him in peace. Day and night run the course appointed by him, in no wise hindering each other. The sun and moon, with the companies of the stars, roll on in harmony according

to his command, within their prescribed limits, and without any deviation. The fruitful earth, according to his will, brings forth food in abundance, at the proper seasons, for man and beast and all the living beings upon it, never hesitating, nor changing any of the ordinances which he has fixed.[26]

What is striking here is the calm confidence of the writer, who perceives order and harmony from the largest to the smallest beings of the cosmos, under the authority of God, who has become known. The cosmos is not perceived as an accidental assemblage of events, or the uncaring work of a capricious deity or deities, or the operation of some vast, impersonal mechanism that is impossibly beyond our grasp. On the contrary, the letter of Clement (above) hints at a new confidence that will, in time, give rise to projects to investigate the natural order of the cosmos with an expectation of success.

Of course, over time the broader impact of the Christian faith on natural philosophy, which eventually gave rise to science, remains a matter of vast historical complexity and conflicting narratives. But assuming that there is an impact of some kind, which seems plausible, is this also a matter for consideration within natural theology? The answer, I think, is that there are points of overlap, but it is probably more appropriate to place the supernatural understanding of natural matters within the theology of nature rather than what is usually called natural theology.

Conclusions

The Catholic faith defends the legitimacy of natural theology. Although the Catholic Church has never adjudicated formally regarding any particular purported proofs about God, the teaching office of the Church has declared formally that it is part of the Catholic faith to hold that it is possible, by means of natural reason, to know that there is a God, and that God is both Creator and Lord. Although purely natural theology requires the exclusion of matters of faith, or the kind of understanding associated with such matters, examples can be found in pre-Christian or other cultures that lack such influences. Under these circumstances, the study of what is known by persons from these cultures can facilitate the discovery of points of consonance and of dissonance, both of which have propaedeutic value.

Beyond such cases of "pure" natural theology, the situation is complicated by the fact that there is a vast amount of objective material in the world that is associated directly or indirectly with revelation, and that is accessible to more

---

26. From 1 Clement 20.1–5, ed. and trans. Donaldson and Roberts, *Apostolic Fathers*, 10.

or less anyone. Narratives, in particular, play an important role, insofar as they communicate aspects of a supernatural worldview, even if the person hearing them does not yet have that worldview. One may also consider the supernatural understanding of natural matters as another possible extension of natural theology, although these extensions, while sharing some commonalities with natural theology, are more commonly classified under other fields, such as the theology of evangelization, apologetics, and the theology of nature.

What is striking about these extensions, however, is that the key issue is understanding rather than knowledge or reasoning. Such understanding, as either an intellectual virtue or a gift of the Holy Spirit in the life of grace, arguably remains one of the key areas of research for further progress in natural theology. But it is also challenging since there is little consensus about what understanding is or even whether it is really important. On this point, there is a parallel with another long-standing controversy. Those who consider the Turing Test to be adequate to test artificial intelligence might be relatively inclined to consider the issue of understanding to be unimportant for supernatural theology, as long as one reasons to correct conclusions. On the other hand, those who consider John Searle's Chinese Room[27] to be a valid counterexample to Turing would probably consider, along with Aquinas, that reaching correct conclusions is not, by itself, adequate to show that one is a genuine supernatural theologian.

What, then, can be said about the problem raised at the beginning, namely, that of the demons calling Jesus the "Son of God"? Assuming that the demons lack the supernatural understanding associated with divine love, this absence does not preclude them from remembering divinely revealed knowledge from their prelapsarian state, such as that God is a Trinity, or acquiring knowledge of facts connected to what is being revealed in the world, such as what is being said by Jesus or about Jesus by others. These possibilities serve to underline that knowledge of facts and reasoning about facts connected with revelation are not enough to identify genuine supernatural theology, the heart of which is the supernatural understanding made possible by the gifts of the Holy Spirit within the divine life of grace. Hence, despite the demons apparently boasting, at times, of their cognitive abilities,[28] even the most powerfully endowed natural intellects cannot cross that gap to the divine understanding made possible by grace.

Ultimately, therefore, although the Catholic faith defends natural theology, it is important to remember its radical insufficiency and the need, also from a

27. Searle, "Chinese Room Argument."
28. See, e.g., Mark 1:23–24: "Immediately there was in their synagogue a man with an unclean spirit; and he cried out, 'What have you to do with us, Jesus of Nazareth? Have you come to destroy us? I know who you are, the Holy One of God.'"

Catholic perspective, for all human beings in this life to enter into the divine life of grace. Only in the context of this life of grace is the understanding of supernatural matters possible from a supernatural perspective, including, most importantly, the capacity to know and love God with the divine love of friendship. I therefore finish with a warning about the limitations of natural theology by theologian and canonized saint John Henry Newman, whose early life and ministry took place in a context in which natural theology was popular: "Religion, it has been well observed, is something *relative to us*; a system of commands and promises of God *towards* us. But how are we to be concerned with the sun, moon, and stars? Or with the laws of the universe? . . . They do not speak to sinners at all. They were created before Adam fell. They 'declare the glory of God,' but not his will."[29] Newman here warns that the study of nature alone, while showing the handiwork of God, cannot enable us to know the purposes or the will of God, let alone to bridge the unthinkable gap between God and ourselves. Only what God has revealed provides a bridge, namely Jesus Christ, and the means for us to cross that bridge, the life of grace, bearing its ultimate fruit in eternity.

29. See Newman, "Sermon XXIV."

Contemporary Response

CHARLES TALIAFERRO

We are in Andrew Pinsent's debt for laying out a Roman Catholic view of natural theology and his nuanced analysis of the relevant work of Thomas Aquinas distinguishing the natural and the supernatural. While I am an Anglo-Catholic, not a Roman Catholic, and more attuned to Christian Platonism (especially the Cambridge Platonists) than Aquinas's Christianity with his extraordinary transformation of Aristotle, I am much more in harmony with Thomas than, say, Karl Barth. If you are looking for a ruthless critique of Pinsent's chapter, you'd best skip this response. In an effort to make this "response" not a waste of your time, I offer comments not on the idea of baptizing babies in beer but on the use of the term "supernatural" today, the nature of religious conversion, the idea of infused ideas or grace or virtue, and an observation about demons.

The Supernatural

While the Latin term *supernaturalis* may have an elegant usage (and definition) in the work of Aquinas and his contemporaries, the term "supernatural" in English has a much broader usage. In the writings of Thomas Hobbes and David Hume, the supernatural includes ghosts, fairies, witches, and a host of paranormal entities. In the context of popular culture today, we may easily see that the supernatural includes not just demons and angels, but also vampires, goblins, and the kinds of bizarre creatures that appear in the modern dark-fantasy television series *Supernatural*. In philosophical circles today, the term "supernatural," like the term "apologetics," is often used derisively, along with the claim that "we" have a clear-headed notion of what counts as "natural" and virtually no idea of what would count as being supernatural.

I suggest that theists today would be better off not using the term "supernatural" and instead using the term introduced in the seventeenth century by the Cambridge Platonists: "theistic." This avoids confusing theism with the paranormal, and it can also be in concert with developing a challenge to those naturalists who assume we have a problem-free concept of nature, or what it is to be physical. I have spent most of my career challenging contemporary naturalism and resisting the effort to depict the God of theism as nonnatural or (to use a phrase of Fiona Ellis) philosophically "too spooky."[1] For the record, I agree with Pinsent that the belief in God is natural and, even more importantly, that God is not just natural but also the creator and sustainer of this contingent cosmos / the creation.

Conversion

I am not certain Pinsent would disagree, but I suggest that in the vast number of cases the conversion from unbelief or from one religion to another religion involves the conviction that there is a fact about reality that is new or different, which they had not recognized in the past. The famous duck/rabbit figure can be telling, so long as it is used as an analogy of how two persons can look at the same thing (a drawing), and one person sees it as a duck while the other sees it as a rabbit. The relevant analogy is that a theist and a naturalist can look at the same thing, and one sees it as godless while the other sees it as the creation of God. But the difference between them is not just in terms of *ways of seeing*, but on the grounds of *what is the case*. As a friend once observed: If he saw something in the distance and he wanted to know if it was a duck or rabbit, he would run toward it. If "it" flew away, he would conclude it was a duck, whereas if it hopped away, he would conclude it was a rabbit. Analogy: in my view, engaging in natural theology is one way to discern that it is more likely we live in a theistic or naturalistic cosmos.

Divine Infusion

I do not know what to think about God infusing ideas or grace or virtue. In English, the term "infusion" suggests (as an analogy) pouring something (like water) into a container or injecting something (medicine) into one's body. I suppose we might say that Pinsent infused this volume with some

1. See Ellis, *God, Nature, and Value*, introduction and chap. 1.

expert findings from the Angelic Doctor. I may be wrong, but I am inclined to think that, today in English, to refer to God *infusing* ideas, grace, virtue, even love, sounds Pickwickian. I think it more sensible (or less odd) to claim that in meditation, prayer, or corporeal acts of mercy, one senses (or experiences or perceives) God's love. If I convince you that I love you platonically (whether or not you are a Barthian or Roman Catholic Thomist), I think it would suffice to acknowledge that you trust my expression of love and not resort to the language of infusion.

The Demonic

Skeptics might be uneasy with Pinsent speculating about demons and what they may or may not know. Not me. I highly recommend spending at least a little time thinking about life from a demonic point of view, as C. S. Lewis did in his classic *Screwtape Letters* (1942) and *Screwtape Proposes a Toast* (1959). If you are wrestling with the hiddenness-of-God literature (a hot topic in philosophy of religion advanced by John Schellenberg and debated by tout le monde), look at why Screwtape (an older demon) explains to a younger demon why demons should be hidden.[2] From the vantage point of hell, they can do more damage to souls if they disguise their reality. Reversing things to heaven, I am inclined to think that God's being overwhelmingly evident to creatures would overshadow our free will, but for God to be partially discoverable in natural theology and then, on the grounds of religious experience (or even infusion), to come to Paul Moser's I-Thou relationship with our Creator and Redeemer would be a great, even awesome gift.

---

2. For an overview and analysis of this debate, see Howard-Snyder and Green, "Hiddenness of God."

Classical Response

ALISTER E. McGRATH

ndrew Pinsent's engaging and thoughtful reflections on a Catholic approach to natural theology situate the enterprise within a broad historical and cultural context, establishing a positive yet critical relationship between theology and philosophy, while clearly delineating their distinct (and occasionally divergent) approaches to the question of what we can know of God and how we can hope to find this. As Pinsent rightly points out, Catholicism takes the view that, through the exercise of "natural reason" alone, it is possible to know of the existence of God and that God is Creator. Pinsent's focus on Aquinas provides a helpful window into this rich tradition of theological reflection and the way in which it frames a broad approach to natural theology.

As a historical theologian, I think it is helpful to set Aquinas in context by noting his predecessor Albertus Magnus's formulation of the distinction between the realms of the natural and supernatural, arguing that philosophy offers an appropriate means of studying the former, and theology the latter. The breadth of his intellectual vision was such that he was able to hold together philosophy and theology while delineating their respective realms of authority and inquiry. For Albertus, no special divine illumination is required to gather a reliable knowledge of the natural world by using intrinsic human powers of reasoning. The study of natural things (*naturalia*) can be conducted by using a "natural light"; the study of revealed truth, however, requires divine grace and illumination.[1] This approach envisages a progression from what

1. Führer, "Albertus Magnus' Theory of Divine Illumination."

can be known about God through intelligent reflection on the natural world (such as the idea that God is Creator), and specifically Christian insights into God (such as knowledge of God as Trinity). This approach, of course, is expanded and given added conceptual depth by Aquinas.

This approach is, in my view, seen at its most winsome in recent times in John Paul II's 1998 encyclical letter *Fides et ratio* (Faith and reason), which declares that faith and reason are like "two wings on which the human spirit rises to the contemplation of truth."[2] So can reason on its own lead humanity to this truth? *Fides et ratio* pays a handsome tribute to philosophy as "one of the noblest of human tasks" and "driven by the desire to discover the ultimate truth of existence." Yet it insists that unaided human reason cannot fully penetrate to the mystery of life or the character of God. For this reason, God graciously chose to make these things known through revelation, things that would otherwise remain unknown. "The truth made known to us by Revelation is neither the product nor the consummation of an argument devised by human reason."

Here, I think, we see a move away from the position of the First Vatican Council (1869–70), which declared that reason can lead us to a knowledge of the existence of God as the source and goal of all things. Though positive about the capacity of natural human reason, Vatican I was somewhat cooler about the merits of philosophy as an intellectual discipline. Perhaps this reflected the *Zeitgeist*, in that the philosophies of the mid-nineteenth century were widely seen as promoting rationalism and agnosticism. The situation has changed, of course, not least because of the remarkable recovery of confidence in Christian philosophy since then, aided to a significant extent by Leo XIII's encouragement to engage Aquinas as a model of Catholic theology and philosophy in 1879. Pinsent's engagement of Aquinas is a good example of the depth and range that this has brought to Catholic thinking on issues of faith and reason, including natural theology. It is important to note here that Aquinas is now being read with increasing interest and respect in Protestant and evangelical theological circles, particularly in relation to the question of the rationality of faith and the nature of theological language.[3]

Pinsent's exploration of Catholic approaches to natural theology opens a rich range of issues for further exploration as we reflect on the past, present, and potential futures of natural theology. So how would I respond to Pinsent's lucid account of such a significant tradition of reflection on the place and purpose of natural theology? I welcome it, while seeing it as part

2. For an excellent analysis, see Dulles, "Reason, Philosophy and the Grounding of Faith."
3. This development can be traced back to Vos, *Aquinas, Calvin, and Contemporary Protestant Thought*.

of a spectrum of possible approaches. It represents a careful and extended synthesis of faith and reason, which can function as the basis of a theologically informed public engagement.[4]

I think it is also important to note a shift away from the somewhat rationalistic tone of the First Vatican Council's statements on natural theology to the "more expansive treatment" of natural theology found in the *Catechism of the Catholic Church* (1992), which clearly recognizes "a role for imagination alongside reason, in terms of 'openness to truth and beauty.'"[5] This is a point at which I would have welcomed amplification of Pinsent's analysis, perhaps engaging the "aesthetic turn" that is so evident in Hans Urs von Balthasar's approach to natural theology.[6]

Yet it is fair to ask some critical questions. One is inevitable, given the historical diversity of approaches to natural theology that are evident within the long tradition of Christian theology: Why give priority or precedence to *this* understanding of natural theology when others might be taken into consideration? Pinsent would, I think, point out that this is a distinctively Catholic approach to the topic and that his task was to delineate the basic assumptions and characteristics of this approach. This, I gladly concede, he does with grace and insight. His careful exploration of the dialectic between the "natural" and "supernatural," and his emphasis on the importance of divine grace in enabling the perception of deeper truths than those of reason alone, help distinguish his approach from that of many philosophers of religion, who make little use of the dialectic between the natural and supernatural, or nature and grace.

A second point of discussion could concern what Protestants and evangelicals might learn from—or express unease about—Catholic approaches to natural theology. To what extent does this approach depend on assumptions about human nature and divine grace that they might feel to be problematic? While I concede that a Barthian critic would find cause for anxiety in the approach outlined in Pinsent's overview, a historical theologian would point out that it shares some themes with some forms of Reformed theology of the late sixteenth and early seventeenth centuries—evident, for example, in the careful analysis of the relation of faith and reason found in the Genevan theologian and successor to John Calvin, Theodore Beza.[7]

4. This is a major theme in the works of the Australian lay Catholic theologian Neil Ormerod. See, e.g., Ormerod, "In Defence of Natural Theology."

5. Pickering, "New Directions in Natural Theology." For the application of such a natural theology of beauty, see Viladesau, "Natural Theology and Aesthetics"; Caldecott, *Beauty for Truth's Sake.*

6. Murphy, "Hans Urs von Balthasar."

7. Mallinson, *Faith, Reason, and Revelation in Theodore Beza,* especially 99–141.

Yet many contemporary evangelical theologians would express concern about whether the fundamentally sinful disposition of humanity renders them incapable of reasoning toward God in the first place, or leads them into distorted understandings of God in the second. Some theologians within the Reformed tradition would formalize this concern in terms of the noetic consequences of sin.[8] Recent discussions of the "hiddenness of God"—an important theme for natural theology—have highlighted the potential importance of the noetic impact of sin;[9] it would be helpful to know how Pinsent would respond to this concern.

8. For a representative statement of this issue, see Helm, "Calvin, the *Sensus Divinitatis* and the Noetic Effects of Sin."
9. For a good introduction to this issue, see Ebrahim, "Divine Hiddenness and Human Sin."

Deflationary Response

PAUL K. MOSER

ndrew Pinsent draws from Thomas Aquinas to elucidate a Roman Catholic approach to natural theology. I largely agree with his interpretation of Aquinas, but I recommend a more critical approach to Aquinas on pure natural theology. Aquinas, I suggest, has failed to make a convincing case for pure natural knowledge of God's existence.

Pinsent's Taxonomy

Pinsent recommends a "distinction of natural and supernatural theology . . . in terms of subjective understanding, especially the understanding associated with the gift of the Holy Spirit in the life of grace. Progress in natural theology today will need to focus on this difficult topic of understanding, while recognizing that natural theology alone can never bridge the gap between God and ourselves." It is unclear what "bridge the gap" means here, but Pinsent is *not* claiming that natural theology alone fails to yield knowledge that God exists.

Pinsent quotes Aquinas with agreement: "There are certain things to which even natural reason can attain, for instance that God is, that God is one, and others like these, which even the philosophers proved demonstratively of God, being guided by the light of natural reason."[1] He then notes:

> One of the canons of the First Vatican Council [of the Roman Catholic Church] in 1870 states, "If anyone shall have said that the one true God, our Creator

1. Aquinas, *Summa contra Gentiles* 1.3.

and our Lord, cannot be known with certitude by those things which have been made, by the natural light of human reason, let him be anathema (DZ 1806, cf. 1785)." In other words, according to this canon, one places oneself outside the Catholic faith if one denies that it is possible to know by natural reason alone that there is one true God. This definition makes no judgment about any specific proofs for the existence of God, or whether there are in fact any adequate proofs. But the canon does define that the existence of God can be known with certitude from created things and by the light of natural reason, placing the existence of God firmly within natural theology.

Let us be more precise. Aquinas does not claim simply that "it is possible to know by natural reason alone that there is one true God." He claims, in the quotation above, that "the philosophers proved demonstratively of God, being guided by the light of natural reason, . . . that God is, [and] that God is one." This takes us beyond merely a claim of possible knowledge to a claim of demonstrative proof (and knowledge) of God's existence by natural reason alone.

Pinsent develops the theme that "Aquinas uses the term 'supernatural,' not to refer to what is distinct and separate from nature, in the modern sense, but principally to refer to a divine gift that is implanted within a nature to transform that nature. . . . What is at stake, principally, is not what is beyond nature but what is implanted by God into the natural world, a divine act that is not wholly dissimilar to, and is indeed associated with, the transformation of a created personal nature." Such transformation, he explains, is part of a life of "grace," a life "characterized by infused theological and moral virtues, interwoven with gifts, beatitudes, and fruits of the Spirit." I have no objection to this side of Aquinas's story, as long as we allow for a genuinely voluntary human role in receiving the kind of grace that reconciles a person to God. Aquinas himself seems at places to be a compatibilist who does not allow for genuine human freedom in this area, but we cannot digress.

Pinsent interprets Aquinas to allow for direct human knowledge of God, which is "not discursive, or argumentative, but absolute and simple, to which that knowledge is likened which is a gift of the Holy Spirit, since it is a participated likeness thereof."[2] Pinsent adds that "a distinction must be drawn between a subjective understanding and objective knowledge in regard to theology. . . . While reasoning power can be of service in clarifying and defending revelation, on Aquinas's account, the gift of understanding is more a matter of the harmony of the alignment of one's soul with God, a stance that is ultimately a matter of the response of one's will to grace."

2. Aquinas, *Summa Theologiae* II–II.9.1 ad 1.

Pinsent identifies the relevant options as follows: "(1) a natural under-standing of natural matters; (2) a natural understanding of supernatural matters; (3) a supernatural understanding of natural matters; and (4) a supernatural understanding of supernatural matters. By the term 'natural,' I mean, here, the absence of what is supernatural in regard to matters or under-standing. Unaided natural sources or cognitive powers encompass the first of these four possibilities." He adds that "even if one excludes all knowledge of supernatural matters or the understanding associated with the life of grace, the [Roman] Catholic Church formally defends the position that it is pos-sible to know of the existence of God, and that God is Creator and Lord, from natural reason alone, hence making possible at least a limited kind of natural theology."

According to Pinsent, the Roman Catholic Church "defends the study of natural theological knowledge acquired by others, especially those living in pre-Christian cultures. In practice, for most Catholic clergy and teachers, this purely natural theological knowledge is most frequently encountered in the study of classical philosophy, notably the works of Plato and Aristotle." By way of a contrast between "purely natural" and Christian approaches to God, Pinsent remarks that "Aristotle describes God as good, eternal, and living, but he never addresses God as 'you,' let alone in the manner of Augustine's 'Late have I loved you.' The contrast highlights the covenantal aspect of the relationship with God made possible only by a response to divine grace." He adds that "the study of purely natural theological matters from a natural understanding is therefore important for communication of the gospel, both to facilitate the discovery of points of consonance to establish some common ground, and also to highlight differences that can assist by means of a foil or contrast in communicating the newness of the gospel."

The following claim seems to be question-begging in the present context: "Purely natural theological knowledge is most frequently encountered in the study of classical philosophy, notably the works of Plato and Aristotle." On the one hand, many inquirers doubt that Plato and Aristotle had genuine knowledge of God; they thus will demand specification of the evidence needed for such knowledge in Plato and Aristotle. We gain nothing by begging the key issue here. On the other hand, some inquirers will grant that Plato and Aristotle did have genuine knowledge of God but deny that it was "purely natural." They may have had a religious experience of God, and that experi-ence need not have been "purely natural." Indeed, it seems more plausible that God self-presents to people in the situation of Plato and Aristotle than that they had a "purely natural" argument or evidence for God. In any case, we cannot begin to evaluate or cogently to endorse Pinsent's claim of "purely

natural theological knowledge" with no specification of the relevant supporting evidence or argument. More explanation is needed here if natural
theology is to convince us.

If the term "God" is a perfectionist title, requiring worthiness of worship and thus moral perfection, Pinsent's claim to "purely natural theological
knowledge" of God will be a tall order, at best. Appeals to evidence for a "first
cause" or a "designer" of nature will fall short, because they do not require or
deliver a being who is worthy of worship and thus morally perfect. As a result,
they do not confirm the reality of the kind of God in question, including the
God of traditional monotheism found in Judaism, Christianity, and Islam.

Pinsent does not limit "purely natural theological knowledge" of God to
knowledge of God's existence. He claims that it includes knowledge of God
as Creator and Lord. Thus: "The teaching office of the Church has declared
formally that it is part of the [Roman] Catholic faith to hold that it is possible,
by means of natural reason, to know that there is a God, and that God is both
Creator and Lord. Although purely natural theology requires the exclusion
of matters of faith, or the kind of understanding associated with such matters, examples can be found in pre-Christian or other cultures that lack such
influences." So, our question becomes: What specific evidence or argument,
within "natural reason," yields the existence of a God who is Creator and
Lord of the universe? We have no cogent first-cause or design argument to
serve this purpose. Where, then, should we turn? Pinsent does not answer.
So, we lack needed support for his bold claim about natural knowledge of
God as Creator and Lord.

Citing Clement of Rome, Pinsent comments regarding "the natural order
of the cosmos": "What is striking here is the calm confidence of the writer,
who perceives order and harmony from the largest to the smallest beings of
the cosmos, under the authority of God, who has become known. The cosmos
is not perceived as an accidental assemblage of events, or the uncaring work
of a capricious deity or deities, or the operation of some vast, impersonal
mechanism that is impossibly beyond our grasp. On the contrary, the letter
of Clement (above) hints at a new confidence that will, in time, give rise to
projects to investigate the natural order of the cosmos with an expectation
of success." The key claim is that Clement "perceives order and harmony"
throughout the universe, from large to small objects. Perceiving such order
and harmony, however, is not perceiving *God*. The perceived order and harmony may arise from a source other than God, and its source may not be
intentional or intelligent. More to the point, we have not been given adequate
evidence to say that the perceived order and harmony are "under the authority of God, who has become known." So, we are not in a position, from a

cognitive point of view, to say that they stem from an intelligent agent who is a candidate for being God.

Pinsent introduces John Henry Newman on a limitation of natural knowledge of God: "How are we to be concerned with the sun, moon, and stars? Or with the laws of the universe? . . . They do not speak to sinners at all. They were created before Adam fell. They 'declare the glory of God,' but not his will."[3] Pinsent explains: "Newman here warns that the study of nature alone, while showing the handiwork of God, cannot enable us to know the purposes or the will of God, let alone to bridge the unthinkable gap between God and ourselves. Only what God has revealed provides a bridge, namely Jesus Christ, and the means for us to cross that bridge, the life of grace, bearing its ultimate fruit in eternity." Even if "the study of nature alone . . . [shows] the handiwork of God," it is still an open question whether it shows *the reality of God*. A study of nature alone could show the handiwork of God (*de re*) without showing (*de dicto*) that nature is the handiwork of God. It thus could leave unsettled the issue of whether God exists.

Newman adds to the problem for purely natural knowledge of God with his claim that such knowledge may "'declare the glory of God,' but not his will." Pinsent adds that the study of nature alone "cannot enable us to know the purposes or the will of God, let alone to bridge the unthinkable gap between God and ourselves." It is unclear, however, what kind of "bridge" of "the unthinkable gap between God and ourselves" Pinsent seeks. Perhaps he has in mind at least a *cognitive* bridge between God and ourselves that delivers knowledge of "the purposes or the will of God." If so, I concur that the study of nature alone does not supply any such bridge. Here we have a serious limitation on any purely natural knowledge of God.

A far-reaching problem arises now for natural theology in its pure form. If it "cannot enable us to know the purposes or the will of God," it will fall short of knowledge of God *as God*, that is, as a being with a good will who is worthy of worship and thus morally perfect. In that case, it will yield at most knowledge of something inferior to God, strictly speaking—that is, God as worthy of worship. It then will be doubtful that natural theology in its pure form gives us knowledge of *God*. It still could give us knowledge of some *effects* of God, but such knowledge does not add up to knowledge of *God as God*. The limitation on natural knowledge of God's will endorsed by Newman and Pinsent evidently blocks, then, the claim that humans can have purely natural knowledge of God, including such knowledge of God as Creator and Lord.

---

3. See Newman, "Sermon XXIV."

Concept and Experience of God

Part of the difficulty for natural theology stems from proceeding with an indefinite conception of "God." Many writers, including many philosophers and theologians, work with an indefinite conception of God, especially when supporting natural theology. Aquinas is one example, but we find the same shortcoming in Newman and Pinsent. It is easy to make sweeping claims about natural knowledge of God as long as we have an indefinite conception of God. Once we clarify the concept of God being used, however, trouble typically arises.

If our concept of God requires that God is, inherently, worthy of worship and thus perfectly morally good, we have a definite constraint on our pertinent evidence for God's reality. We then will need evidence for God's reality to be evidence of the reality of a *morally good* intentional agent, that is, an intentional agent with a morally good will. This will block purely natural knowledge of God if, as Newman and Pinsent hold, such knowledge falls short of God's will. The pressing issue then becomes: What kind of evidence would indicate the reality of an intentional agent who has a morally good will and is worthy of worship?

I see no hope for purely a priori evidence, arising from thought and inference alone, yielding or otherwise confirming the existence of a God with a morally good will. Evidence from *moral experience* is arguably a different story. Many humans testify to experiencing what is morally good, including wills that are morally good, and they arguably are pointing to something real rather than illusory. I recommend that we look to moral conscience for the relevant kind of moral experience. Perhaps this is where Socrates, Plato, and Aristotle *ultimately* found God, if they did, rather than in any argument of natural theology. At least this option seems more promising than the familiar arguments of natural theology.

We sometimes find in moral conscience, if we pay due attention, moral challenges and features that present a will superior to our own. We thus speak of being "convicted" in our conscience to have our previous intentions overridden by a morally superior will. We sometimes find that superior will to challenge us with righteous love, even such love toward our enemies. Indeed, we sometimes talk of our "being led" to what is morally good by our conscience, in virtue of the morally superior will at work there.

The apostle Paul, I have suggested in reply to John McDowell and Alister McGrath, points us in the direction suggested. If Paul thinks of moral conscience in terms of the human moral center called "the heart," his following remark is relevant: "Hope [in God] does not disappoint us, because God's love has been poured into our hearts through the Holy Spirit which has been given to us" (Rom. 5:5). Paul has in mind a human religious experience of God's moral character and will of righteous love, and this experience is irreducible to a theology or a belief. It is a self-presentation of God's distinctive character and will to a human. Its qualitative features enable it to serve as experiential evidence for a person of God's reality. Such evidence has no need for the traditional arguments of natural theology, and that is a benefit, from an evidential point of view.

Paul ties the experience in question to moral leading from an intentional agent, thus remarking: "All who are led by the Spirit of God are children of God" (Rom. 8:14 NRSVue). This is intentional leading toward what is good, in relation to God and to other people, but it requires human cooperation. So, it is not coercive. God's aim is to lead people to conformity to God's moral character, in relation to God and to other people. The relevant evidence comes in human moral experience, and it comes to its intended fruition as a human cooperates with it, in moving toward moral goodness. If a person does not cooperate, the moral power of the evidence in experience will not be experienced in its fruition and may even be overlooked. So, a human response to moral conscience can form one's evidence for God's reality, at least regarding its clarity from coming to its fruition intended by God.

If we follow Paul's suggestions, we can have grounded hope and faith in God, courtesy of a distinctive religious experience and intentional moral leading. We then can avoid both mere dogmatism toward belief in God and dubious inferences from natural theology. We then can ask what best explains our moral experience in conscience. If a God of righteous love figures in this matter, we can hope and believe in God without disappointment, from an evidential point of view. I recommend exploration of this live option, as a replacement for traditional natural theology.[4]

---

4. For relevant discussion, in connection with Jesus, see Moser, *Divine Goodness of Jesus*.

Barthian Response

JOHN C. McDOWELL

In a brief discussion explaining why it is useful to study ethics, Herbert Mc-Cabe provides an analogy with the study of grammar and suggests two reasons why the latter is a fitting topic for reflection. The first reason provided is that "it is always satisfactory to see the reasons and principles and patterns behind what we do."[1] This we might term "practice-seeking-understanding." The second reason involves a more critical mood concerning grammatical rules: "Even though we speak quite grammatically for the most part, there may be times when we make mistakes or are puzzled about some linguistic form. And a study of grammar will help us to avoid mistakes in these cases."

When dealing with "natural theology," the question of what constitutes a "mistake" becomes not only crucial but also considerably more complicated. As McCabe's work on ethics suggests, "The norms of traditional morality . . . are never stable, and never quite adequate to deal with new forms of human behaviour. So we need some way of determining what is a growth in our understanding and what is merely decay."[2] It is not theology just because it mimics the language of the past, since discursive conditions shift. Within contemporaneity there is a contest for adducing what counts as theological grammar, as well as a distinctive avoidance of the question of whether there can be a mistake. This reticence too should be a cause for theological concern. For McCabe, "if a word is to be meaningful there must be at least something that it doesn't mean, however open-ended it may otherwise be."[3] Even if "God" is the most expansive of terms (within a Christian context speaking

1. McCabe, *Good Life*, 3.
2. McCabe, *Good Life*, 4.
3. McCabe, *Law, Language, Love*, 20.

of, among other things, the creative agency of all existents, without itself being one of the existents, as McCabe continually reminds with reference to Thomas Aquinas) there must be uses of "God" that cannot count as linguistically recognizable, and therefore as not "meant" by the term if it is to be linguistically usable. Otherwise, God becomes, in the terms of Michael Buckley's description of contemporaneity, "so sentimentally amorphous that it admits any statement of meaning, even quite contradictory statements."[4]

That Thomas undergirded Karl Barth's sense of the trouble with, or the mistakenness of, the "gods" of modernity hardly needs to be said. Barth's error in this represents a failure to pay sufficient attention to a Thomas free from his neo-Thomistic captivity.[5] Of course, as a historical reading, Barth's reading has to be situated within certain formative conditions, not least his critical engagement with Eric Przywara. For a theologian normally acutely aware of cultural conditioning, Barth's treatment of Thomas duly suffers when read in the light of recent Thomistic scholarship. Barth's interactions with the likes of Gottlieb Söhngen, however, encouraged a rethink. Citing Söhngen's claim that "there is no *theologia naturalis* that can be unmoored from salvation history," Barth declares that, should this be the case for Roman Catholicism, "he would have to withdraw his famous remark that the notion of *analogia entis* [analogy of being] is 'the invention of anti-Christ' and the root of all Roman Catholic deviations from true Christian doctrine."[6]

Thomas, simply put, looks distinctly bent out of shape when configured in terms of modern theism. Theistic definitions of God, predicated on theolinguistic univocity, would strike Thomas as being idolatrous since they locate God ontologically within talk of being (even if "being" is capitalized when used of God as though setting God at the apex of being simply solves the problem), adding a supersensible realm to the sensible one. Famously, Thomas denies that God is part of a class, even if that be a class of things called "gods." This is not a minor matter either, not a critique driven by intellectual pedantry. On the contrary, this denial is a way of resisting speech's propensity to idolatry. Fergus Kerr explains, "For Thomas, however, it was vital to head off the thought that was tempting in his day, and certainly is in ours, that God is an item in the world, on however grander a scale than the rest of us. That would be idolatry: equivalent to making God a creature."[7] The appropriate contrast,

---

4. Buckley, *At the Origins of Modern Atheism*, 13.
5. Even if he be acknowledged as *the* Catholic theologian, reading Thomas is a contested matter. Simply put, as the subtitle of Fergus Kerr's study *After Aquinas* suggests, to speak of a singular Thomism (never mind a singular Catholicism) is counterfactual.
6. Kerr, *After Aquinas*, 35, referring to Barth, *Church Dogmatics* I/1, preface.
7. Kerr, *After Aquinas*, 43.

then, is not between envisaging God to be either a *thing* or *nothing*. Instead, God is *no-thing*, that which does not appear under any identifying category of thing or nothing. Thomas is not utilizing Aristotle's ontology and his categorization of things without exposing it to a significant overhaul of what it is on which Aristotle can assist knowledge (as a handmaiden for clarificatory purposes). Frederick Christian Bauerschmidt explains, "What Aristotle gives us are conceptual tools with which we can understand the natural world. Our understanding of that world can provide hints and intimations of the God who is its cause, but Aristotelian philosophy itself attests to its radical inadequacy to the task of speaking of God. . . . What Aquinas learned from Aristotle was a certain habit of mind regarding the making of distinctions."[8]

Here is where Andrew Pinsent's recognition of the way in which Thomas handled the *naturalis/supernaturalis* distinction is helpful. The supernatural is not a supplement to the natural, something standing over against it that then inserts itself into it, or that requires a discontinuation of natural processes and their integrity in order to be known. It is not something that can be defined in a straightforwardly contrastive way with the natural, as if it is something immaterial in contrast to the material. The intellectual confusion on this among some philosophies of religion sets the terms of their whole approach to developing a rational theology. Jerome Gellman, for instance, illustrates the muddle when he defines "religious experience" as "an experience purportedly granting acquaintance with, or supporting belief in the existence of, realities or states of affairs of a kind not accessible by way of sense perception, somatosensory modalities, or standard introspection and having religious meaning for the subject."[9] This object of so-called "religious experience," Kai-Man Kwan argues, could be "an experience of God or some supernatural being."[10] The experience is of some paranormal entity that fits a category of being, even if it is not a category of usually perceivable physical matters. Developing Przywara's and Austin Farrer's perspectives on the matter, Rowan Williams, in contrast, explains that what is meant by "supernature" is the unconditioned, which also functions "to transform the finite from within." The refusal to read this in terms of simple contrastive categories on a plane of ontological equivalence is crucial.

> Thus the supernatural is neither an exalted version of the finite—the finite with certain constraints removed—nor a reality alongside the finite. Its difference is absolute—which is why it is possible for the infinite to be present in and as the

8. Bauerschmidt, *Thomas Aquinas*, 73.
9. Gellman, "Religious Experience," 155.
10. Kwan, "Argument from Religious Experience," 251.

finite, since . . . it is never the case, as with discrete finite substances, that more of one entails less of the other. In thus informing, subtending, permeating the finite, the infinite Word shows once and for all equally the non-*duality* of God and the world and the non-*identity* of God and the world.[11]

The significance of this is pronounced, and not merely as a way of reading Thomas or much of the variety within the Catholic tradition. For instance, Thomas's Five Ways come to be read in a fashion that mitigates the more neo-Thomistic sense of them arguing evidentially, as if they move from what is known (nature) to an additional (supernatural) unknown entity that becomes known. Thomas is no Richard Swinburne, despite the decontextualized readings of innumerable philosophy-of-religion textbooks. Kerr takes the five arguments to be "the first lesson in Thomas' negative theology," by which is meant the protection of "God's transcendence."[12] "God is much stranger than those who see his presence everywhere realize. That an argument is needed for the existence of God is Thomas's first move in resisting idolatry."[13] According to Bauerschmidt, Thomas assumes "we know God's effects better than we know God, since the human mind's natural object is the *quidditas* of material things. . . . This is something different from the kind of evidence-gathering that goes on in modern empirical science, since the method remains deductive rather than inductive."[14] Rudi te Velde recognizes that the being of Thomas's God, "as such, cannot be known."[15] Accordingly, the *Quinquae viae* do "not make the truth of his being knowable to us. God's being is not subject to a demonstration, nor to a definition, nor to any other form of rational knowledge. The arguments lead the human intellect to the insight into the truth of the proposition that God is, not into the truth of God's being."[16] For Lubor Velecky, Thomas's arguments are those "of an 'insider,' and they aim to give content to the notion of divinity by suggesting" to Christians "different ways of seeing their experience as pointing to a transcendent being, which is worshipped by them as the God of Christian revelation."[17]

Inquiry into the grammar of the ground and end of all that exists is not to render God self-evident, or to claim that God can be known if only we look

11. Williams, *Christ*, 226.
12. Kerr, *After Aquinas*, 58. Denys Turner argues that Thomas's approach undermines that of Bonaventure, for whom the mind naturally ascends to God and from there comes to know the world (*Thomas Aquinas*, chap. 2).
13. Kerr, *After Aquinas*, 58.
14. Bauerschmidt, *Thomas Aquinas*, 94.
15. Te Velde, "Understanding the *Scientia* of Faith," 71.
16. Te Velde, "Understanding the *Scientia* of Faith," 71–72.
17. Citation from te Velde, "Understanding the *Scientia* of Faith," 57–58, referring to Velecky, *Aquinas's Five Arguments*.

a little bit harder. True, te Velde recognizes, "'God exists' is, considered in itself, a self-evident truth (since God is his being)." However, it is "not self-evidently known by us."[18] Thomas's Five Ways make a claim that the world, when looked on in a certain way, discloses its contingency. The nub of the matter, then, is this "certain way," of what can be seen of the vestigial.

It was hardly contested that a well-functioning reason could, in practice, lead to truthful claims about its dependency: that should not be a surprise. The fifteenth-century thinker Nicholas of Cusa (hereafter referred to as Cusanus) declares that "there is only one essence of all, which is participated differently."[19] However, when this is combined with the argument that the world is that which it should be to direct the journey of seeking God, and that "all beings participate in being," he appears to be committed to the kind of *analogia entis* that Barth was particularly anxious about.[20] It would be a rhetorical assertion to proclaim with Cusanus that "no sound mind can reject what is most true," if what is meant by the "most true" is God as the ground and condition for all knowledge.[21] After all, as Alasdair MacIntyre observes, Thomas's account of *natural* law is immediately preceded by an Augustinian-inspired discussion of sins and vices.[22] Article 1 of question 2 in the first part of *Summa Theologiae* is "pervaded by theological assumptions" and addresses the issue of the "ignorance of God's nature," which is sin.[23] Accordingly, Karen Kilby observes, "If one supposes the five ways to be Thomas' attempt, no matter how brief, to lay down a rational philosophical foundation for his theology, one would have to say that he goes about his business in a confused, sloppy, embarrassingly bad way."[24] Moreover, for Cusanus at least, divine *illumination* is needed to help the seeker on her way. Only in this context can he declare that the proper seeking of God occurs, and so he urges his readers to "strive to seek God with the most diligent vision, for God who is everywhere is impossible not to find if God is sought in the right way."[25] It is difficult to entertain how Cusanus's journey could make sense to a John Locke or a William Paley. Cusanus's discursive process is frequently punctuated by an admission of the ineffability of God, that the "infinite as infinite is unknown,"[26] so that what one is seeking is not the objectification of an

18. Te Velde, "Understanding the *Scientia* of Faith," 70.
19. Nicholas of Cusa, *On Learned Ignorance* ¶ 48.
20. Nicholas of Cusa, *On Learned Ignorance* ¶ 51. Cf. Nicholas of Cusa, *On Seeking God*, 18.
21. Nicholas of Cusa, *On Learned Ignorance* ¶ 2.
22. MacIntyre, *Ethics and Politics*, 82.
23. Kerr, *After Aquinas*, 58.
24. Kilby, "Philosophy," 64.
25. Nicholas of Cusa, *On Seeking God*, 223.
26. Nicholas of Cusa, *On Learned Ignorance* ¶ 3.

existent being at a distance, or the reinforcement of the handle on revelation, but the reformative purgation of the seeker in *constant* transit. What Cusanus calls "learned ignorance" is not the cumulative result of all other forms of ignorance but the very ground and setting for the recognition of the incomprehensibility of God as the maximal. "There is," he explains, "no proportion between the infinite and the finite."[27] Accordingly, the difference between God and creature is not one that can be defined and measured, so that the naming of God is a complex matter in which "the affirmative names we attribute to God apply to God in an infinitely diminished way. . . . For no affirmations, as if positing in God something of what is signified, can apply to God, who is not any one thing more than God is all things."[28] God is not comprehensible, and this darkness is not lifted, even eschatologically. Instead, by being God, God "surpasses every concept," even the "name *Theos*."[29] Likewise, for Thomas, revelation intensifies any sense of divine incomprehensibility rather than relieves it.[30] Thomas is not predicating a notion of reason-come-to-its-limits with revelation topping it up, supplementing what it can know, or pushing into the territory of faith. This is why, unlike Immanuel Kant, Thomas does not predicate God-talk as that beyond the boundary of reason's knowing as an article of faith stripped of reason. Nor does he generate a philosophical method that founds, grounds, and sustains the subsequent operations of *sacra doctrina* or holy teaching. This Thomas, however, is lost on the likes of Richard Swinburne, who anachronistically projects his own theism back onto Thomas: "The opening questions of St Thomas Aquinas's *Summa Theologiae* provide the paradigm of medieval philosophical theism."[31]

If *theologia naturalis* is a useful category it is so, first, as a refusal to denaturalize the world in its relations with God (as if the natural ascends out of itself and into the supernatural); second, as a rejection of a failure to acknowledge that all existents are effects; and third, as a denial that God can be relegated to an idle or uneventful beyond-the-worldly that engages creatures by intruding into, and suspending, the natural. Showing how reason stands in relation to God, here, is where Thomas is particularly intellectually interesting. On the one hand, he resists removing God-talk to its own special and world-secluded (or privatized) religious sphere as a transcendental supernatural, and on the other, he prevents the world from being intelligible to itself in and of itself. "Each of the five ways turns on a claim about what

27. Nicholas of Cusa, *On Learned Ignorance* ¶ 9.
28. Nicholas of Cusa, *On Learned Ignorance* ¶ 122.
29. Nicholas of Cusa, *On Seeking God*, 19.
30. See Turner, *Faith, Reason and the Existence of God*, 76.
31. Swinburne, "Philosophical Theism," 4.

we might call the world's insufficiency: nothing moves itself; nothing causes itself; nothing is the source of its own necessity; nothing measures itself; the universe as a whole does not guide itself."[32] Yet argument does not get one very far in Thomas's work. After all, as Denys Turner explains, "He simply asks the question: *Utrum Deus sit*, 'whether there is a God,' without any discussion at all as to how we would know that what the arguments prove is, after all, 'God.'"[33] Thomas's talk that this is "what we mean by God" functions as a rejoinder to the "fool" from Psalm 53:1, whose heart or shaping of living is in misalignment with the tongue, which can all too readily confess belief in God. In Thomas's hands, reason is figured as the movement of scientific categorization, doctrinal reasoning, and so on, that remain perennially conducive to the practices of inquiry, deliberation, disputation, and wise living within and toward the *archē* and *telos* of all things.

32. Bauerschmidt, *Thomas Aquinas*, 95.
33. Turner, *Thomas Aquinas*, 115.

A Catholic Reply

FATHER ANDREW PINSENT

What emerges from the comments on my chapter is the central question of the meaning of the term "nature" in contrast to the life of grace, a question that is central to prospects for natural theology. Alister McGrath draws attention to the heart of the issue in the final paragraph of his commentary by raising the issue of whether "the fundamentally sinful disposition of humanity" might be seen, at least by some, as invalidating any possibility of understanding or reasoning about God. Behind this concern is, of course, the tendency of the original minds of the Reformation to undercut any stable ground between grace and sin. This tendency has had a parallel in Catholic theology, at least in the interval between the implosion of a desiccated neo-Thomism in the 1960s and a limited recovery of Aquinas today.[1] Only today are we beginning, tentatively, to recover and reinterpret the theological understanding of nature.

What, then, is this state of nature? From the Christian perspective, it is the natural human state *without* sanctifying grace, and the mere stating of

---

1. The Catholic Church gave priority to the work of Aquinas after the encyclical *Aeterni Patris* in 1879. Yet many students in Church institutions in subsequent decades, including the recently deceased Pope Benedict XVI, received a desiccated presentation of Aquinas through a neo-Thomist perspective. This theme is also reflected in McDowell's comment on my chapter, that Barth failed "to pay sufficient attention to a Thomas free from his neo-Thomistic captivity," drawing attention to the many significant differences between Aquinas and his purported disciples. As McGrath remarks, Aquinas is being read far more widely today. Moreover, I add that the advent of information technology, with an extraordinary investment by IBM in digitizing all the works of Aquinas (the world's first great digital humanities project), has enormously facilitated direct engagement with his work. See Jones, *Roberto Busa*.

that definition implies all kinds of interesting conclusions. First, the state of nature is "unnaturally" natural, in the sense that this state is not one that we were ever meant to experience, according to God's will for prelapsarian humanity. As well as the Blessed Virgin Mary, we were all meant to be full of grace forever. Second, for all human beings who can cease to resist grace, there is at least some sin involved if one remains, obstinately, in a state of nature without grace. Moreover, there is certainly sin involved if someone in a state of grace rejects that grace, a rejection that is possible only through sin, especially deadly sin. In these senses it is perfectly true that there is no stable ground between grace and sin. Nevertheless, Aquinas differs from many theologians, especially but not exclusively within the Reformed tradition, in at least the following point: even though this state of nature is inaccessible without sin, the state of nature itself is not sin. On this interpretation, there is in fact a third state, the state of *pure nature*, between sin and grace.

What, then, are the implications of this state? At first glance, it might seem that a state of pure nature resembles one of hypothetical "superheavy elements" in nuclear physics. Heavy atomic nuclei, such as uranium, tend to fall to pieces easily, and their instability generally increases with the atomic number. But it has long been speculated that even heavier, relatively stable elements, so-called superheavy elements, might exist in islands of stability beyond the reach of present technology. At the time of this writing, such elements have never been observed, but they have a peculiar status within empirical science insofar as it is possible to make some theoretical investigation of their properties. Perhaps a state of pure nature resembles these superheavy elements, insofar as one might be able to investigate the characteristics of this state even if it is unachievable and unobservable. But why would one want to make this study? How can it be helpful for theology to speculate about a purportedly unattainable state?

One answer is the state of pure nature is in fact very relevant to those many human persons who are conceived but never come to term, let alone reach the age of reason. What fate is there for this vast multitude of souls, beyond the extremes of an easygoing universalism or consignment to the fires of hell? As I have argued extensively elsewhere, drawing especially from Aquinas, *Disputed Questions on Evil (De malo)* 4–5, there is a third possibility: limbo.[2] Admittedly, the term "limbo" has all kinds of negative connotations, including neglect or oblivion. Aquinas, however, argues that this state could be one in which all natural desires are fulfilled. Furthermore, beyond even Dante's

2. Pinsent, "Limbo and the Children of Faerie."

building of the Elysian Fields within hell, Aquinas argues that this is a state completely without regret or any sense of loss.[3] One may elaborate further by speculating that these sinless souls at the resurrection see King Jesus in his human nature and accompany and experience the joy of seeing the faces of those who see the face of God. The crucial point is that although one cannot choose to enter or obstinately remain in a graceless state without sin, we all begin in this state of nature, without the state of grace but also without actual sin. Since this limbo is also a state in which one lacks any personal culpability, natural theology offers an account that is considerably more attractive than consigning these innocents to hell.

A second answer is that the possibility of pure nature allows Christianity to engage with non-Christian societies with a degree of nuance. A pertinent example in Roman Catholic culture in the Americas is the image of *Our Lady of Guadalupe*, a hugely influential image of the Virgin Mary clothed in an Aztec style. Of course, one should not be naive, and there were good reasons why the Spanish missionaries of the seventeenth century did not choose to use the name of Huitzilopochtli, the Father of the Aztecs, as the Aztec transla- tion of "God." But the recognition of a state of comparatively sinless nature, at least as a theoretical possibility, has long allowed Christian thinkers to engage fruitfully with the natural theology of Plato and Aristotle, among others. As one consequence, the single most important word of the Nicene Creed, which the vast majority of self-identifying Christians accept today, is *homoousios*, meaning "consubstantial," or "of one being," to describe the relation of the Father and Son. As is well known, *homoousios* is not found in Scripture but is adapted from Greek philosophy, which would have been even more difficult if early Christians did not have at least some appreciation for natural theology and philosophy. On this point, Paul Moser, in his commen- tary on my chapter, raises pertinent doubts about the kind of knowledge, if any, that Aristotle and Plato had of God, but we have the testimony of their own texts, such as *Metaphysics*, book 12; and *Republic*, book 7. Of course, the language and imagery of God in these texts should not be assumed to equate with the Christian understanding of God, but that is largely the point of the distinct category of natural theology. As another example, when St. Augustine of Canterbury landed in England in 597 to convert the Saxons, Pope Gregory advised him to adapt rather than destroy the pagan temples, a policy followed in many other times and places.[4] I can also repeat the modern

3. The souls in Dante's limbo (*Inferno*, canto 4) are described as sighing (line 26), but Aqui- nas argues that they have no regret, since one cannot regret the loss of a love that one does not know (*De malo* 5.3).

4. Pope Gregory I, *Letter to Abbot Mellitus*.

example of Father Anthony Barrett, who spent many years living with the
Turkana people of northwest Kenya. Barrett would never dream of simply
labeling the rich natural theology of the Turkana people as wrong, but he
would consider it a foundation that has provided a point of dialogue and
exchange with Christian revelation.

A third answer is that the state of nature protects the genuine gratuity of
the state of grace. Charles Taliaferro is perfectly correct in his commentary
on my chapter, stating that the term "supernatural" is problematic today. In
my own work, I mostly use the phrases "life of grace" or "state of grace,"
and Eleonore Stump refers to "life in grace."[5] I also note in passing that
many contemporary Christians have recovered at least some of this meaning
in their self-description of being "born again." Nevertheless, I do not want
to lose the medieval term *supernaturalis* entirely, given that its etymology
underlines how the terms "natural" and "supernatural" developed symbioti-
cally. Both terms are at least in part understood as contrasts, and it is hard
to have a sense of the gratuity of grace in the absence of a coherent account
of nature. In the history of theology, when a sense of the state of nature has
been lost, the sense of grace has also decayed. The challenge is to understand
the anthropology of these states, but the hard work has been done. Aristotle
provides us with an insightful account of nature from nature's perspective in
his *Nicomachean Ethics*. Aquinas provides us with an insightful account of
the life of grace from a perspective of grace in *Summa Theologiae* II-II.1–170.[6]
I have argued extensively elsewhere that the novelty and root metaphor of
Aquinas's theological anthropology is second-person relatedness to God.[7]
On this account, although one must be extremely careful in using this metaphor, the state of grace is like losing our spiritual autism to God, beginning
a new life in which the key relationship is "I" to "Thou," in the manner of
Augustine's *Confessions*.[8] This transfiguration is due to the unmerited gift
of grace, with a revealed theology that is distinct from the natural theology
of the state of nature.

5. Stump, *Atonement*, 197.
6. Aquinas's commentary on the *Nicomachean Ethics* is a third option: nature from the
perspective of grace.
7. Pinsent, *Second-Person Perspective in Aquinas's Ethics*.
8. I have been criticized for the phrase "spiritual autism," so let me reiterate how this phrase
should be qualified. First, this phrase is a metaphor, just as the Bible sometimes uses the word
"blindness" to refer to lack of physical sight or, metaphorically, to a lack of spiritual insight.
Second, it is probably the most suitable metaphor since autistic spectrum disorder, as a physical condition, is characterized by atypical or reduced second-person relatedness. Finally, on a
Catholic reading and with just a handful of exceptions, everyone comes into existence with this
condition in relation to God, which is scarcely a matter of singling out a minority.

For all these reasons, I conclude that natural theology is not simply a rich, optional extra for revealed theology but is essential for understanding revelation. I am very grateful to my interlocutors and the editors of this volume for challenging me to think deeply about these matters.

3

A Classical View

ALISTER E. McGRATH

The term "natural theology" is rich and evocative, hinting at a relationship of disclosure or insight between the world of nature and the transcendent reality of God. On the one hand, it expresses the deep human intuition, given theological warrant by the Christian belief in humanity bearing the "image of God," that the created order points beyond itself, inviting us to explore what lies past its limiting horizons.[1] In reminding us that the world is the "theater of God's glory," John Calvin was pointing to both the work of God in redemption and the work of God in creation as means through which God could be known and worshiped.[2] Many find in God a "repository for our awestruck wonderment"[3] at the complexity of our world, given added importance through the Christian doctrine of incarnation, which affirms that God did not merely create this world but also entered into it in Christ in order to redeem it. A full trinitarian vision of God inspires both worship and intellectual reflection, especially in grasping the rational, imaginative, and affective threads of connection between God and the created order.

The term "natural theology," though not itself biblical, can certainly be used cautiously to describe certain thoroughly biblical lines of thought, not least concerning the capacity of the complexity and immensity of nature to point toward God. The historical and prophetic traditions of the Old Testament point to God being disclosed in both the great act of redemption—such as the exodus from Egypt—and the act of creation and its outcomes. Indeed, it is possible to consider Old Testament theology as the proclamation of the acts of God—including creation—along with its inferences and consequences.[4]

The Wisdom literature of the Old Testament is particularly important in highlighting the role of the created order in illuminating the character of Israel's covenant God.[5] There is no question here of nature "proving" the existence of the God of Israel; there is, however, a constant insistence that

1. Vidal and Kleeberg, "Knowledge, Belief, and the Impulse to Natural Theology."
2. Schreiner, *Theater of His Glory*.
3. Rushdie, *Is Nothing Sacred?*, 8.
4. C. Barth, *God with Us*, 5–6.
5. J. Collins, "Biblical Precedent for Natural Theology." For reflections on how the Wisdom literature fits into the "acts of God" approach to Old Testament theology, see Belcher, *Finding Favour in the Sight of God*, 1–15.

aspects of the natural order can illuminate and inform the human quest for wisdom—and hence ultimately for God.[6] At several points, the New Testament indicates the capacity of the visible world to disclose or intimate the existence of God—for example, in the opening chapter of Paul's letter to the Romans, or Paul's Areopagus speech in Acts 17.[7] Although Romans 1:19–20 is widely interpreted as aiming to demonstrate the "incontrovertible and universally recognizable conclusion of humanity's eschatological culpability,"[8] this conclusion sits uneasily with Paul's statements elsewhere—such as his questioning the capacity of the world's wisdom to inform us about God (1 Cor. 1:18–29). There are clearly some hermeneutical issues that need to be resolved here.

Dictionary definitions fail to do justice to the complexity of natural theology, as this has been understood and practiced within the Christian tradition. Too often they reduce natural theology to a clinical exercise in intellectual dissection that cannot give an adequate account of the beauty of nature or our sense of wonder at its complexity. A purely rational account of natural theology, such as that found in many works of systematic theology, can only give a superficial rendering of its conceptual depth. Modernist hostility toward the imagination still affects the way we think about natural theology, which offers us both a rational account of how God can be found in or through nature and an imaginative framework that allows us to see and experience nature in a new manner—what we might describe as "a theological re-imagining of nature."[9]

The Theological Foundations of Natural Theology

As Emil Brunner rightly noted back in the 1930s, any approach to natural theology ultimately rests on an explicitly or implicitly assumed *theological* understanding of human nature.[10] For Brunner, a Christian understanding of human nature, especially the all-important insight that humanity bears the image of God, when set alongside the doctrine of God as Creator (so that the created order bears some "permanent capacity for revelation"), produces the intellectual matrix from which the classic project of natural theology

6. Lefebure, "Wisdom Tradition in Recent Christian Theology"; J. Collins, "Natural Theology and Biblical Tradition"; Barr, *Biblical Faith and Natural Theology*, 58–79. The role of the divine speeches in Job 38–42 is especially interesting; see Clines, *Job 38–42*, 1039–242.

7. On which see Campbell, "Natural Theology in Paul?"; Gärtner, *Areopagus Speech and Natural Revelation*; Barr, *Biblical Faith and Natural Theology*, 21–38.

8. Campbell, "Natural Theology in Paul?," 234. Cf. Watson, *Text and Truth*, 256–62.

9. Vidal, "Extraordinary Bodies and the Physicotheological Imagination." I explore this theme in more detail in McGrath, *Re-Imagining Nature*.

10. For what follows, see McGrath, *Emil Brunner*, 90–148.

emerges. There is no such thing as a neutral account of human nature; inevitably, every theory of human nature embodies certain assumptions and beliefs. Christianity provides a capacious and rich vision of our world and humanity, which creates intellectual space for the enterprise described in this chapter as "natural theology" by showing that it is *natural* for human beings to want to undertake natural theology.[11] The doctrine of the *imago Dei* represents a theological formulation of what we might call the "preparedness" of humanity for divine disclosure, in effect shaping our interpretation of nature.[12] While God is disclosed through the created order, which bears the divine imprint, a natural theology rests on human beings possessing some created capacity to recognize this limited disclosure for what it really is, whether through the training or disciplining of their natural capacities, or through the healing or expansion of those capacities through grace.[13]

A classic Christian theological framework—articulated by writers such as Athanasius, Augustine, Aquinas, and Calvin—thus enables us to account for the existence of the natural human activity of seeking to find God within or through the world of nature. For Athanasius, a Christian anthropology leads directly into a natural theology. God created humanity as bearing the "image of God" in order that God might be known through the "works of creation."[14] Calvin affirmed the importance of revelation through nature, while emphasizing the importance of Scripture in clarifying, interpreting, and expanding this limited revelation. "The knowledge of God, which is clearly shown in the ordering of the world and in all creatures, is still more clearly and familiarly explained in the Word."[15] Although this fundamental insight is deeply ingrained within the Reformed theological tradition,[16] it is something common to most Christian traditions.

Christian theology thus lays a general foundation for natural theology, both in terms of the divine origins of nature and of humanity bearing the "image of God"; it does not, however, prescribe what specific forms it should take. For example, does such a natural theology elicit a rational recognition of the reality of God? Or is the response to the natural world better framed in terms

11. See especially the analysis in Haldane, "Philosophy, the Restless Heart, and the Meaning of Theism."

12. For the importance of the "image of God" in recent discussions of natural theology, see D. Robinson, *Understanding the "Imago Dei."*

13. For this theme in Augustine, see Couenhoven, *Stricken by Sin, Cured by Christ*, 19–105.

14. Athanasius, *De incarnatione* 3.12.

15. Calvin, *Institutes of the Christian Religion* 1.10.1. See further Grabill, *Rediscovering the Natural Law*, 70–97.

16. For this theme in Calvin, see Husbands, "Calvin on the Revelation of God"; E. Adams, "Calvin's View of Natural Knowledge of God."

of an imaginative embrace of God, or a relational loving of God? Christian theology provides us with a starting point for the colligation of our experience of the world and God, while leaving us to fill in the fine details—a process of enrichment that is shaped to no small extent by the context within which such a natural theology is developed, with its envisaged tasks.

Some may want to raise a question at this point. Is too much weight being given to the context within which natural theology is located? After all, the Enlightenment tended to think that rationality was historically and culturally invariant. The intellectual context within which natural theology was located was thus a constant. However, human patterns and norms of reasoning are now known to be shaped, at least in part, by cultural forces.[17] Alasdair Mac-Intyre argues that writers of the Enlightenment believed it was possible to engage the natural world in an empirical, presuppositionless way, so that a natural theology could be constructed independently of "social and cultural particularities." This project failed, partly because it adopted "an ideal of rational justification which it has proved impossible to attain."[18] MacIntyre thus urges the recognition of the role of tradition and communities in rational discourse, arguing that "there is no standing ground, no place for enquiry, no way to engage in the practices of advancing, evaluating, accepting and rejecting reasoned argument apart from that which is provided by some particular tradition or other."[19] Christianity provides such a tradition-mediated rationality that provides a "standing ground" for the interpretation of the natural world.[20]

Natural Theology: The Problem of Definition

The default definition of natural theology today, uncritically repeated in both popular and scholarly accounts of the notion, is that it designates the "branch of philosophy which investigates what human reason unaided by revelation can tell us concerning God."[21] This locates the enterprise within the discipline of philosophy and establishes its purpose as essentially apologetic. Yet a study of the historical development of natural theology indicates that this is only one of several forms it has taken during its trajectory.[22] This specific

---

17. See McGrath, *Territories of Human Reason.*

18. MacIntyre, *Whose Justice?*, 6.

19. MacIntyre, *Whose Justice?*, 350.

20. For a defense of such an approach, see Seipel, "In Defense of the Rationality of Traditions."

21. Joyce, *Principles of Natural Theology*, 1.

22. Note the important comments on this diversity of approaches in Re Manning, Brooke, and Watts, *Oxford Handbook of Natural Theology*: "It is one of the primary aims of this *Handbook* to highlight the rich diversity of approaches to, and definitions of, natural theology" (1).

understanding of natural theology dates from the late seventeenth century and reflects the cultural and intellectual context of that period, particularly the growing sense of a rift between scientific and religious ways of thinking.[23]

Some would raise a concern here, noting the large scholarly literature dealing with the "natural theology" of Thomas Aquinas or other patristic or medieval writers. A good example is Norman Kretzmann's informed and engaging account of Aquinas's "metaphysically based natural theology," as this is set out in his *Summa contra Gentiles*.[24] Yet Kretzmann's exploration of Aquinas's way of framing natural theology raises a difficult question, which has generally been overlooked in such discussions: where in the *Summa contra Gentiles* does Aquinas explicitly discuss "natural theology" *by that name*? What Kretzmann actually does is offer an account of Aquinas's views on what philosophers of religion now understand by natural theology—an understanding of "natural theology" that we do not find in Aquinas himself.

In preparation for writing this article, I reread Aquinas's *Summa contra Gentiles* in the original Latin, to great profit. My reason for doing so, however, was to confirm that the Latin phrase *theologia naturalis* is conspicuously absent from the text of this work. Kretzmann is thus unable to adduce Aquinas's own definition of natural theology, in that Aquinas, in common with the Western theological tradition at this stage, simply does not use this term. Instead, Kretzmann uses Aquinas as a dialogue partner in a retrojective discussion of natural theology, predicated on the modern understanding of what "natural theology" might be, thus imposing a modern interpretive and evaluative framework on Aquinas. It is a worthwhile undertaking; it nevertheless creates the impression that Aquinas sets out an understanding of natural theology identical to that characteristic of contemporary philosophy of religion.

Historically, it is quite easy to show that the term "natural theology" (*theologia naturalis*) was known to theologians of late classical antiquity, such as Augustine of Hippo,[25] who drew on themes found in the "tripartite theology" of the philosopher Marcus Terentius Varro (d. 27 BCE).[26] Yet Augustine did not consider the notion of natural theology, as Varro presented it, to be particularly helpful, and he made little use of it. Given the high regard in which Augustine was held during the theological Renaissance of the Middle Ages,[27]

23. For a detailed study, see Mandelbrote, "Uses of Natural Theology in Seventeenth-Century England."

24. Kretzmann, *Metaphysics of Theism*, 23–29.

25. Dihle, "Die Theologia tripertita bei Augustin." The three elements of this theology are *theologia naturalis, civilis, et mythica*.

26. On Varro's approach, see van Nuffelen, "Varro's Divine Antiquities."

27. Colish, "Sentence Collection and the Education of Professional Theologians."

this lack of interest in the notion of natural theology appears to have been carried over into the worlds of thought of his medieval successors. Although the Latin term *theologia naturalis* was used in late classical antiquity, it did not secure philosophical or theological traction in the West until the time of the Renaissance, largely through the influence of the fifteenth-century Catalan scholar Raimundo de Sebonde (c. 1385–1436).

As the Oxford scholar C. C. J. Webb rightly noted in the early twentieth century, historical scholarship indicated that the term "natural theology" was rarely used during the patristic and medieval periods, and it came into wider use only in the sixteenth century, mainly on account of Sebonde's *Liber creaturarum* (The book of the creatures), thought to have been written in the final two years of his life.[28] A posthumous sixteenth-century editorial decision led to the addition of the subtitle *seu theologia naturalis* (or natural theology) to the second Latin edition of this work—and hence to the adoption of this term to describe the broad form of theological engagement with nature that Sebonde commended. This work was widely imitated, with multiple publications appearing from French and Spanish publishers in the sixteenth century developing its method and approach, shaping expectations of what a "natural theology" looked like, in theory and practice. Sebonde's approach was recognized as a classic, despite concerns in some quarters about its emphasis on revelation through creation.

The form of natural theology found in Sebonde's work, however, bears little relation to modern understandings of the concept, which emerged two centuries later.[29] Sebonde does not interpret *theologia naturalis* in purely cognitive terms but rather understands it to involve an *affective* engagement with the natural order, seen from the perspective of faith. Sebonde's treatise, while including some later catechetical sections dealing with dogmatic theology, is really a work of spirituality rather than theology.

Decades later, the Renaissance philosopher Michel de Montaigne published an influential French translation of Sebonde's work as *La théologie naturelle de Raymond Sebon* (The natural theology of Raymond Sebon, 1569), which did much to popularize Sebonde's approach and the term "natural theology" in the later Renaissance, particularly as a way of affirming the intrinsic rationality of faith. While Sebonde's work was clearly not written for apologetic purposes, aiming to counter skepticism or unbelief, such an agenda influenced Montaigne's decision more than a century later to translate Sebonde's

---

28. Webb, *Studies in the History of Natural Theology*, 1–83. For the history and influence of Sebonde's work, see Bujanda, "L'influence de Sebond en Espagne au XVIᵉ siècle."

29. For further discussion, see de Puig, *La filosofia de Ramon Sibiuda*.

work into French and to append an essay on Sebonde's wider significance. By this time, apologetic issues were becoming increasingly important, leading Montaigne to note the potential application of Sebonde's approach to the criticisms of theistic belief that were then securing a hearing within French humanist circles.[30]

This historical reflection must give us cause to reflect on what we understand by "natural theology" and on what its "classic" form might be. Sebonde's way of framing the relation of God and creatures has a strong claim to represent a "classic" approach to natural theology; yet his approach has little connection with the understandings of natural theology regnant in the twenty-first century. For this reason, it is probably best to use historical inquiry to explore how the concept has been understood within the Christian tradition, rather than impose modern definitions (significantly shaped by the cultural debates of modernity) onto the past. The recovery of the rich Christian understanding of a natural *theology*—as opposed to a philosophy affirming the rationality of belief in God—depends critically on allowing writers of the past to shape our understandings of the notion, rather than imposing our own views on them. For this reason, we shall turn to consider what history discloses concerning the past understandings and applications of the concept.

A Genealogical Approach to Natural Theology

The most appropriate research tool for uncovering what Christian theology has understood by the term "natural theology" is a description of the contexts in which such an enterprise appears to be envisaged and the manners in which it was undertaken. It is important to appreciate the historical context in shaping the character and objectives of approaches to natural theology. The recognition that notions such as "nature," "science," and "religion" are historically situated social constructions[31] suggests that there is unlikely to be any predetermined essential form of either "nature" or "natural theology"; these are, rather, open to cultural revision and ideological reconstruction, reflecting the social and cultural location in which they emerge, often in response to a perceived need. We cannot exclude the possibility that new forms of natural theology will develop in the future, as a result of new apologetic situations that cannot at present be determined.

In such a fluid and complex situation, offering a priori definitions of what natural theology ought to be unhelpfully restricts (and potentially distorts) the

---

30. For a detailed account, see Habert, *Montaigne traducteur de la Théologie naturelle*.
31. E.g., see Harrison, *Territories of Science and Religion*, 1–19; Gerber, "Beyond Dualism."

notion. It is something that calls out to be *described* by considering its history of use and application. Such a genealogical approach is a prominent feature in the writings of philosophers such as Friedrich Nietzsche[32] and has clear potential for theological application. A careful historical study discloses multiple ways in which the notion of natural theology has been understood.[33] In what follows, we consider four such approaches that are part of this genealogy of natural theology and reflect the ambiguity of the Latin term *theologia naturalis* as designating both "a natural theology" and "a theology of nature."[34]

First, natural theology designates a theology that comes "naturally" to the human mind, thus without the aid of divine revelation. It can be considered as a demonstration of the intrinsic rationality of the Christian faith using natural forms of reasoning. Anselm's so-called ontological argument for the existence of God is a good example of such an approach. Anselm makes no appeal to revelation in justifying the rationality of faith in the *Proslogion*, and he does not engage with the natural world, focusing instead on human reasoning patterns and pointing to their implications.[35]

Second, natural theology refers to a form of reasoning, independent of revelation, that reflects on the theistic entailments of the beauty or complexity of the natural world. This specific understanding of natural theology is widely called "physicotheology" (Greek: *physikos*, "natural") and emerged as a significant intellectual presence in eighteenth-century England.[36] The trajectory of thought here is from observation of the natural world to inference of the existence of God, without presupposing or establishing a relationship of dependence on revealed ideas. Because of its appeal to the publicly accessible world of nature, this approach avoids the "scandal of particularity"[37] that arises from modernism's insistence that knowledge of the divine must be universally accessible rather than historically located at some specific (and now past) moment in time.

Both of the two approaches to natural theology just outlined relate the world of nature to a generic divinity, which then requires correlation with the Christian God. Yet some approaches to natural theology are specifically

32. Lightbody, *Philosophical Genealogy*.

33. See the different lists in McGrath, *Re-Imagining Nature*, 18–33; Fergusson, "Types of Natural Theology."

34. See the argument in Padgett, "*Theologia Naturalis*."

35. Schumacher, "Lost Legacy of Anselm's Argument."

36. Zeitz, "Natural Theology, Rhetoric, and Revolution"; Harrison, "Physico-Theology and the Mixed Sciences."

37. Although this general idea is developed by the Enlightenment writer G. W. Lessing, the specific term "Ärgernis der Einmaligkeit" appears to have been coined by the biblical scholar Gerhard Kittel in 1930.

Christian, originating from within the Christian community of faith, and are informed by its core beliefs. We shall consider one such approach in what follows.

Third, natural theology is to be understood primarily as a "theology of nature," as a specifically Christian way of seeing or understanding the natural world, reflecting the core assumptions of the Christian faith: this is to be contrasted with or opposed to secular or naturalist accounts of nature.[38] The movement of thought here is from within the Christian tradition toward nature, rather than from nature toward faith (as in the second approach identified above). This approach presupposes divine revelation and reflects the specific understanding of nature that results when it is viewed from this perspective. It originates from within the Christian tradition and enacts a specifically Christian mode of seeing the natural order.

Fourth, natural theology is the intellectual outcome of the natural tendency of the human mind to desire or be inclined toward God. This approach traditionally makes an appeal to the "natural desire to see God," developed by Aquinas and others,[39] although it can be formulated in a number of ways—such as Bernard Lonergan's assertion of an innate tendency of the human intellect to understand being.[40] On this approach, it is natural for the human mind to seek for God; natural theology is the outcome of this quest, grounded in some intellectual or imaginative "homing instinct" within humanity.

Other approaches can, of course, be discerned within the rich and complex history of Christian theology. Limiting the scope of natural theology to one or more of these for the sake of intellectual neatness or argumentative precision has certain advantages. Yet this conceptual tidiness is achieved at the cost of excluding certain approaches that the Christian theological tradition has found to be legitimate and helpful; it needlessly impoverishes the range of resources we can bring to deploy on the complex question of how we explore and represent the relation of the natural world and God, and how we present this within the community of faith and in conversation with a wider culture.

Yet while this genealogical approach to natural theology maximizes its intellectual possibilities, it also raises difficult questions, which cannot be overlooked. Are these different implementations or conceptualizations of natural theology essentially *disconnected*, so that the task is simply to identify them and set them out for individual evaluation and application? Or is there some deeper or richer vision of natural theology that can enfold them all within a

38. Morley, *John Macquarrie's Natural Theology*, 97–120; Gunton, "Trinity, Natural Theology, and a Theology of Nature," 98–103.

39. Feingold, *Natural Desire to See God*; Kerr, *Immortal Longings*, 159–84.

40. Lonergan, "General Character of the Natural Theology of *Insight*."

single theoretical framework? There is no firm agreement on this issue. Some argue that the diversity of natural theology is an indication of its fundamental conceptual incoherence;[41] others argue that a Christian metanarrative, grounded in a trinitarian vision of God, provides a larger vision of reality that holds these multiple visions of natural theology together.[42]

A Brief Description of Natural Theology

The complexity of the historical location and use of "natural theology" makes it improper to offer a precise definition of the notion: this would both limit and distort a broad enterprise of engagement and reflection with the natural world, which is ultimately more theological than philosophical in character. In this section, I offer a brief description of natural theology that respects its historical roots and the multiple contexts in which it has been put to use.[43]

Natural theology designates a multifaceted intellectual enterprise, resistant to definition but rich in applications, that explores possible connections between the world of nature and a transcendent reality, such as the Christian concept of God. Those connections are multiple and complex. Traditionally, these focus reflection on God as an explanation for the beauty and regularity of nature, using inductive, abductive, and deductive modes of argumentation.[44] Yet other approaches must be noted, particularly the classical Renaissance metaphor of "God's two books," the origins of which can be tracked back to the early medieval period.[45] This strongly visual metaphor invites us to see God as the author or creator of two distinct yet related "books," the Book of Nature and the Book of Scripture, and thus to imagine nature as a readable text that requires interpretation,[46] in a manner comparable to the Christian interpretation of the Bible.

Although natural theology is sometimes understood as an approach to nature and divinity based on a reading only of the Book of Nature, it is possible to frame it in terms of the outcomes of reading these two books side by side, allowing them to enrich and interpenetrate each other. More recently, there has been a move to develop a "natural semiotics," which considers the natural order as a system of embedded signs, an order signifying and pointing beyond

41. This is the view of Graham Oppy. See, e.g., Oppy, *Arguing about Gods*. For further discussion, see Siniscalchi, "Atheist Criticism of Thomistic Natural Theology."

42. For this latter view, see McGrath, *Re-Imagining Nature*, 25–40.

43. For a "thick" description of natural theology, see McGrath, *Re-Imagining Nature*, 22–25.

44. McGrath, *Territories of Human Reason*, 154–81.

45. For its medieval roots, see Mews, "World as Text." For its later development, see Howell, *God's Two Books*.

46. On this, see Blumenberg, *Die Lesbarkeit der Welt*.

itself to God.[47] In both cases, natural theology aims to show that a Christian imaginative or semiotic framework is able to interpret the complexities more satisfactorily than its secular alternatives.

Yet this general intellectual enterprise is conducted within a variety of contexts and for several purposes; those contexts and purposes shape the form that it takes. Natural theology is a bidirectional process: it can designate the process by which one begins from reflection on nature and concludes in belief in God; it can equally designate the process by which one begins with belief in God and ends with reflection on the natural world in the light of this belief. This helps us understand how natural theology can take different forms and why it is misleading to treat any one of them as normative or characteristic.

One family of approaches emphasizes the consonance or congruence of the vision of reality articulated by the Christian faith alongside our observations or experience of nature. Joseph Butler's *Analogy of Religion* (1736) develops a form of natural theology aimed at engaging the questions prompted by the rise of skeptical forms of rationalism in the early eighteenth century. Its basic approach is to affirm the "analogy" or intellectual resonance between the human experience of nature and the intellectual framework offered by the Christian gospel. This approach to natural theology does not seek to prove God's existence from an appeal to nature or reason, but rather to demonstrate a coherence or congruence between the specific claims of Christian faith and a knowledge of the world derived from other disciplines or areas of life.

In much the same way, William Paley's *Natural Theology* (1802) set out to demonstrate how the idea of God as an "artificer," someone who designs and constructs, chimes in with our observations of the world, particularly the complexity of the biological world.[48] A similar approach is taken in the *Bridgewater Treatises* (1833–36).[49] The argument again does not attempt to prove God's necessary existence but seeks to show how the Christian faith is able to accommodate or "fit in" what is actually observed in the world of nature.

This family of natural theologies is clearly bidirectional in its approach. The intention lying behind all the works just noted is twofold: first, to reassure religious believers that their faith is indeed able to make sense of their world of experience; and second, to affirm the rationality of faith to those outside the church, thus neutralizing or at least blunting some of the criticisms of the intrinsic incoherence or irrationality of the gospel that were then making

---

47. See, e.g., A. Robinson, *God and the World of Signs*.
48. Sweet, "Paley, Whately, and 'Enlightenment Evidentialism.'"
49. Topham, "Biology in the Service of Natural Theology."

their appearance.[50] This helps us understand why the rich spectrum of natural theology is deployed in different ways to different envisaged audiences.

Other approaches to natural theology, however, go beyond cognitive or analytical reflection on nature and aim to identify and cultivate the affective and imaginative aspects of our engagement with the natural world.[51] As the study of the Christian theological tradition makes clear, there is a rich heritage of correlating doctrine and the imagination that needs to be applied to theological reflection on the natural world.[52] The American Puritan theologian Jonathan Edwards developed an approach to natural theology that both safeguarded and highlighted the affective aspects of the believer's encounter with the world of nature. For Edwards, the regeneration of the believer "establishes a new vision, radically different from that of natural understanding and sight." As a result, nature is seen in a new way, its beauty being highlighted and exhibited by the new vision of reality resulting from conversion.[53] This is particularly evident in one of Edwards's most lyrical descriptions of nature:

> When we are delighted with flowery meadows and gentle breezes of wind, we may consider that we only see the emanations of the sweet benevolence of Jesus Christ; when we behold the fragrant rose and lily, we see his love and purity. So the green trees and fields, and singing of birds, are emanations of his infinite joy and benignity; the easiness and naturalness of trees and vines [are] shadows of his infinite beauty and loveliness; the crystal rivers and murmuring streams have the footsteps of his sweet grace and bounty.[54]

The Christian vision of reality allows us to see nature in such a way that its beauties, as Edwards goes on to say, "are really emanations, or shadows, of the excellencies of the Son of God."

Natural Theology and Apologetics

The big-tent approach to natural theology sketched in this chapter is motivated by intellectual and imaginative delight.[55] Psalm 19:1 is thus understood

---

50. For a reflection on the cultural significance of such criticisms, see Jager, "Mansfield Park and the End of Natural Theology."

51. Smith, *Imagining the Kingdom*, 103–49.

52. See Zahl, "On the Affective Salience of Doctrines."

53. Lane, "Jonathan Edwards on Beauty, Desire, and the Sensory World."

54. Edwards, "Miscellanies, no. 108," in Edwards, *Works*, 13:279.

55. Note the discussion of the "allure" of natural theology in Bork, "Natural Theology in the Eighteenth Century."

not as a proof of God's existence but as affirming the capacity of our experience of the natural world, when rightly interpreted, to imaginatively enhance and affectively enrich our appreciation of God as creator of the world. Most of us, when looking at our complex and wonderful universe through the lens of the Christian faith, find our vision of God enriched and extended by reflecting on God's works. It is a theme that is widely explored in the writings of great medieval theologians, such as Bonaventure, who emphasize the capacity of the natural world, when rightly seen, to intensify our sense of delight and wonder at God's wisdom in creation.[56]

It is generally agreed that Karl Barth's critique of natural theology still remains potent within Protestant theology, even to the point where some now regard natural theology as a form of heresy.[57] For Barth, natural theology represents an improper assertion of human autonomy, which seeks to encounter and characterize God under terms of our own choosing.[58] It is an important concern, and Barth is right to raise it. Yet Barth's legitimate objections actually correlate with only a somewhat restricted region of the spectrum of possible natural theologies and are best seen as identifying possible risks attending the enterprise of natural theology, rather than systematically discrediting the notion. The 1934 disagreement between Barth and Brunner fundamentally concerns the general question of the relation of nature and grace, rather than the specific notion of natural theology.[59]

Yet Barth's concerns about natural theology are also entangled with a deeper suspicion of the purpose and place of apologetics, which is reflected in his criticisms of Brunner's notion of the "other" task of theology—namely, the critical engagement with culture. While valid criticisms can be made of attempts to try to prove God's existence or to bypass God's self-disclosure, it is entirely proper to aim to show a wider public, beyond the realm of the church, that Christianity is rationally plausible and deserves further consideration.

Apologetics has always been an essential aspect of the church's ministry, particularly when the gospel has faced intellectual challenges—as, for example, in the period of the early church.[60] There are, of course, various approaches to apologetics, including those that propose to demonstrate the rationality of faith by direct argumentation.[61] Yet there are other forms of

56. Cullen, *Bonaventure*, 119–29.
57. A point highlighted throughout Kock, *Natürliche Theologie*.
58. Kock, *Natürliche Theologie*, 23–102.
59. For a critical account of this debate and detailed engagement with the original German-language sources, see McGrath, *Emil Brunner*, 90–132. Barth clearly misunderstands Brunner at several important points.
60. Pelikan, *Christianity and Classical Culture*, 22–39.
61. Dulles, *History of Apologetics*.

apologetics that do not take such an approach but rather assert the consonance or resonance between the Christian faith and what is observed in the world and experienced within us. C. S. Lewis's apologetic method, for example, is based primarily on the capacity of Christianity to "fit in" our experience and observations of the world.[62] Some theologians consider apologetics to be illegitimate, arguing that what is required is merely the proclamation of the gospel. Others, however, argue that apologetics is a constructive and appropriate method for preparing the ground for evangelism, partly by affirming the trustworthiness of Christianity, and partly by helping outsiders grasp something of the quality of its rendering of reality—including the natural world. This is seen particularly clearly in the early modern period in Western Europe, as new challenges to the comprehensiveness and coherence of Christianity were raised through the emergence of a scientific culture.

It is widely agreed that the emergence of physicotheology in the eighteenth century reflects apologetic considerations specific to that historical period, especially in England. It was held to represent an apologetic means of ensuring that a religious culture remained in contact with an increasingly scientific culture during a period of transition, allowing the ongoing vitality of traditional religious ideas to be affirmed in a rising scientific culture, and emerging scientific approaches to be affirmed in an ongoing religious culture.[63] Yet such a natural theology ran the risk of becoming imprisoned within its cultural context. Two points are of particular importance.

First, the "god" disclosed by such a natural theology was essentially a creator who had no necessary connection with the ongoing governance of the world (a theological idea traditionally expressed in terms of divine providence) or with the redemption of humanity. The god of physicotheology corresponded in some loose ways with the somewhat impersonal and inactive divinity proposed by various forms of Deism. This form of natural theology created a workable alliance between science and religion in the late seventeenth and early eighteenth centuries, allowing them to coexist in relative harmony; it became clear that it was possible to dispense with this god without undue difficulty. By the end of the eighteenth century, natural theology was seen by its critics as encouraging various forms of atheism, by presenting an inadequate concept of God.[64]

Second, the emerging rationalism of this period reduced natural theology to rational categories, particularly through the suppression of the imagination.

62. McGrath, "Reason, Experience, and Imagination."
63. Mandelbrote, "Uses of Natural Theology in Seventeenth-Century England."
64. Odom, "Estrangement of Celestial Mechanics and Religion."

This form of natural theology emphasized the importance of rational explanation—but in doing so, failed to capture the imaginative and emotive aspects of religious faith, thus impoverishing our vision for an enterprise that is both rational and imaginative.[65] Neither the academy nor the church can be allowed to become trapped within a restrictive conceptualization of natural theology that reflects the specific social and cultural situation of the early modern period. Yet these difficulties can be resolved—not by abandoning natural theology, but by ensuring that neither Christian theology nor apologetics is needlessly restricted to this one specific implementation of the practice of natural theology.

Some might make the entirely reasonable point that the broad approach to a Christian natural theology briefly sketched here seems to confuse the descriptive and normative, in effect presenting such a natural theology both as an apologetic approach that is to be tested, and as an established way of thinking that is capable of testing and assessing other perspectives and outlooks. While I concede this concern, it is important to appreciate that the plurality of contexts within which natural theology operates makes such a diversity of functions inevitable. As Ludwig Wittgenstein pointed out, one and the same proposition or idea may be treated at one point as something that is *to be tested* and at another as a *rule of testing*.[66] As I have stressed, natural theology is bidirectional, engaging audiences within and beyond the churches. Yet what might seem to be conceptual incoherence or an inappropriate plasticity of approach is actually a reflection of the remarkable versatility of the broad notion of natural theology, affirming its capacity to engage in multiple conversations and enterprises. Those conversations will continue and are likely to become more important.

Science and Religion: A Catalyst for Natural Theology

Perhaps the most significant contemporary interface between Christian theology and the natural world is the broad area designated by the term "science and religion." Growing cultural interest in engaging nature led to the emergence of three significant terms in the seventeenth and eighteenth centuries, each of which developed quite distinct resonances and associations: "natural science," "natural theology," and "natural philosophy."[67] What holds them together in this early modern context is the shared assumption that an engagement with the natural world is intellectually significant,

65. Note the points made in Caldecott, *Beauty for Truth's Sake*, 37–52.
66. Wittgenstein, *On Certainty*, 98.
67. See, e.g., Dear, "Reason and Common Culture in Early Modern Natural Philosophy."

morally improving, and religiously enriching.[68] In due course, these three concepts became freighted with various assumptions. In the twenty-first century, "natural science" is now widely understood to mean the empirical investigation of nature, without reference to philosophical or theological assumptions; "natural theology" has come to be seen as a subdivision of the philosophy of religion; and "natural philosophy" has generally ceased to be used.

Both the natural sciences and Christian theology reflect a sense of wonder at the world around us and within us,[69] a realization that our conceptual categories are simultaneously stretched and enriched by the vastness of nature on the one hand, and the immensity of God—so often expressed using the notion of "glory"—on the other. It is well known that there is an important historical link between the emergence of certain types of natural theology (especially physicotheology) and the increasingly important cultural role of the natural sciences in the early modern period.[70]

Natural theology created an important—though often loosely conceived—intellectual and imaginative bridge between a scientific and a religious culture, particularly in England during the late seventeenth and early eighteenth centuries. Several nonscientific factors apparently helped to shape this new interest in natural theology and the related notion of natural religion at this time in England.[71]

1. The rise of biblical criticism called into question the reliability or intelligibility of Scripture and hence generated interest in the revelatory capacities of the natural world.

2. A growing distrust of ecclesiastical authority led some to explore sources of knowledge that were seen to be independent of ecclesiastical control, such as an appeal to reason or to the natural order.

3. A dislike of organized religion and Christian doctrines caused many to search for a simpler "religion of nature," in which nature was valued as a source of revelation.

These factors served to maximize the plausibility of physicotheology at the time, allowing the scientific uncovering of regularity in the universe to

68. Isaac Newton is an excellent example of a scientist who brings together these three potentially disparate lines of thought; see Iliffe, *Priest of Nature.*

69. Tallis, *In Defence of Wonder,* 1–22.

70. Brooke, "Science and the Fortunes of Natural Theology"; Bork, "Natural Theology in the Eighteenth Century."

71. Westfall, "Scientific Revolution of the Seventeenth Century."

be correlated with some core themes of Christian theology.[72] The forms of natural theology that emerged from within the Newtonian synthesis tended to emphasize the regularity of the natural order. The existence of laws (or principles) of nature was often held to indicate, possibly even prove, the existence of a lawgiver—easily identified with, or assimilated to, the Christian notion of God.[73] Although teleological notions could be embedded within this conceptual matrix without difficulty, its prime emphasis rested on the ordering and rationality of nature, rather than on the purposes for which such ordering and rationality might have been devised. Yet the growing tendency to think of the universe in mechanical terms made it increasingly plausible to argue from the demonstration of a cosmic mechanism to an affirmation and appreciation of its designer—an approach characteristic of English physicotheology.

More recently, the British quantum physicist and theologian John Polkinghorne has argued for both the renewal and revision of natural theology, in response to natural scientists' growing interest in grander questions that lie beyond the scope of the sciences to answer. Polkinghorne rejects the idea of natural theology as a way of proving the existence of God, arguing that natural theology rightly belongs within "the fold of general theological inquiry" and that it aims to offer enhanced insight into the structure, function, and significance of our universe by complementing or supplementing the sciences, rather than by seeking to displace them.[74]

Polkinghorne develops an approach to natural theology that makes no claims to *prove* the existence of God but rather aims to offer a more satisfying account of nature than its atheist alternatives. Natural theology is thus to be seen as supplementing the natural sciences, rather than considering itself as a rival or competitor in the matter of explanation. While science itself does not appear to need any theological supplementation within its own distinctive domain, it nevertheless raises questions it cannot answer via its own working methods. "There are metaquestions, which arise from our scientific experience and understanding but which point us beyond what science by itself can presume to speak about."[75]

So what "metaquestions" does Polkinghorne have in mind? A good example is this: Why is the physical universe so rationally transparent to us, so that we can discern its pattern and structure, even in the quantum world,

---

72. For a good analysis, see Peterfreund, *Turning Points in Natural Theology*.

73. For the development of this idea, see Osler, *Divine Will and the Mechanical Philosophy*, 118–46.

74. Polkinghorne, "New Natural Theology," 50.

75. Polkinghorne, "New Natural Theology," 43.

which bears little relation to our everyday experience?[76] Why is it that some of the most beautiful patterns proposed by pure mathematicians are actually found to occur in the structure of the physical world? Natural theology offers an explanatory framework that supplements—but does not displace—the framework of the natural sciences, allowing a fuller and deeper grasp of their potential and limits. This explanation of the deep intelligibility of the universe that arises from natural theology must therefore be seen as an insight rather than a demonstration.

As Polkinghorne suggests, natural theology has a particularly significant role to play in the theological engagement with the natural sciences by providing a credible rational and imaginative challenge to naturalist or materialist accounts of nature. One of the most basic and significant functions of a Christian natural theology is to set out a theology of nature: a compelling, comprehensive, and fundamentally *religious* vision of the world as God's creation that can illuminate our minds and excite our hearts,[77] the quality of which calls into question the adequacy of secular approaches.

Wittgenstein's famous remark that "a *picture* held us captive" highlights how easily our understanding of our world can be controlled by a worldview or metanarrative that has, whether we realize it or not, come to determine what we perceive within this world.[78] This "picture" causes us to interpret experience in certain manners as natural or self-evidentially correct, while blinding us to alternative ways of understanding it. Peter de Bolla, drawing on this image, has noted how someone viewing a work of art might become locked into "a set of expectations and beliefs," so that the reading of that work merely reiterates its "grounding ideology"[79]—in this case, materialist naturalism. Wittgenstein's metaphor invites us to imagine a picture gallery of worldviews, stepping into each and assessing the quality of its rendering of the texture of our world. A Christian natural theology can thus be seen as a specific way of beholding and engaging the natural order, displaying a rational, imaginative, and affective rendering of reality that eludes secular mythologies and materialist naturalisms. A natural theology makes possible a Christian reading of nature, enriching a scientific narrative by preventing it from becoming a "dull catalogue of common things" (John Keats).[80]

76. Polkinghorne, "New Natural Theology," 44.
77. Gunton, "Trinity, Natural Theology, and a Theology of Nature."
78. Wittgenstein, *Philosophical Investigations*, §115.
79. De Bolla, *Art Matters*, 97.
80. While significant intellectual criticisms have been directed against a "natural atheology"—e.g., Sosa, "Natural Theology and Naturalist Atheology"—these are often limited to challenging its rational depth and coherence and do not engage with its obvious failure to connect

Conclusion: The Future of Natural Theology

This chapter has set out an expansive vision of natural theology as a practice of exploring the interface between nature and God by using the human faculties of reason, imagination, and emotion. It recognizes and respects the rich diversity of approaches to, and definitions of, natural theology. This classic understanding of natural theology inevitably and necessarily enfolds a variety of ways of envisaging and enacting a correlation and connection of the natural world and God. Although I have raised some concerns about the specific notion of natural theology as "the enterprise of providing support for religious beliefs by starting from premises that neither are nor presuppose any religious beliefs," my concern here is not to criticize this specific approach: I seek merely to point out that it is part of a spectrum of possibilities and is thus neither the *only* approach to natural theology nor its normative form.[81]

Throughout, I have made it clear that I see no legitimate place for a view of natural theology that seeks to subvert revelation or to offer a demonstrative proof of the existence of God. There nevertheless remains a legitimate apologetic role for natural theology, in that it exhibits the distinct intrinsic rationality of faith to those outside the church, thus preparing the way for a deeper and transformative encounter with the gospel itself. It also remains important for Christian believers to be reassured of the intellectual resilience of their position, particularly in cultures that privilege the methods and outcomes of the natural sciences.

The whole enterprise of natural theology rests on a fundamental *theological* belief that the God who created the world is also the God who is disclosed in and through the Christian Bible, nested in a set of equally theological beliefs concerning the transformative impact of grace and the nature of revelation. Without this underlying and informing assumption, God and nature are disconnected entities. The viability of the range of natural theologies is established and safeguarded by the Christian theological assumption of a creator God, revealed in Scripture, whose imprint is embedded within the natural world. A natural theology rests on the core belief that the natural world is actually a created order. While this chapter sets out the case for recognizing and deploying a rich and deeply satisfying range of understandings of natural theology, it is perhaps best seen as a plea to rediscover natural theology as an authentically and characteristically *theological* practice, rather than merely as an aspect of the philosophy of religion.

---

meaningfully with the human imagination, affections, and emotions. The phrasing by Keats is from his poem "Lamia" (1819).

81. Alston, *Perceiving God*, 289.

Contemporary Response

CHARLES TALIAFERRO

Alister McGrath has made excellent contributions to the relationship of science and religion, and so the high quality of his chapter on natural theology is not surprising. If anything might be surprising, it would be my offering a brilliant response to his "classical view." Without any claim to brilliance, I will use this space to reinforce the understanding of natural theology—as I believe it is generally understood by philosophers today. I then invite us to consider whether all forms of natural theology must assume (presuppose) some kind of theological anthropology. Finally, what sort of cultural, social context is likely to foster the practice of natural theology?

I take it that *The Blackwell Companion to Natural Theology*, edited by William Lane Craig and J. P. Moreland, is respectable; it received some good reviews and is endorsed by Quentin Smith, John Haught, and Justin Barrett. It contains chapters on the Leibnizian cosmological argument, the kalam cosmological argument, the teleological argument, the argument from consciousness, the argument from reason, the ontological argument, and the moral argument. As I noted in my chapter, although natural theology is customarily treated as not assuming the authority of revelation, it now is taken to encompass theistic arguments from religious experience, so the *Companion* includes an outstanding chapter, "The Argument from Religious Experience," by Kai-Man Kwan. I submit that "natural theology" today encompasses (at the least) the arguments in this *Companion*.

Do any of the arguments in the *Companion* presuppose at the outset a theological anthropology? I think none of the chapters ask readers to assume, for example, that humans are created in God's image or that natural theology can or should only (or principally) be done in the context of Christian belief and practice. This is not at all an issue in my chapter in the volume, "The Project of Natural Theology," in which I reply to the critique of natural theology attributed to Kant, Hume, and others. Speaking autobiographically, my own journey to Christian faith was like C. S. Lewis's: I first became a theist based on arguments (for me it was a combination of a broadly teleological argument and the argument from reason). This was not a matter of my beginning with the Bible or joining a faith community or studying German theology. When it came to my becoming a professing Christian, it was a matter of religious experience and a case for the resurrection.[1]

Some years after my conversion, I became convinced of a theistic cosmological argument based on the version defended by Richard Taylor in his book *Metaphysics*. Maybe my being a theist inclined me to accept that argument (since refined by William Rowe, Bruce Reichenbach, T. O'Connor, and R. Koons), but there are no premises or claims of a religious nature in Taylor's argument. He would be horrified if there were since Taylor thought all religions are based on superstition and fear.

A question arises: If the theistic cosmological argument is so impressive, why don't more people endorse it? To begin, the argument is not the kind of thing that the majority of educated adults encounter. And even philosophically trained adults may not be exposed to it. Moreover, while statistics on such matters are a bit foggy, I can report that those of us who are professional philosophers are not always the best guides to life; for many years one of my professors (Peter Unger) argued that he did not exist. Today it is rare for any philosopher to claim to have a proof for some position; rather, we refer to arguments that are good or bad, persuasive or unconvincing, and so on. From my perspective, the theistic cosmological argument is on a par with other arguments I accept: a phenomenological argument against physicalism, a case for moral realism, reasons to accept a Platonic view of abstract objects.[2]

What about the cultural, social context for natural theology? Natural theology probably would be unlikely to flourish in communities that are in dire poverty, communities subject to pandemics and violence, secular totalitarian societies that censure philosophical theology, and the like. A better

1. Incidentally, the *Companion* concludes with an excellent chapter on the resurrection: T. McGrew and L. McGrew, "Argument from Miracles."

2. For an excellent critical analysis on how contemporary philosophers assess the evidence of their theses, see Lycan, *On Evidence in Philosophy*.

setting would be what Karl Popper referred to as an open society: a site providing freedom of thought and speech, occasions for respectful arguments and objections, and time to debate and to change one's mind without ridicule.[3] And perhaps even time to read and discuss with friends the viewpoints and responses to be found in this book.

3. See Popper, *Open Society*.

Catholic Response

FATHER ANDREW PINSENT

Alister McGrath's chapter on a classical view of natural theology offers an exceptionally rich and broad-ranging account of the field. A major focus of his chapter is the problem of defining natural theology and the need for historical inquiry to avoid the retrospective and frequently distorting imposition of an exclusively modern perspective. He points out, for example, that although "natural theology" is not a biblical term, it can describe a variety of biblical lines of thought. One example is the Wisdom literature of the Old Testament, which is particularly important in highlighting the role of the created order in illuminating the character of Israel's covenant with God. Another example is the way in which the New Testament points to the capacity of the visible world to disclose or intimate the existence of God (Rom. 1:18–20). McGrath further explicates how a broad classic theological framework—articulated by, for example, Athanasius, Augustine, Aquinas, and Calvin—has built on these foundations.

One theme that emerges from this survey is the need for and value of a broad understanding of natural theology to encompass bidirectionality, from the God of revelation to the world, as well as from the world to God. In other words, on McGrath's view, natural theology should include the theology of nature, offering a Christian reading of nature, as well as what is frequently understood by natural theology in the modern sense: proofs or intimations of the existence of God from nature alone. Other themes that emerge include the role of imagination and context, the value of affective as well as cognitive engagement, and natural theology as a loosely conceived imaginative bridge between a scientific and religious culture in the late seventeenth through early eighteenth centuries. This last observation introduces his concluding theme: the field of science and religion as a catalyst for natural theology.

Given the wealth of valuable insights in this chapter, it seems to me almost churlish to make any criticism, but there is one aspect that I would like to see expanded. McGrath briefly mentions the negativity of Barth to natural theology, an attitude that is, at least in part, grounded in Barth's Reformed theology. This grounding is one of the topics of John McDowell's chapter. Nevertheless, some Catholic authors have also been, at least in part, somewhat negative about natural theology. One example is Augustine, whose negativity is mentioned but not examined in McGrath's chapter. Another example, not mentioned by McGrath, is the newly minted Catholic saint John Henry Newman, who warned, in effect, of the limitations of natural theology in the following quotation, with which I conclude my chapter: "Religion, it has been well observed, is something *relative to us*; a system of commands and promises of God *towards* us. But how are we to be concerned with the sun, moon, and stars? Or with the laws of the universe? . . . They do not speak to sinners at all. They were created before Adam fell. They 'declare the glory of God,' but not his will."[1] As I noted previously, Newman here warns that the study of the sun, moon, stars, and laws of the universe, while showing the handiwork of God, cannot enable us to know the purposes or the will of God, let alone bridge the unthinkable gap between God and ourselves. But in the absence of revelation and grace, exactly what is the character of our separation from God?

This problem is articulated with the greatest eloquence in one of the most important texts of what might be called natural theology in the Bible, Job 38–41, which begins as follows:

> Then the LORD answered Job out of the whirlwind:
> "Who is this that darkens counsel by words without knowledge?
> Gird up your loins like a man,
> I will question you, and you shall declare to me.
> Where were you when I laid the foundation of the earth?
> Tell me, if you have understanding.
> Who determined its measurements—surely you know!" (Job 38:1–5)

At first glance, the main issue of this and subsequent verses is the ignorance of Job, but I read them differently, a point of difference highlighted in the words, "Where were you?" These words seem to parallel Genesis 3:9, when the

---

1. See Newman, "Sermon XXIV."

Lord God asks, "Where are you?"[2] In both cases the questions seem rhetorical at best, since God knows the answers, but their significance is highlighted by the remainder of Job 38–41, which includes verses like these:

> "On what were its bases sunk,
> or who laid its cornerstone,
> when the morning stars sang together,
> and all the sons of God shouted for joy?" (38:6–7)

> "Has the rain a father,
> or who has begotten the drops of dew?
> From whose womb did the ice come forth,
> and who has given birth to the hoarfrost of heaven?" (38:28–29)

> "Can you lift up your voice to the clouds,
> that a flood of waters may cover you?
> Can you send forth lightnings, that they may go
> and say to you, 'Here we are'?" (38:34–35)

The impression I gain from these chapters is that God has an intimacy—one might almost call it playfulness—with his creation, in which stars sing; in which it is suggested that God begets rain, dew, ice, and hoarfrost; and in which lightning converses with God. Indeed, the scenario seems almost like a dance or party, but with one of the guests missing, namely, Job, who may also stand for humanity in general. More specifically, as implied by Genesis 3:9 and Job 38:4, as well as my analysis of Thomas Aquinas's account of the life of grace (see my chapter), what is missing is the second-person relationship to God. This loss of second-person relatedness to God, due to sin, is a rupture that also severs humanity from intimacy with creation. Under these circumstances, it is not surprising that humans can come to view creation as just dead stuff to be manipulated.

These considerations underscore the limitations of natural theology without grace yet also emphasize the value of a theology of nature from the perspective of grace, along the lines of McGrath's account. Moreover, the reference to a kind of solemn play between God and creation in Job 38–41 suggests another kind of solemn play that has been part of most Christian

2. God's question to Adam in Hebrew in Genesis 3:9 consists of the single word *'ayyekkah?* The precise construct form is a hapax legomenon in the Hebrew Bible. The phrase is not exactly "Where are you?" but "Where do you exist?" or "What has become of you?" or "What is your spiritual state?" What is clear is the loss of the relationship with humanity from God's perspective. I am grateful to Rabbi Shabtai Rappaport, from Bar-Ilan University in Tel Aviv, for discussions on these points.

experience across diverse cultures and history—namely, liturgy and all manner of associated disciplines, such as art, architecture, and music. Rather than creation being dead stuff, in liturgy all kinds of created beings are directly or indirectly caught up into the act of giving praise to God. Examples include the flowers for the altars, the bees that make the wax for the candles, works of art that evoke the concretely given supernatural, and inspiring music and architecture. Such matters, which go far beyond what most people would think of as natural theology, illustrate the extraordinary potential of a broad understanding of this field.

Deflationary Response

PAUL K. MOSER

Alister McGrath offers a historical taxonomy of natural theology, thereby illuminating some of the prominent motives behind natural theology in history. I have no quarrel with his taxonomy, but I contend that we should be more candid about the limitations of natural theology in its persuasive value.

McGrath's Proposals

McGrath rightly acknowledges that the Wisdom literature of the Jewish Scriptures does not use a natural theology to argue for God's existence. He remarks: "There is no question here of nature 'proving' the existence of the God of Israel; there is, however, a constant insistence that aspects of the natural order can illuminate and inform the human quest for wisdom—and hence ultimately for God. At several points, the New Testament indicates the capacity of the visible world to disclose or intimate the existence of God—for example, in the opening chapter of Paul's letter to the Romans, or Paul's Areopagus speech in Acts 17."

Even if parts of the New Testament point to "the capacity of the visible world to disclose or intimate the existence of God," we can ask some pressing questions for many inquirers about natural theology. (1) If parts of the New Testament point in this direction, is their pointing *accurate* rather than misleading? (2) *How* exactly does the visible world "disclose or intimate the existence of God," *if* it does so? (3) Is not the visible world too mixed with evil and good to merit the honorific status of disclosing or intimating the

129

existence of God? If God is perfectly good, the morally mixed visible world does not seem up to the task. Perhaps *God* could reveal God through nature somehow, but that would be a separate topic.

McGrath aims to accommodate a role for human imagination in natural theology. He thus comments: "Modernist hostility toward the imagination still affects the way we think about natural theology, which offers us both a rational account of how God can be found in or through nature and an imaginative framework that allows us to see and experience nature in a new manner—what we might describe as 'a theological re-imagining of nature.'" Such a "re-imagining of nature" is a live option as a *coherent* perspective. It should be acceptable as coherent even to agnostics and atheists so long as it avoids disputed claims to truth or knowledge of reality. Imagination is one thing; evidence of reality, another. If we maintain this sound distinction, we can allow for natural theology as something coherently imagined, with no threat to what is reasonable or evidentially grounded with regard to reality.

McGrath adds: "Christianity provides a capacious and rich vision of our world and humanity, which creates intellectual space for the enterprise described in this chapter as 'natural theology' by showing that it is *natural* for human beings to want to undertake natural theology." It is unclear how it is "natural," if it is natural, for humans to pursue natural theology. Even so, we can grant the claim for the sake of argument. What is gained if the claim is true? Perhaps we then can say that we should have expected what is a reality: many humans do pursue natural theology, regardless of the rate of success in their adequately defending theism. Our empirical evidence supports the latter claim, but it is simply a claim of sociology that is evidently true. It does not follow, however, that the *natural theology* being pursued is true or evidently true. So, the cognitive or evidential issue behind natural theology is not thereby settled.

McGrath moves beyond sociology with his following claim: "While God is disclosed through the created order, which bears the divine imprint, a natural theology rests on human beings possessing some created capacity to recognize this limited disclosure for what it really is, whether through the training or disciplining of their natural capacities, or through the healing or expansion of those capacities through grace." We are no longer in the domain of mere "imagination" if we accept McGrath's claim that "God is disclosed through the created order, which bears the divine imprint."

McGrath's claim is a truth claim about *reality*, beyond a domain of "imagination." Careful inquirers thus will ask: What evidence, if any, supports the *truth* (beyond the imaginability) of the claim about divine disclosure and the divine imprint? In addition, is this evidence available to all inquirers, and can it be stated without begging key questions from agnostics, atheists, and other dissenting inquirers? If not, what is the lesson about the epistemic reasonableness of belief that God exists? A natural theology should attend to such pressing questions. Without cogent answers, we can rightly be suspicious of the natural theology on offer.

McGrath fittingly asks, "Does such a natural theology elicit a rational recognition of the reality of God? Or is the response to the natural world better framed in terms of an imaginative embrace of God, or a relational loving of God? Christian theology provides us with a starting point for the colligation of our experience of the world and God, while leaving us to fill in the fine details—a process of enrichment that is shaped to no small extent by the context within which such a natural theology is developed, with its envisaged tasks." A retreat from "a rational recognition of the reality of God" to "an imaginative embrace of God, or a relational loving of God," would be troubling from a cognitive point of view. If "an imaginative embrace of God" is to be a genuine embrace of *God*, we will need to face a straightforward question: Is our "imaginative embrace of God" (whatever the details or the phenomenology) an *actual* embrace of God rather than a counterfeit?

Imagination, as we know, often leaves us at odds with reality, or at least doubtful about reality. While half asleep recently, I imagined with due regret that I had contracted COVID-19, but I came to recognize, quickly and gladly, that my imagination had misled me. My imagination did not match reality: it went against my overwhelming evidence to the contrary. A related consideration arises for talk of "a relational loving of God." Is it an *actual* loving of *God* rather than a counterfeit? Imagination will not settle this matter. We can grant the imagination and even find it "enriching" in some sense, but, as responsible inquirers, we need relevant evidence for the relevant truth claims. We need a truth indicator of some sort to ground our imagination about its *accuracy* regarding reality. So, we have not actually sidestepped concerns about "a rational recognition of the reality of God." Even an imaginative natural theology must face such concerns.

McGrath observes that "the intention lying behind [the natural theology of Butler and Paley] is twofold: first, to reassure religious believers that their faith is indeed able to make sense of their world of experience; and second, to affirm the rationality of faith to those outside the church, thus neutralizing or at least blunting some of the criticisms of the intrinsic incoherence or irrationality of the gospel that were then making their appearance." This seems right to me, regardless of the success of their intentions. There are relevant "criticisms" and challenging questions in circulation about theistic belief, and a merely dogmatic response will seem arbitrary in the face of positions that compete with one's favorite theology.

My response to John C. McDowell in this book identifies some serious problems with Karl Barth's dogmatic approach to theology. As a result, I do not find benefit now in McGrath's following claim: "It is generally agreed that Karl Barth's critique of natural theology still remains potent within Protestant theology, even to the point where some now regard natural theology as a form of heresy. For Barth, natural theology represents an improper assertion of human autonomy, which seeks to encounter and characterize God under terms of our own choosing. It is an important concern, and Barth is right to raise it." In my response to McDowell, I have noted that we have no reason to suppose that natural theology must rely on "an improper assertion of human autonomy." I identify a fitting concern of natural theology to develop a rationale for theistic belief, in terms of evidential support, with avoidance of as much question-begging as possible in response to dissenting inquires. Barth misses the importance of this concern; thus he leaves us with an unconvincing dogmatism in theology.

McGrath holds out for natural theology as "an enterprise that is both rational and imaginative," and he recommends against "a restrictive conceptualization of natural theology that reflects the specific social and cultural situation of the early modern period." We can grant that, but we still need to wonder how the "rational" side of natural theology should proceed. McGrath considers natural theology as a supplement to science, following a suggestion of John Polkinghorne regarding certain "metaquestions" for science. He explains:

> So what "metaquestions" does Polkinghorne have in mind? A good example is this: Why is the physical universe so rationally transparent to us, so that we can discern its pattern and structure, even in the quantum world, which bears little relation to our everyday experience? Why is it that some of the most beautiful patterns proposed by pure mathematicians are actually found to occur in the structure of the physical world? Natural theology offers an explanatory framework that supplements—but does not displace—the framework of the natural sciences, allowing a fuller and deeper grasp of their potential and limits. This explanation of the deep intelligibility of the universe that arises from natural theology must therefore be seen as an insight rather than a demonstration.

It is wise of McGrath to disown a "demonstration" here, given that we seem not to have one available. As for the retreat to "an insight" about "the deep intelligibility of the universe," the plot thickens. Does this alleged insight rest on supporting evidence for endorsing an *intelligent source* of the "deep intelligibility"? If so, can that evidence be affirmed without begging key questions against inquirers who dissent from theism? If not, our natural theology may end up simply preaching to the choir. If, however, there is such evidence, we need to state it convincingly. McGrath has not discharged the latter duty.

We can put the relevant issue as follows: Is there actually the "deep intelligibility of the universe" alleged by McGrath? We would gain nothing by suggesting, under the influence of Barth, that belief in it is "axiomatic." That would simply beg the key question against dissenting inquirers, including many scientists. It is at least logically coherent to deny that there is "deep intelligibility" requiring a divine source of intelligence, and many scientists withhold judgment on whether there actually is such intelligibility. If a natural theology endorses such intelligibility and its divine source, it owes us a rationale for its endorsement, if it is to be cogent. That rationale will not serve adequately if it simply begs key questions about the matter. Here, with the need for such a rationale, we have an unfulfilled task for McGrath's approach to natural theology.

McGrath does not retreat from his "rational" component of natural theology: "A Christian natural theology can thus be seen as a specific way of beholding and engaging the natural order, displaying a rational, imaginative, and affective rendering of reality that eludes secular mythologies and materialist naturalisms. A natural theology makes possible a Christian reading of nature, enriching a scientific narrative by preventing it from becoming a 'dull catalogue of common things' (John Keats)." Even if "a natural theology makes possible a Christian reading of nature," rationality does not settle for what is "possible." It calls for what is *adequately supported from an evidential point of view*. The adequate evidential support cannot leave the "Christian reading" as merely "possible," as axiomatic, or as question-begging regarding familiar questions about truth, trustworthiness, and reliability.

McGrath explains:

> I have made it clear that I see no legitimate place for a view of natural theology that seeks to subvert revelation or to offer a demonstrative proof of the existence of God. There nevertheless remains a legitimate apologetic role for natural theology, in that it exhibits the distinct intrinsic rationality of faith to those outside the church, thus preparing the way for a deeper and transformative encounter with the gospel itself. It also remains important for Christian believers to be reassured of the intellectual resilience of their position, particularly in cultures that privilege the methods and outcomes of the natural sciences.

The key issue now concerns what the alleged "distinct intrinsic rationality of faith" consists in. Once we get an answer to that issue, we can ask whether

Christian faith actually has support from such rationality. In the absence of an answer, we should withhold judgment, and we are now in that position. It is one thing to recommend in general the "distinct intrinsic rationality of faith"; it is something else—something more difficult—to explain what that rationality is and how it arises for Christian faith. An important question is whether the alleged rationality is "intrinsic." A prior question concerns what that term means in this context. We are left wondering.

McGrath concludes: "The whole enterprise of natural theology rests on a fundamental *theological* belief that the God who created the world is also the God who is disclosed in and through the Christian Bible, nested in a set of equally theological beliefs concerning the transformative impact of grace and the nature of revelation. . . . A natural theology rests on the core belief that the natural world is actually a created order." This conclusion is misleading in two ways. First, natural theology need not be linked with "the Christian Bible." It can be Deist, Jewish, Islamic, or Hindu, without a connection with "the Christian Bible." We have no good reason, given the actual history of natural theology, to link it in general with "the Christian Bible." Second, natural theology does not rest on "the core belief that the natural world is actually a created order." It may *lend support* to such a belief, but it does not "rest on" it. For instance, a natural theology could be (neo-)Platonic in supporting a designer who forms the world's material in some way but does not create it. We do well, then, not to wed natural theology in general to Christian theology.

Whither Religious Experience?

Barth and Emil Brunner, notoriously, overreacted to Friedrich Schleiermacher on subjective religious experience; thus they generally neglected the value of religious experience in theology. In a late work, Brunner commented: "Faith [in God] really and exclusively is dependent on the Word [of God], which against all empirical reality, supported by no experience, is in itself enough; the Word . . . is only to be grasped in the event in which that affirmation is uttered."[1] The misleading language is this: "supported by no experience." It stems from Barth's kind of exclusive contrast between the Word of God and human experience. The result is a divorce of religious inquiry from human experience, as if such experience were irrelevant.

The overreaction of Barth and Brunner to Schleiermacher devalues human experience and psychology in a way that makes them negligible by religious inquiry and commitment. It thus does not fit with much of religious inquiry

---

1. Brunner, *Christian Doctrine of the Church*, 201.

and life, and it opens the door to a misleading kind of dogmatism. Brunner's full position, including his view of the role of God's Spirit in human experience, does not fit with this extreme position. He did make some troublesome claims about experience, however, that stem from Barth's misplaced fear of giving human experience a role in religious inquiry and commitment. A robust theology, including any robust natural theology, will need to correct that overreaction of Barth and Brunner.

McGrath leaves us wondering about a role for religious experience in his approach to natural theology. His silence does not help the case for his approach, which could benefit from attention to the apostle Paul on religious experience. In my reply to John McDowell in this book, I note Paul's concern to avoid disappointment, including cognitive disappointment, in hope and faith in God. Paul, I suggest, identifies a basis for distinguishing *grounded* hope and faith in God from the "disappointment" of ungrounded, wishful thinking: "Hope [in God] does not disappoint us, because God's love [*agapē*] has been poured into our hearts through the Holy Spirit which has been given to us" (Rom. 5:5). Paul, I propose, has in mind evidential disappointment that arises from ungrounded hope, leaving us with wishful thinking. I suggest, on the basis of Romans 5:1, that Paul's thinking here bears on faith as well as hope in God.

If a person has experienced the kind of righteous *agapē* mentioned by Paul, we can ask what best explains that experience. In doing so, we can ask about a role of causal influence from *God* in that experience. Paul thought of it as including intentional *leading* by God, and this feature emerges in his remark that "all who are led by the Spirit of God are children of God" (Rom. 8:14 NRSVue). Such leading relies on a religious experience of God's distinctive character of righteous *agapē*. That experience, according to Paul, is a current down payment on a divine promise of full redemption. It thus saves Christians from mere dogmatism, wishful thinking, or dubious reliance on theology as "axiomatic" or "independent of experience." It saves us from the harmful overreaction of Barth and Brunner to Schleiermacher on religious experience.[2]

The general approach of the apostle Paul to grounded hope and faith in God enables us to talk of an evidential basis for such hope and faith. Such a basis relies on distinctive religious experience that calls for a best explanation. I cannot find a corresponding basis in the approaches of Barth, Brunner, or McGrath. So I recommend focusing attention on Paul for a needed improvement. I am confident that we will not be disappointed, cognitively or otherwise.

---

2. For development of this kind of view, see Moser, *God Relationship*; Moser, *Understanding Religious Experience*.

Barthian Response

JOHN C. McDOWELL

n *Oration* 28, composed in the mid-fourth century, Gregory the Theologian provides a striking image of the theological task.[1] The Theologian allusively likens his seeking God to Moses's ascent of Mount Sinai. This notion of ascent functions metaphorically to depict the kind of rigorous purificatory process that the disciple seeking God needs to undergo. On the mountain, however, as Exodus 33:20–23 makes clear, the person who ascends is denied sight of God and thereby a form of contemplation that gazes at God unimpeded by anything. The essence of God is *thoroughly* incomprehensible. One of the images used by Gregory is of God as the light that is too bright for the creature's gaze. The task becomes not that of describing God's essence, which is simply impossible to do since God is the highest and unapproachable and ineffable light. Instead, in and through the illuminative enlightening of God, or the power to understand, God is known in and through God's creatures. In other words, the result is not an activity limited to identifying and describing the divine nature, since *all things* are God's. The range of what is to be known and understood, then, is limited to everything that exists. The epistemic task is, we might say, a hermeneutical one that offers a way of looking at everything in relation to God. In this vein, Sergius Bulgakov, for instance, argues that "the createdness of the world can only be an object of faith."[2] In Rowan Williams's words, "Theology should be equipping us for the recognition of the parabolic in the world."[3]

1. Norris, *Faith Gives Fullness to Reasoning.*
2. Bulgakov, *Bride of the Lamb*, 8.
3. Williams, *On Christian Theology*, 42.

Accordingly, care must be taken not to put too much store by the little conjunctive word "and" in a phrase such as "revealed theology and natural theology" (or even "theology and the sciences"). For Gregory, these would properly not be discrete activities that can be defined over against each other in such a way as to require reflection on how to piece them together in some kind of engagement. Both human activities operate through the illuminative grace of God and are in need of appropriately transfigurative purging so that they may reflect God's light.

The way Gregory theologically uses nature and culture here, or rather creatureliness and creaturely activities, is suggestive of what is commendable about Alister McGrath's account and what would need considerable pressure exerted on it. The opening material on the "classical" witness to the non-human creature signifying God, in some way, is not theologically interesting. The important question comes in seeking what this vestigial *quality* is.

First, Gregory's *theological reading* of all things frames the interpretive context. God illuminates so that everything can be seen for what it is, according to its nature. Here is where McGrath's indication of the multiple ways in which, and purposes for which, natural theology operates is helpful lest critiques of natural theology bypass their targets. As McGrath claims elsewhere, "The enterprise of natural theology is thus one of discernment, of seeing nature in a certain way, of viewing it through a particular and specific set of spectacles."[4] The image of a perceptual aid is developed by John Calvin's account of the role of Scripture. What the Reformer does when he specifically speaks of "the first evidence in the order of nature" is suggest a context for understanding in terms of faith's purchase on teleology. He is "mindful that wherever we cast our eyes, all things they meet are works of God, and at the same time to ponder with pious meditation to what end God created them."[5]

Second, that Gregory regards creatures as disclosive of God is certainly true, even if it is only a minor note in his work, given that his focus is elsewhere, on explicating how the world looks when illuminated by God, something the Eunomians in his critique, with their separation of the mystery of God from the creativity of the Logos, could not do. This highlights the interpretive context needed to purge *distorted readings*. Not all reading contexts or readings are equal. In this regard, and more interestingly, McGrath approvingly refers to Jonathan Edwards's claim that the appropriate reading of nature requires a regenerated vision.

4. McGrath, *Open Secret*, 3.
5. Calvin, *Institutes of the Christian Religion* 1.14.1.

In this regard, it would be helpful if McGrath had provided a more developed sense of how and why the differences matter between the versions of natural theology he identifies. After all, despite attempting to indicate that the ignorance of God is inexcusable, Calvin quickly moves to delineate the way in which *idols* are generated, idols that then provide the conditions for further acts of deprivation requiring vivification for now-mortified consciousness. On the one hand, he can exude "pious delight in the works of God open and manifest in this most beautiful theatre."[6] Yet, on the other hand, he declares, "Such is our feebleness [that], unless Scripture guides us in seeking God, we are immediately confused."[7] With regard to the significance of the shifts in the very approaches taken by several trajectories within modernities, Michael Buckley critiques modern theisms and their atheistic rejections as *theologically* significant matters.[8] The critique in McGrath's chapter, instead, reduces concerns to what he elsewhere calls the Age of Reason's "attenuation of" natural theology's "scope."[9]

In addition, to speak of human beings as being *capaciously* fitted for divine revelation is unhelpful. Does this language do any interesting theo-rational work beyond, at best, what can be claimed about the divine commitment to loving the creature? Or does it distract from the way that creaturely fittingness itself is a given, something that is misdirected *post lapsum*, and that properly requires reeducation in perception?

It is certainly possible to argue that it is *natural* for creatures to read all things as vestigial in their very creatureliness. Yet McGrath's language of bearing the "divine imprint" is too flat and static to describe what is going on here. After all, for a lover, a photograph of the beloved is not a momentary capture or an immobilizing imprint of the image of the beloved, a stationary form of presence. Instead, it is a commemoratively provocative sign, something that generates a series of images, events, feelings, and so on, of a history together. Moreover, the image of "imprint" is an external one, like imprinting one's thumb onto a painting or tagging it, placing one's name on a book manuscript, and so on. After production, the artifact comes to have a presence of its own, and the imprint is as much a sign of absence as presence. That is certainly not what an apophatic theology means by divine mystery: it is not the darkness of absence abated only by moments of enlightening presence but is instead an indication of the sheer excess of divine plenitude

6. Calvin, *Institutes of the Christian Religion* 1.14.20.
7. Calvin, *Institutes of the Christian Religion* 1.14.1.
8. Buckley, *At the Origins of Modern Atheism*. McGrath speaks of "modernism" rather than "modernities," but this is largely a term reserved for an *artistic* period.
9. McGrath, *Open Secret*, 6.

in the thoroughness of God's presence that can be received only as a darkness of overwhelming light. It is not that the "disclosure" is "limited" in and through the creaturely signs, as McGrath's Brunnerian adaptation suggests, but rather that the sign itself is limited for iconizing the repleteness of God's being in God's self-disclosive presence.

Talk of "created capacity," or of the *imago Dei* as "'preparedness' of humanity for divine disclosure," is designed to depict the nature of human consciousness as interpretive—able to perceive, read, and fittingly act in the light of the created existent's determinative end. However, once again, it can misconstrue complex realities, since its appeal is to something human creatures qua creatures are now said to *possess* as agents. The language, even when it does come with an acknowledgment that God is continuously giving the conditions for knowing God, does not handle well, or at least not without significant qualification, the ongoing presence of divine action in and through all things as a *concursus* and creaturely response as that which involves divinely *illuminated* perception. According to Vladimir Lossky, "I am as I am given to be," and it is only through "participatory adherence to the presence of Him Who reveals Himself" that there comes the thinking of faith that "gives us true intelligence."[10] "It is," Lossky argues, "a matter of the internal reconstruction of our faculties of knowing, conditioned by the presence in us of the Holy Spirit."[11] To speak of nature's bearing witness to God when nature is read well is to ground the claim in absolute dependence on the prevenience of divine agency as gifting action, as an agency that provides the terms for the nature of all things to be beloved creatures, and for their proper end in the communicativeness of God.

Yet there is something missing from the chapter that is more substantive: this is the third point that can be broadly developed from Gregory's Moses-like theologian. The pentateuchal source text underlying Gregory's theological ascent not only denies Moses any sight of God but also forces him down the mountain for the sake of the covenanted people (Exod. 19:20–21), to destroy their idol and repair their lives within the covenantal law (32:7–8). In other words, the text removes worship from the kind of contemplative gaze that is distracted from worshipers' social responsibility, from evading engagement with corporate flourishing.[12]

McGrath's categories are epistemic (understanding) and aesthetic (wonder). For instance, the conversation between the sciences and theology is couched in terms of the theologians' supplementary contributions of aiding

10. Lossky, *Orthodox Theology*, 16.
11. Lossky, *Orthodox Theology*, 17.
12. See McDowell, "Ascent of Theological Reading."

in the "realization that our conceptual categories are . . . stretched and enriched by the . . . immensity of God," and therefore of offering "a more satisfying account of nature than its atheist alternatives . . . that can illuminate
our minds and excite our hearts." The cultured despisers are encouraged to
be provoked by natural splendor to the shock and awe of wonderment as
witnessing to God. Using Edwards's lyrical description of the excellence of
"flowery meadows and gentle breezes of wind," McGrath attempts to restore
the imagination to the way natural theology functions.[13] The question of
what difference God makes here circles back to the gap of the imagination
and affectivity that it can aesthetically fill.

Speaking of a "classical" (again, as I noted in my own chapter, the singularity of this is too neat) account of the nature, or *esse*, of the creature provides
an opportunity for a nontrivializing reflection on modernities' instrumental
rationality, to use the concept of Max Horkheimer, and the process of objectification that has taken place with the disenchantment of the world. This
links to serious questions regarding environmental engagement, abuse, and
responsive repair—scientific projects shaped by public value that can contribute, and have contributed to, ways that damage or repair, distract from
or refocus on, global conditions for flourishing together.

It would be problematic to suggest that McGrath is unsympathetic to such
political/ethical concerns, or that, on another occasion, these would remain
absent from his work.[14] After all, he speaks elsewhere about "the capacity of
the Christian faith to bring about a radical change in the way in which we
understand and *inhabit* the world."[15] But the need to refuse compartmental-
ization, to resist separating considerations of the creature qua creature from
considerations of hamartiology and the redemptiveness of God's pneumatic
agency in Christ, interrupts the aesthetic mood as its transfigurative necessity. That the chapter, reflecting the concerns of McGrath's *Re-Imagining
Nature* book, does not spend time with these matters, displacing them with
the ascent of understanding and affectivity, requires interrogation as to what
subject formation is possible from this piece of work. The challenge, then,
lies in evaluating what it leaves out as much as what it says.

To press this question, it is worth contrasting Gregory's purgative ascent
with another form of ascent. In the development of the modern Romantic
sensibility, hill walking and mountain climbing became activities of a *leisured
class*. A residual Romantic temperament was the very ground for the kind
of splendor and awe felt deep within the interiorized affections of modern

13. Edwards, "Miscellanies, no. 108," in Edwards, *Works*, 13:279.
14. For instance, see McGrath, *Reenchantment of Nature*.
15. McGrath, *Open Secret*, 4.

bourgeois selves. The Romantics' contemplative gaze of wonder in the act of ascending and the view from the summit reflect the development of what the Italian political philosopher Giorgio Agamben identifies as a growing tendency "in the course of the seventeenth and eighteenth centuries."[16] It was then that "authors began to distinguish a faculty that proclaimed the judgment on and enjoyment of the beautiful as its specific concern."[17] He claims that here the notion of "taste" was transformed from having been firmly grounded in rational intelligence, with aesthetic judgment being disciplined by habits developed from learning to discern truth. Seventeenth- and eighteenth-century writers began to identify "taste" as the faculty that was specifically concerned with the enjoyment of the beautiful. What emerged was a form of judgment that sat alongside, but disengaged from, other forms of knowledge. Aesthetics, Agamben argues, was born as a distinctive mode of perception. "From beginning to end, taste thus presents itself as that of 'another knowledge.'"[18] In fact, for Gottfried Wilhelm Leibniz, for example, taste as aesthetic judgment "is something close to an instinct."[19] The sense of the aesthetic, and of taste as its mode of appreciation, is an excess that appears as a transcendental immediate. Accordingly, Immanuel Kant's *Critique of Judgment* functions as an aesthetic supplement to his *Critique of Pure Reason* and *Critique of Practical Reason* only by way of *paralleling* them. Here, Agamben observes, is "aesthetic pleasure as an excess of representation over knowledge."[20] Its transcendentalism has its theological reflection in the vacuous divine sublimity of Rudolf Otto and his sense of the numinous, his taste for the infinite.

This is not a theologically innocent matter. The context for the early modern redevelopment of the aesthetic, and of taste as the primary condition for aesthetic judgment, appears to be political. According to Terry Eagleton, aesthetics develops from the failing bourgeois political struggle, securing a sphere of pure autonomy and intuition. Among several casualties of this move is the artist's genuine social function *as an artist*, and art thereby loses its capacity to contribute to a social language that is more interesting and significant than a reduction to matters of private preference and affection would have it.[21] Eagleton maintains, "The construction of the modern notion of the aesthetic artefact is . . . inseparable from the construction of the

16. Agamben, *Taste*, 4.
17. Agamben, Taste, 5.
18. Agamben, *Taste*, 6.
19. Leibniz, cited in Agamben, *Taste*, 27.
20. Agamben, *Taste*, 40.
21. Eagleton, *Ideology of the Aesthetic*, 93, 96.

dominant ideological forms of modern class-society, and indeed from a whole new form of human subjectivity appropriate to that social order."[22] That means, Eagleton continues, that "the aesthetic is . . . a bourgeois concept in the most literal historical sense, hatched and nurtured in the Enlightenment."[23]

At the very least, there is a question over whether reducing "natural theology" to aesthetic affectivity functions as a mode of distraction. According to Grace Jantzen, certain activities are bourgeois and politically complacent. Pressing this into her critique of modern philosophy of religion, she complains about "the blinkered privilege of western philosophers of religion," and one should add many theologians to that. In contrast, "there are many millions of people for whom just getting enough to eat is of much more pressing concern."[24] Likewise, and more acerbically, James Cone argues, "Since most professional theologians are the descendants of the advantaged class and thus often represent the consciousness of the class, it is difficult not to conclude that their theologies are in fact a bourgeois exercise in intellectual masturbation."[25] Therefore, he explains, "Because white theologians [in particular] are well fed and speak for a people who control the means of production, the problem of hunger is not a theological problem for them. That is why they spend more time debating the relation between the Jesus of history and the Christ of faith than probing the depths of Jesus' command to feed the poor."[26] To return to Eagleton's analysis, to be able to affectively gaze with wonder on the splendor of the divine is prone "to become an isolated enclave within which the dominant social order can find refuge from its own values of competitiveness, exploitation and material possessiveness."[27] After all, "the ultimate binding force of the bourgeois social order, in contrast to the coercive social habits of absolutism, will be habits, pieties, sentiments and affections. And this is equivalent to saying that power in such an order has become *aestheticized*."[28]

There is an issue that results from this line of questioning, and that can be sharpened by reflecting on David Hume's critique of the design argument. It postulated that this theistic argument is problematically selective. What would happen to the argument if it were expanded to include phenomena less evidently complex (arguably not designed) or even sufficiently unconducive to talk of design (chaos, catastrophe, etc.)? What would happen to

22. Eagleton, *Ideology of the Aesthetic*, 3.
23. Eagleton, *Ideology of the Aesthetic*, 8.
24. Jantzen, *Becoming Divine*, 79.
25. Cone, *God of the Oppressed*, 47.
26. Cone, *God of the Oppressed*, 52.
27. Eagleton, *Ideology of the Aesthetic*, 9.
28. Eagleton, *Ideology of the Aesthetic*, 20.

the transcendental production of wonder if beautiful sunshine and fields of flowers were not taken as straightforward cases for theological reflection but instead read in the contexts of observations on the relative unlivability of particularly hot and dry environments; or on the enclosures of common land and the pressure on the livelihoods of people; or on the harvesting of plant life for the drug trade; or on the demolition of rainforests for the sake of undercutting the processing of timber by industry competitors. The point here, as Hume makes evident, is that examples are not value-free and innocent but rather play a role in an interpretive act that selects some examples for particular purposes and deselects others. While a private garden may provide emotional relief for one person, for another it may be a display of opulence by a landowner who condemns tenants to cramped and unsanitary conditions.

Should one respond that the aesthetic, the imaginative, is but one dimension of the natural, then the appeal to partiality should in turn produce the question Why this part? The selectivity in this guise appears unduly beholden to the bourgeois temperament. Thus Calvin's image of the world as a "theatre" of divine glory is useful in indicating conditions that allow for the performance of living. The world, one could add, does not reflect God as a moment for contemplation as much as provide the very ecology for sustainable flourishing together. "A God who is sought, or celebrated, or obeyed, *elsewhere* than in the everyday (in religion, for example) is a figment of our imagination destructive of our common humanity—and thereby destructive of our relations with God."[29] Nicholas Lash consequently theologically engages "in denying that there are any particular districts, or places, or times, in which God is more likely to be met than in any others."[30] The *political* significance of the aesthetic is not a supplement to the aesthetic entertainment or pleasure value of nature appreciation that may be expressed affectively as astonishment. It is not a third transcendentalist way added to the dehistoricized epistemic and aesthetic sensibilities. Instead, it functions as a theo-materialist hermeneutical context that allows for discourse's celebratory mood to be consistently chastened by, and dialectically ordered with, the interrogative mood. Hence, Lash argues, "A Christian account of the 'experiences that matter most' should be derived from a consideration of the ways in which Jesus came to bear the responsibility of his mission and, especially, of how it went with him in Gethsemane."[31] The *theologia gloriae* looks considerably different when run through the stigmatic discipline of the *theologia crucis*. If theology is to engage in schooling responsible attention to the parabolic in the world, it

29. Lash, *Easter in Ordinary*, 181.
30. Lash, *Easter in Ordinary*, 251.
31. Lash, *Easter in Ordinary*, 251.

does so as the theological science of *life*: that life is distorted but *made anew* in Christ through the redemptive presence of God's Spirit. The question is whether McGrath's chapter is sufficiently attuned to this, or whether it could encourage the formation of a different and depoliticized social subject. To reconfigure Karl Marx's famous criticism of the right-wing Hegelians in his "Theses on Feuerbach," we are called not to interpret or feel astonishment over the world but to change it.

A Classical Reply

ALISTER E. MCGRATH

I am very grateful to my colleagues for their thoughtful responses to my reflections on natural theology. My thinking on this question continues to develop, and this is due in no small part to others engaging my ideas and offering criticisms that clearly lead to their refinement and improvement.

Let me begin with Andrew Pinsent, who offers a very focused and perceptive critique of my approach, rightly highlighting the importance of John Henry Newman's critical assessment of natural theology. The section of Newman's sermon that Pinsent offers in support of his concern is representative of Newman's anxieties about natural theology, which are expressed at several points, including the important "Idea of a University."[1] As I read Newman's critique of natural theology, I sense a parallel with Barth, in that Newman's concerns seem to relate to a specific form of natural theology, exemplified in William Paley's *Natural Theology* (1802), which was highly influential in England in the middle of the nineteenth century.[2] Newman's concerns about this work target its excessive rationalization of faith, which is inattentive to the importance of mystery and lacks engagement with the human imagination.[3] Newman rightly discerned that Paley's emaciated divinity would not evoke worship or capture the imagination but would reduce God to an irrelevance. Newman famously quipped, "I believe in design because I believe in God, not in a God because I believe in design."[4]

1. Fletcher, "Newman and Natural Theology."
2. Fyfe, "Publishing and the Classics."
3. Mongrain, "Eyes of Faith"; Dive, *John Henry Newman and the Imagination*.
4. Newman, "Letter to William Robert Brownlow," 25:97.

I here take Newman to offer a criticism of a culturally dominant version of natural theology; he makes some significant criticisms that I find persuasive. Happily, other forms of natural theology are available that remedy Paley's shortcomings and deficiencies. Newman, as Pinsent hints, is a perceptive critic of problematic approaches to natural theology, and his concerns need to be taken seriously. I often wonder how Newman would respond to the affectively and imaginatively rich forms of natural theology that we find in the works of Hans Urs von Balthasar, or the notion of *theōria physikē* that we find in Maximus the Confessor.[5]

This neatly leads me to John McDowell's response to my article, which opens with some reflections on Gregory Nazianzen, for whom we both clearly share an admiration. Gregory rightly points to the importance of a theological reading of the created order, which helps to set what the Western tradition has come to know as "natural theology" in a helpfully informing perspective. It would have been excellent if I had had space to develop this point in my article: this tradition is clearly highly important for reflections on the nature, scope, and affective aspects of natural theology. I would add that Hans-Georg Gadamer's important retrieval of the Aristotelian notion of *theōria* as enfolding what would now be termed both "theory" and "practice" opens the way to creating practices that embody this vision of nature.

I am sure that criticisms could be made of my emphasis on the importance of both "understanding" and "affectivity" in relation to the natural order. McDowell is certainly correct in pointing out that much more could be said about the relation of natural theology and bourgeois culture. However, my analysis needs to be framed in terms of a wider theological concern about excessively objective approaches to theology, which continue to dominate many discussions of natural theology. My concern here is to restore an awareness of the need for, and indeed propriety of, an *affective* approach to Christian theology, building on Simeon Zahl's excellent accounts of the need to recognize the "affective salience" of doctrine.[6] This is important in correcting the excessive objectivity of some accounts of the natural world, such as its landscapes, with their perceived importance. My interest in my essay for this volume lay partly in ensuring that the affective aspects of a theological reading of the natural world are noted and respected, given the worrying trends toward detached spectatorial attitudes to natural theology that remain influential.

---

5. For a good account of the latter, see Wirzba, "Christian *Theoria Physike*."
6. See especially his early work, Zahl, "On the Affective Salience of Doctrines." For my own reflections on this theme, see McGrath, "Place, History, and Incarnation."

McDowell rightly notes that I fail to engage political and ethical concerns in my essay, and he happily provides a generous catena of writers who have remedied this deficiency. This is a fair concern, which I have addressed in my recent monograph on natural philosophy: there I stress the importance of learning both about nature and from nature, using Gadamer's "Praise of Theory" to offer an intellectual bridge between reflection, contemplation, and action in relation to nature.[7] Yet while I can see the importance of political analysis in this context, other dialogue partners are clearly appropriate. For example, I can see the importance of poetry in maintaining a proper balance and comprehensiveness in any account of the human response to nature.[8]

Paul Moser's response to my paper makes some interesting points, particularly in relation to his concerns about Karl Barth's approach to natural theology. While I share some of Moser's misgivings, I can nevertheless see the force of Barth's political concerns during the 1930s about how a natural theology could be abused or exploited by those with ideological agendas. However, I shall focus on some specific concerns Moser notes about my own approach since these will hopefully lead to an interesting discussion. Moser is worried about my use of terms such as "rational" and "rationality" and their implications for how I frame natural theology. Rationality, Moser suggests, "calls for what is *adequately supported from an evidential point of view*."

I understand what he means and see his point, but I don't consider this to be a major concern. The terms "rational" and "rationality" are used within different communities of discourse with quite distinct understandings of what it means to be "rational." When I was working on my monograph on the empirically observable diversities of concepts of rationality and their implementation across disciplines,[9] I came across the "Beyond Rationality" program established by the Centre for the Philosophy of Natural and Social Science at the London School of Economics. This attempted to map domain-relative practices and discourses relating to rationality, making it clear that we must speak of rationalities *in the plural*. We have to learn to live with there being one generic human reason, yet many rationalities.[10]

My approach to natural theology can be seen as an attempt to identify what patterns of reason might be considered normative or "best practice" within Christian communities, and how this enables the various forms of

---

7. McGrath, *Natural Philosophy*.

8. I am particularly impressed by the analysis in McLeish, *Poetry and Music of Science*. For a more philosophical approach, see Midgley, *Science and Poetry*.

9. McGrath, *Territories of Human Reason*.

10. This is the theme explored in Apel and Kettner, *Die eine Vernunft und die vielen Rationalitäten*.

natural theology that have emerged within Christianity to correlate with other instantiations of rationality. It is certainly true that some of those rational approaches begin with evidence and proceed to the formulation of theories; others, however, begin with the proposal of theories, which are then judged against their capacity to interpret the observations, before leading to the development of research programs to extend this analysis.

Moser also raises questions about my statement that the "whole enterprise of natural theology rests on a fundamental *theological* belief that the God who created the world is also the God who is disclosed in and through the Christian Bible." He argues that natural theology "can be Deist, Jewish, Islamic, or Hindu, without a connection with 'the Christian Bible.'" Indeed it can. Yet the term "natural theology" is open to many interpretations, and my own conception of natural theology, about which I had been asked to write, is rooted in the specifics of the Christian faith. Perhaps Moser does not share this understanding of the term, but it is one of many legitimate manners of framing this issue, and I was addressing a specifically Christian way of formulating and applying this idea. This uncertainty about terminology is one of the reasons why I have now moved the framework of my more recent discussion away from "natural theology" to "natural philosophy," which allows me to explore Christian, Jewish, Islamic, and Confucian approaches to natural philosophy[11]—which, I may add, is a fascinating topic. My book *Natural Philosophy* arose from earlier discussions with colleagues, which helped me to see how some of the themes of natural theology could perhaps be accommodated and further developed more appropriately through reviving the early modern tradition of natural philosophy.

A similar issue arises in Taliaferro's generous response to my article, which suggests that *The Blackwell Companion to Natural Theology* (2009), edited by William Lane Craig and J. P. Moreland, can be seen as an exemplary formulation of natural theology. I share his esteem for this work, having regularly encouraged my students to draw on its rich resources. But it is an exemplar of a *specific approach* to natural theology, located within a specific disciplinary tradition, which may helpfully be contrasted with *The Oxford Handbook of Natural Theology* (2013), edited by Russell Re Manning, John Hedley Brooke, and Fraser Watts, whose opening chapter emphasizes the diversity and pluriformity of "natural theology" and cautions against definitional foreclosures of how this is to be understood. Once more, we encounter the difficult question of determining what the term "natural theology" means, when there is little agreement about the criteria to be used in this judgment.

11. McGrath, *Natural Philosophy*, 36–38, 150–53.

Yet, while there are divergences of interpretation and varieties of implementation across the five views gathered in this volume, they clearly indicate the continuing importance of natural theology in philosophical and theological discussion. It has been a pleasure to interact with my colleagues and hopefully open up a wider discussion of the issues, including whether we need to live with a plurality of understandings of natural theology or are able to impose a preferred definition.

4

A Deflationary View

PAUL K. MOSER

Introduction

How do humans get knowledge of God, if they do? Proposed answers are legion, but some are more defensible than others. Having a correct answer matters, because if God exists, knowledge of God matters. God would be a source of value for humans, in a way that would make human knowledge of God valuable.

Some philosophers and theologians have wondered if humans can gain knowledge of God on the basis of justified premises that are "natural" rather than supernatural regarding their content. Such premises would not claim or presuppose that God exists but still yield, with due cogency, the conclusion that God exists. It is a matter of dispute what these premises are, along with what kind of inference would enable them cogently to deliver the conclusion that God exists. Indeed, no particular instantiation of such natural theology enjoys widespread acceptance among philosophers and theologians. The same holds for the general enterprise of natural theology based on natural premises: it fails to attract anything near consensus support. I shall use "natural theology" to include the various ontological arguments as well as familiar arguments for God's existence from design and fine-tuning, causation and first cause, historical uniqueness (e.g., resurrection), moral factuality, and human (moral) consciousness.

William James comments bluntly on the traditional arguments of natural theology: "The bare fact that all idealists since Kant have felt entitled either to scout or to neglect them shows that they are not solid enough to serve as religion's all-sufficient foundation. Absolutely impersonal reasons would be in duty bound to show more general convincingness. . . . They prove nothing rigorously. They only corroborate our preexistent partialities."[1] Is James correct about what natural theology corroborates? Only "preexistent partialities"?

Some philosophers remain unmoved by James-style doubts. They offer arguments of natural theology, for apologetic purposes, and they expect reasonable inquirers to concur with their arguments. I aim to deflate the pretensions of natural theology, at least if a God worthy of worship is our concern. I contend that the dispute over natural theology reduces to the issue of what

1. James, *Varieties of Religious Experience*, 428–29.

153

kind of God is in view. If we have in mind a God worthy of worship, particularly the God of Abraham, Isaac, Jacob, and Jesus, then we cannot get there from here, that is, from the premises of a natural theology. If, however, we have in mind a lesser god, the dispute can continue, but natural theology does not yield or otherwise ground the existence of a God worthy of worship. As a result, I conclude that natural theology lacks conclusive or even confirmatory value regarding such a God. I allow for its *interrogatory* value, however, in prompting questions about God, but this falls short of what advocates of natural theology claim. As a result, my approach is deflationary toward natural theology. I also outline an alternative based in moral experience.

Representative Arguments

Proponents of natural theology have offered an abundance of arguments for God's existence, but the sheer number has not helped their cause. Quantity of arguments, of course, does not deliver the rational cogency of arguments: the latter requires soundness and rational credibility for any agent having the relevant evidence and needed intelligence. A key issue is whether natural premises can provide an argument that cogently yields the conclusion that a God worthy of worship exists. Typically, the devil is in the details of the arguments of natural theology, but not only in the details, as we shall see. So for present purposes, we need not get lost in details. We turn to some common failures of natural theology.

Ontological Arguments

There is no such thing as "the" ontological argument. Many ontological arguments are in circulation, from Anselm to Descartes to Leibniz to various contemporary philosophers and theologians. It is hard to identify what the arguments have in common that makes them "ontological" arguments, if something does. In any case, we cannot assess the range of ontological arguments in a single chapter. For illustration, we shall identify a common problem in one of Anselm's arguments. It might seem that his arguments are promising for yielding a God worthy of worship because they are concerned with maximal perfection, including moral perfection. We shall see why any initial promise falls short.

The argument in question infers, just from our having a *concept* of a maximally perfect being, that such a perfect being *actually exists*. The ground offered is that without the actual existence of its represented object, such a concept would not genuinely be that of a *maximally perfect* being. Allegedly, the lack of the existence of the object represented would block the concept from representing a maximally perfect object. Some philosophers and theologians offer such an argument for the existence of a being worthy of worship, not just a being adequate to account for some empirical or moral feature of the world.

Plausible doubt arises and remains. We should distinguish (a) an *existence-affirming* concept of a maximally perfect being and (b) an *existence-guaranteeing* concept of such a being. An existence-affirming concept of a maximally perfect being includes, if by implication, either *correct* or *incorrect* affirmation of the existence of that being. It does not by itself, however, guarantee the existence of that being. We could have the concept while the represented perfect being does not exist. For instance, a represented perfect world need not exist and, as we know, does not exist.[2]

An existence-guaranteeing concept of a maximally perfect being would logically preclude *incorrect* affirmation of the existence of that being. It thus would secure the existence of that being. A concept of a being can affirm, if by implication, the existence of that being, but this affirming may be incorrect. In that case, the concept is misleading in what it affirms. An existence-guaranteeing concept, in contrast, would not be misleading in that way. The main question is whether there is such a concept corresponding to God. A relevant consideration is that we apparently can imagine coherently that God does not exist. Atheism and agnosticism do not seem to rest on conceptual blunders, even if they sometimes face epistemic problems.

We can imagine an ontological argument that includes an existence-affirming concept of a maximally perfect being. An immediate question is whether its affirmation of the existence of that being is correct. We thus ask whether reality is such that it includes the maximally perfect being in question. We can imagine that reality does not include that being, despite the concept's affirming its existence. So, an existence-affirming concept of a maximally perfect being does not settle the question of whether God exists. We thus do not have here a conclusive step from a concept of a maximally perfect object to its existence.

Perhaps an existence-guaranteeing concept might salvage an ontological argument. Suppose that an ontological argument includes an alleged existence-guaranteeing concept of a maximally perfect being. The supposed ground would be that if the concept's represented object fails to exist, then the concept is not genuinely that of a *maximally perfect* object. We now need

---

2. My talk of "affirmation" by a concept allows that our concept of X affirms the reality of X even though *we* do not.

to ask whether we have a concept of a maximally perfect being that secures the existence of that being. We must ask whether, given the concept, reality necessarily includes a maximally perfect being. This prompts the question of whether the concept is existence-*affirming* but not existence-*guaranteeing* regarding the being in question. We can grant that the concept is existence-affirming, but this leaves open the issue of whether a maximally perfect being actually exists.

A concept typically does not secure the reality of an object whose existence it affirms. An affirmation by a concept typically does not do so: it often is a *mere* affirmation, without the corresponding reality of an object affirmed. This is true even of a concept affirming the reality of a maximally perfect object. Its affirming need not succeed, because reality need not correspond to it. As a result, the ontological argument under consideration is questionable.

It would be question-begging to assume that a concept's affirmation of the existence of a maximally perfect being is correct just by virtue of that affirmation. A concept can be incorrect in its affirmation of the existence of a maximally perfect being, even if that affirmation is essential to the concept. In that case, we would have a concept of a maximally perfect being without a corresponding real object. Such a concept-object separation challenges an alleged existence-guaranteeing concept of a maximally perfect being. It is doubtful, then, that we have a concept of a maximally perfect being that guarantees the existence of that being. So, an alleged existence-guaranteeing concept of a maximally perfect being does not settle the issue of whether God exists. The reality of a maximally perfect divine being is not guaranteed by a concept in the manner alleged.

Ontological arguments do not fit well with the kind of evidential elusiveness that characterizes the Judeo-Christian God. This God supplies *and withdraws* divine presence and evidence relative to humans at various times for redemptive purposes. The evidence consisting of the content of a concept of God, as offered in ontological arguments, is static in a way that the personally interactive evidence of the presence and the reality of the Jewish-Christian God is not. The proposed evidence consisting of the content of a concept is not personally variable relative to the wills of humans toward God. So, the evidence offered in ontological arguments conflicts with the divine self-revelation of intermittent hiding and seeking toward humans. God's self-revelation would aim at the transformation of humans toward God's moral character and therefore would be personally variable and interactive in ways that the content of a concept of God is not. So, the evidence offered in ontological arguments is at odds with the personally and evidentially dynamic God of Jewish-Christian theism. This deficiency applies to ontological arguments generally, not just to Anselm's.[3]

Design and Fine-Tuning Arguments

Some observers infer design and fine-tuning of the world from parts of the world that are apparently ordered. They also infer a Designer or Fine-Tuner to account for the apparent order in question. Whatever notion of a Designer or Fine-Tuner one prefers, it needs special evidence to lead to a God worthy of worship, characterized by moral perfection.

A posteriori arguments from apparent design or fine-tuning in the world confirm at most the existence of causes *just adequate* to yield that apparent design or fine-tuning. Such just-adequate causes, however, fail to confirm the existence of a personal agent who is worthy of worship and thus has a morally perfect character. Some advocates of natural theologians have admitted this, but they have retreated to arguments for something inferior to a God worthy of worship. If the desired conclusion is to yield a personal God worthy of worship, then the a posteriori arguments from apparent design or fine-tuning fail to deliver, either individually or collectively. Those arguments also need some account of the apparent *disorder* in nature that does not leave disorder in God's character.

The problem at hand arises in connection with Thomas Aquinas's teleological arguments in the *Summa Theologiae*[4] and in the *Summa contra Gentiles*.[5] The just-adequate cause in question (as of certain complex, apparently ordered structures in nature) does not deliver the morally perfect Jewish-Christian God, who is a personal agent worthy of worship. We can grant, for the sake of argument, Aquinas's evidence from apparent design, but this would offer no challenge to a morally indifferent source of that evidence. So, Aquinas had no adequate ground in his natural theology for assigning the title "God" to his alleged designer. Recent variations on Aquinas's teleological argument likewise cannot escape this problem while remaining within natural theology and avoiding supernatural revelation. Well-grounded ascription of the perfectionist title "God" to an agent requires evidence of a morally perfect personal agent. An attempt to have natural theology include a *divine call* to humans moves beyond natural theology to *supernatural* theology.

Teleological arguments cannot avoid the problem of divine elusiveness that challenges Aquinas's cosmological argument. Consisting of certain apparently

---

3. For the range of such arguments and their various deficiencies, see Oppy, *Ontological Arguments*.

4. Aquinas, *Summa Theologiae* I.2.3.

5. Aquinas, *Summa contra Gentiles* 1.13.35.

ordered structures in nature, Aquinas's evidence is static in a way that evidence of the presence and the reality of the Jewish-Christian God is not. His evidence from nature is not personally variable relative to the wills of human agents toward God. So, his evidence does not fit with God's hiding and seeking relative to humans for their redemption. In seeking to transform humans morally, divine self-revelation would be personally variable and interactive in ways that complex structures in nature are not. So, the evidence offered in Aquinas's teleological argument does not fit with the personally and cognitively interactive Jewish-Christian God.

First-Cause Arguments

Arguments to a first cause, on behalf of endorsing God's existence, face straightforward versions of the problems at hand. Consider, for instance, Aquinas's cosmological argument in the *Summa Theologiae*.[6] It identifies an order of efficient causation in the sensory world, then affirms that nothing is either the efficient cause of itself or part of an infinite causal chain, and concludes that it is necessary to acknowledge "a first efficient cause, to which everyone gives the name of God."[7] For the sake of argument, we can grant Aquinas's inference that there is a *first* efficient cause, despite the philosophical controversy raised by this inference.

A problem facing Aquinas is that his inference gives us, at most, a first cause that is *just adequate* for the observed causal chains. Such a first cause falls far short of a living personal God who is worthy of worship and thus morally perfect. We have no reason to assign moral perfection to the inferred first cause; that cause offers no challenge to moral indifference in itself or elsewhere. In addition, we have no reason to ascribe redemption-seeking *personal agency* to this first cause. Such personal agency is not required to accommodate the sensory data regarding causal chains. Those data offer no definite indication of a personal agent, let alone a personal agent worthy of worship. P. T. Forsyth appears to make this point in remarking that "nature does not contain its own [moral] teleology."[8] In addition, the first cause in question, so far as our evidence goes, could have ceased to exist long ago.

Aquinas fails to convince in referring to "a first efficient cause, *to which everyone gives the name of God.*"[9] Skeptics rightly balk at that reference to

6. Aquinas, *Summa Theologiae* I.2.3.
7. Aquinas, *Summa Theologiae* I.2.3.
8. Forsyth, "Revelation and the Person of Christ," 100.
9. A similarly dubious reference to God occurs in the related argument in Aquinas, *Summa contra Gentiles* 1.13.35.

God, and we should too, given the exalted demands of morally perfect personal agency for satisfying the title "God." If an argument does not support affirming the existence of a morally perfect intentional agent, then that argument does not confirm that *God* exists. Arguments of natural theology often run afoul of this fact and leave one without evidence for the existence of *God*.

A second problem arises from the elusiveness of the presence and the evidence of the Jewish-Christian God. Aquinas's evidence consisting of efficient causation in the sensory world is static in a way that the evidence for the Jewish-Christian God is not. His evidence involving efficient causation is not variable relative to the volitional tendencies of human agents toward God. So, the evidence in question fails to accommodate the personally interactive character of God's self-revelation that emerges from God's intermittent hiding and seeking relative to humans. Seeking human redemption, God's self-revelation should be expected to be personally interactive, variable, and intermittent in ways that mere efficient causation in the sensory world is not. So, Aquinas's proposed evidence in the cosmological argument is not suited to the evidentially elusive, personally dynamic God of Jewish-Christian theism.

Historical Arguments

Historical arguments from natural theology invoke some feature of history, free of supernatural description, as a basis for concluding that God exists. For instance, the appearances of Jesus to his disciples after his death figure in some of these historical arguments. Such arguments often involve reports about the empty tomb of Jesus and about the recipients of appearances of the risen Jesus.

We have no convincing merely historical case for *God's* raising Jesus, as Emil Brunner,[10] Helmut Thielicke,[11] and others have argued. The New Testament message is not that Jesus survived the crucifixion; instead, it is that *God raised him* from death, in vindication of him. So, any merely historical case would have to confirm God's existence, and that requirement has not been met. In addition, so far as the merely historical evidence goes, Jesus could have been raised and then died. This would not fit, however, with the New Testament message that Jesus is alive now as risen Lord.

The apostle Paul's case for the divine resurrection of Jesus goes beyond the merely historical to the working of God's Spirit. As Paul says: "No one can say 'Jesus is Lord' except by the Holy Spirit" (1 Cor. 12:3). So, he does not offer a case merely on the basis of human testimony regarding appearances.

---

10. See Brunner, "Risen and Exalted Lord."
11. See Thielicke, "Rose Again from the Dead"; Thielicke, "Resurrection of Christ."

Any well-founded human testimony needs a ground in human experience; it needs to be more than a mere report. Paul accommodates this point in Romans 5:5 with an experiential role for God's intervening Spirit: "Hope [in God] does not disappoint us, because God's love has been poured into our hearts through the Holy Spirit which has been given to us" (see also 8:15–16; 2 Cor. 5:14–15). He would identify the same evidential basis for faith in God. This is interpersonal evidence from divine self-manifestation that is irreducible to an argument; it does not need an argument to be genuine evidence of God's reality. We should expect God, as sui generis, to be self-evidencing and self-authenticating for humans in this way. The historicist and other arguments of natural theology fail to bring us anywhere near the self-manifesting and convicting work of God's Spirit.

If Jesus *is* Lord (*now*), then he is not dead and thus did not die after the resurrection. Following 1 Corinthians 15, we can acknowledge testimonial evidence, but the main issue concerns what kind of experience grounds it. In the case of the resurrection of Jesus, it was experience of the risen Jesus (and not just his body). Following Paul, we should consider the claim that we can continue to meet (the Spirit of) the risen Jesus. His Spirit guides the kind of experienced moral conviction to be clarified below. Paul holds that as many as "are *led by the Spirit of God* are children of God" (Rom. 8:14 NRSVue, emphasis added). We shall see that this experience of being led, including moral conviction, is central to our evidence of God's reality, although it is neglected by the arguments of natural theology.

The visual evidence of the appearances of Jesus after his death is insufficient for grounded belief that God raised Jesus. Such appearances need to be accompanied by an experience of God's Spirit. Paul's appeal to testimonies of appearances in 1 Corinthians 15 thus should not be isolated from experience of God's intervening Spirit. Accordingly, simple empirical evidence is inadequate to underwrite Thomas's affirmation, "My Lord and my God!" (John 20:28). We do not see God or the risen Jesus as Lord in the simple empirical evidence, because neither God nor the risen Jesus is a simple empirical object. So, merely historical arguments from the appearances of Jesus after the crucifixion do not salvage natural theology.

Arguments from Morality and Consciousness

Some advocates of natural theology invoke (nonrelativist or objective) moral facts as the basis for an inference to God's existence. Similarly, some advocates cite human (moral) consciousness as the basis for such an inference. Neither strategy avoids the recurring problem for natural theology. The existence of (nonrelativist or objective) moral facts does not confirm the moral perfection of an intentional moral agent. Consider the teachings about moral rightness and goodness offered by any morally responsible group that does not build theology into those teachings. We may suppose, for the sake of argument, that those teachings express moral facts. Even so, those facts give no indication of an intentional agent with a morally perfect character. Such an indication would go well beyond what those facts confirm regarding moral rightness and goodness. They certainly do not logically entail a morally perfect agent, and they offer no challenge to the nonexistence of such an agent. So, the relevant moral facts do not confirm the existence of a God worthy of worship. The familiar realm of moral facts does not supply evidence for such a God unless we insert supernatural theology into the moral facts. Inserting such theology into the evidence, however, goes beyond any argument of *natural* theology.

An argument for God from human (moral) consciousness meets the same fate as an argument from moral facts. It fails to confirm the existence of an intentional agent with a morally perfect character. Human consciousness, while remarkable, gives no indication of the reality of such an agent. It definitely does not logically require a morally perfect agent, and it does not challenge the nonexistence of such an agent. So, the existence of human consciousness does not confirm the reality of a God worthy of worship. If we insert supernatural theology into the facts of human consciousness, we can get a different result. In that case, however, we no longer have an argument of *natural* theology.

Arguments of natural theology from moral facts and human consciousness do not fare well with the biblical theme of divine elusiveness toward humans. Any evidence from moral facts and human consciousness fails to indicate an intentional agent who hides at some times from some humans for redemptive purposes. In that regard, such evidence is static in comparison with the evidence for the God acknowledged by various biblical writers. As a result, we do not find here evidence suited to the biblical portrait of a God who is worthy of worship and thus perfectly moral and redemptive.

The Enduring Problem

The key question becomes clear: *Which* god is in view when one offers an argument of natural theology? The god of some philosophers? Or, instead, the God of Jesus, who is worthy of worship and thus morally perfect? Getting to a morally imperfect god will not bring one close, in terms of required evidence, to a God worthy of worship. Evidence for a morally imperfect god allows for a lack of evidence for a morally perfect God. In addition, if one retreats to the claim that natural theology yields not a God worthy of worship but some morally inferior god, an enduring problem arises. How does one reasonably move from the lesser god to the God of moral perfection? We cannot get there from here on the basis of natural theology. If, however, we try to get there with *super*natural means (say, divine self-manifestation to humans), the presumed underlay of natural theology will be evidentially superfluous and dispensable.

A morally perfect God, I suggest, would not need or rely on the dubious contribution of the familiar arguments of natural theology. Instead, such a God would rely on something more direct and salient.[12] Paul confirms this in Romans 10:20, and he remarks in Romans 1 that *God* shows us God, if at times through nature as a medium. Contrary to some advocates of natural theology, Paul does *not* say or imply that nature by itself (as a purely natural fact) shows us God or grounds an argument for God's reality.

Being sui generis, God alone could give humans evidence of God's reality, by self-revelation in self-manifestation to humans. This is an implication of the biblical theme that God swears by himself, owing to the absence of anyone capable of the task (see Gen. 22:16; Heb. 6:13). A source lacking a morally perfect character will not have the resources, on its own, to indicate the reality of such a character. This is the downfall of the familiar arguments of natural theology. They neglect the need for God's distinctive role in the evidence for God's reality. In particular, they neglect that God alone could be an adequate basis for evidence of God's reality.

Some advocates of natural theology look for relief in distinguishing two senses of "knowledge of God": knowledge *of God's reality*, that is, mere reality; and knowledge of God *as a personal agent of direct acquaintance*. We can grant the distinction, for the sake of argument, but note its ineffectiveness here. The recurring problem concerns inadequate evidence in natural theology for the reality of a God worthy of worship. The problem does not depend on requiring knowledge of God as a personal agent of acquaintance. So, we do not find relief for natural theology here. The thinness of its evidence, relative to a God worthy of worship, is its fatal problem.

The problem at hand is not with arguments in themselves. The problem is that the familiar arguments of natural theology, in terms of the evidence they provide, are inadequate as a reasonable basis to acknowledge a God worthy of worship. I thus have proposed that a morally perfect God would rely on something more direct and salient than the arguments of natural theology.

12. Namely, direct divine self-manifestation to humans at God's opportune time.

The latter arguments not only fail but also tend to divert attention from available direct evidence of God, such as that found in a direct I-Thou encounter between a human and God. Paul has the latter kind of evidence in mind when, following Isaiah, he represents God as saying: "I have shown myself to those who did not ask for me" (Rom. 10:20 NRSVue; cf. Isa. 65:1). Such evidence also figures in Jesus's following interaction with God in Gethsemane: "Abba, Father, for you all things are possible; remove this cup from me, yet not what I want but what you want" (Mark 14:36 NRSVue). God's unique moral character is presented to a person in this kind of direct interaction.

Advocates of natural theology typically insist on *public* evidence for God in arguments. In doing so, they routinely ignore or deflect attention from the nonpublic evidence of a direct I-Thou encounter between a human and God. This results in neglecting the needed evidence of divine self-revelation in the self-manifestation of God's moral character to a person. Such evidence figures in one's knowing God as one's own Lord and God. It thus contrasts with the relatively thin evidence offered by natural theology, which fails to bring one near to a God who first draws near to a person in moral concern. It would be cognitively presumptuous to assume that God must provide public evidence of the sort assumed by natural theology.[13]

Natural theology should prompt us to ask a simple but vital question: What do we value more? Knowing God or knowing an argument regarding God's existence? Natural theology seems to favor the latter, given its emphasis on arguments, and this is a distortion of value regarding God. Perhaps our commitment to relative value here bears on our receptivity to relevant evidence. A misplaced focus on nonpersonal evidence in arguments can hinder our awareness of evidence in interpersonal self-manifestation, such as that found at times in moral conviction in conscience. A more promising focus attends to interpersonal evidence where God supplies self-evidence directly in convicting one in conscience. Such evidence is attributed to God's intervening Spirit by Paul (Rom. 8:15–16) and John (John 16:8). We shall return to this alternative to natural theology.

Many Christian philosophers cannot shake the idea that natural theology plays a role in increasing the probability of theism. They hold that the reality of apparent design in nature, of a first cause, or of human moral agency increases the probability of theism, even if it does not confirm the existence of a God worthy of worship. The matter is complicated, however, by questions about the nature of the relevant probabilities and about how such probabilities are to be assigned. Are they subjective probabilities, determined by a

13. See Moser and Neptune, "Is Traditional Natural Theology Cognitively Presumptuous?"

person's degrees of subjective confidence? If so, they will vary among people and fail to underwrite the broad kind of rational cogency typically sought by advocates of natural theology. If they are not subjective, how are they to be measured without bias or begging of key questions? Is one begging the question whether some of the alleged probabilities are inscrutable? In any case, evidence from apparent design, a first cause, or moral agency will not increase the probability of a God worthy of worship. Such evidence offers no challenge to the nonexistence of a morally perfect agent. In addition, our empirical evidence is highly mixed on the reality of such an agent.

We can support Christian apologetics without the familiar arguments of natural theology, but only if it attends to the right kind of evidence. That would be the kind of experiential evidence invoked by Paul, John, and other New Testament writers. We do not need the dubious arguments of familiar natural theology to support Christian apologetics. Instead, we should focus on the kind of evidence inherent to God's unique moral character, as various New Testament writers do. The focus should be on morally relevant evidence wherein one meets God in interpersonal experience. It should not be on considerations whereby one is left with tenuous support for a belief that a morally questionable god exists. The latter considerations are not a reliable road to the evidence that includes meeting God in experience. As a result, the New Testament writers do not rely on those inadequate considerations.

The arguments of natural theology typically do not lead to a life-guiding commitment to a God worthy of worship. Instead, they usually lead just to (tentative) intellectual commitments about what exists and seemingly endless hand-wringing over those commitments. As a result, natural theology often ignores or obscures the vital experiential evidence of God identified by Paul in, for instance, 1 Corinthians 1–2 and Romans 5–8. It is more promising to start with the robust experiential evidence that indicates the reality of a God worthy of worship.

Experiential acquaintance with God does not automatically give one correct beliefs about God. One still could have beliefs more suited to a god who is not worthy of worship. The key problem regarding natural theology, however, is not a person's belief regarding a lesser god. Instead, the problem concerns proposed evidence that yields at most a lesser god. The *de re* experiential evidence in divine self-manifestation is a God worthy of worship, owing to the *self-manifestation* by *God,* and not just evidence for a lesser, morally inferior god.

Evidence for a creator of the universe can fall short of evidence for a God worthy of worship. We should understand evidence for a creator in terms of what is inherent to being a creator. If intentional agency is inherent, our evidence will invite dispute, because our overall evidence is mixed at best, as even some theists acknowledge. Parts of the universe exhibit apparent disorder (consider various effects of entropy), and such disorder does not require or otherwise recommend a source in intentional agency. Even if we were somehow to get to a creator via natural theology, we still would be left with an equally big task: getting to an on-balance good creator via natural theology. Our actual "natural" evidence, mixed as it is, does not enable our firmly discharging this task. It leaves us at best with tentative surmises and disputed proposals about what is overall probable. An impartial observer, aware of the complexity of the initial conditions, would plausibly suggest that many of the assigned probabilities are actually inscrutable from our limited perspective. We thus would do better to let the relevant evidence for God's reality come from the self-manifestation of God's own character in human experience.

In direct I-Thou acquaintance with God, a person arrives at God himself via God himself first coming in self-manifestation to that person. This leaves the person with a task of *de dicto* interpretation of the acquaintance experience. What exactly does the experience include? Is the intervening Subject (the object of the person's experience) of *this* particular kind rather than *that* kind? Is this experience just an illusion? Is it shared by any other people? And so on. If the experience is shared by others, we should expect a certain amount of disagreement about the relevant features. Does this intervening Subject exist necessarily? Is this Subject self-limiting in knowledge in self-manifesting to humans? And so on. Once God is involved as a Subject in human experience, we can ask about the availability of divine testimony in some cases, so long as the evidence indicates such testimony.

The direct acquaintance in question does get one to God's self-manifested properties *de re*, but the arguments of natural theology do not. Just as you do not know an author *de re* just from reading her book, so you do not know God *de re* just from an experience of God's effects as creator in nature. You may not even know that the book's author exists; she may have died years ago. So, there's a relevant difference between the two cases. A perfectly redemptive God would want cooperative humans to know *God*, via acquaintance with God's will, and this would differ from knowing that God exists.

A problem endures as long as natural theology lacks evidence from direct acquaintance with God. Natural theology then fails to take us to a God who is worthy of worship. This is the source of the enduring problem for the familiar arguments of natural theology. The noted shortcomings in the representative arguments of natural theology indicate their failure. The best available explanation of this failure is that we can arrive at a God worthy of worship only via divine self-revelation in self-manifestation *de re*. We can raise the challenge for natural theology to take us to such a God on its terms, if only to avoid question-begging now. Given the previous misgivings and enduring problem, however, we should be skeptical of the success of natural theology. We shall look a bit closer at an alternative to the familiar arguments of natural theology and then identify where natural theology could serve a question-raising purpose less presumptuous than its typical aim.

I–Thou Evidence for God

Advocates of natural theology, as suggested, typically seek universality of rational cogency in their proposed evidence for God. They thus offer public, nonpersonal reasons in contrast with nonpublic, personal reasons, and they want their reasons to be cogent for all rational inquirers. It is a live option, however, that God prefers to offer nonpublic, personal evidence that focuses, for redemptive reasons, on a first-person perspective. Such evidence would have a *de re* experiential component that is inherently interpersonal between God and a person, and it would not be generalizable to other persons apart from that component. Arguably, God set up this kind of limitation to give the divine will a central place in interaction with humans, and to deflate intellectual pride in the absence of our facing God's holy, righteous will directly. We shall briefly consider this alternative to typical natural theology.

The evidence offered by the apostle Paul for the Jewish-Christian God serves as an alternative to what is found in the familiar arguments of natural theology. Following Jesus, Paul regards God as worthy of worship and thus inherently morally perfect. He therefore deems God to be perfectly loving toward all people, even toward the enemies of God. He also holds that humans can reject any divine offer for humans to be reconciled to God in a cooperative relationship. God, then, does not coerce human cooperation with God; nor does God coerce human acknowledgment of God's reality or goodness. In avoiding such coercion, God preserves human agency and responsibility in our deciding how to relate to God. This allows for intentional love in humans relating to God.

As noted previously, Paul represents God as being self-manifested or self-presented to some humans at some times, and he attributes the following statement to God: "I have shown myself [*emphanēs egenomēn*] to those who did not ask for me" (Rom. 10:20 NRSVue; cf. Isa. 65:1). Paul thinks of this self-manifestation of God as a presentation *de re* of God's moral character to some humans for the sake of their being reconciled to God. In attracting a person's attention *de re*, this self-manifestation figures centrally in the foundational evidence for God's reality and character, and in the guiding religious experience, for that person. It supplies God's self-evidence and self-authentication, with regard to God's reality and moral character, to receptive humans. *God* as an intentional agent is self-evidencing and self-authenticating God's reality and moral character to these humans. So, this is not the self-authentication of a propositional claim or a subjective experience.

Paul states that "all who are led by the Spirit of God are children of God" (Rom. 8:14 NRSVue). As perfectly loving *Lord*, God would try to *lead* people in a way that is best for them, all things considered. Morally perfect lordship offers morally effective leadership, for the good of all involved. We should ask what this intended leading by God would be aimed at. What would be its goal(s), given that it would be intentional or purposive? Paul speaks of being "led by the Spirit" of God in connection with loving others, among other "fruit" of God's Spirit (Gal. 5:18). A perfectly good God who seeks obedient "children of God" thus would want those children to be led by the Spirit of God toward *imitatio Dei* as central to what is best for them, all things considered.

Paul clarifies the divine goal of *leading* in some of his prayers. For instance: "May the Lord make you increase and abound in love for one another and for all . . ." (1 Thess. 3:12 NRSVue). In addition: "This is my prayer, that your love may overflow more and more with knowledge and full insight to help you to determine what really matters . . ." (Phil. 1:9–10 NRSVue). The love (*agapē*) in question, both divine and human, would include a volitional component of *willing* what is best for others, all things considered. So, it would not be just an emotional component. It also would be a basis for human experience and recognition of God's moral character and will. God's redemptive purpose of *imitatio Dei* would be to promote such love by having it figure in human access to the divine will and moral character.

Paul, we have noted, acknowledges the evidential significance of experienced *agapē* in connection with a gift from God to cooperative humans: "Hope [in God] does not disappoint us, because God's love has been poured into our hearts through the Holy Spirit which has been given to us" (Rom. 5:5). The evidential basis for hope and faith in God is something to be received cooperatively from God, in human experience. What is to be received is something integral to God's moral character: divine *agapē*. Paul thus denies evidential disappointment regarding God. Hope and faith in God do not evidentially disappoint people with such hope and faith, because God has given needed evidence to them in the self-manifestation of divine *agapē* to them. God thereby self-evidences and self-authenticates God's reality and character.[14]

---

14. For further explanation of Paul's epistemology, see Moser, *Severity of God*, 138–66; Moser, *God Relationship*, 210–27, 288–300; Moser, "Paul the Apostle."

Divine *agapē* is morally and volitionally robust, because it is *righteous* (that is, holy) love.[15] It thus is morally *convicting* toward unselfish love in the conscience of a cooperative human, as it challenges a selfish human will. The experiential reality of being thus convicted is evidence of God's reality, and it receives attention in John's Gospel: "When [the Spirit of God] comes, he will convict [*elenxei*] the world concerning sin and righteousness and judgment" (John 16:8, using "convict" from RSV margin). A related idea emerges in Revelation 3:19: "As many as I love, I convict [*elenchō*] and instruct [*paideuō*]" (my translation).

Conviction can be a challenge of a person *against* sin, but it also can be a challenge of a person *toward* righteous love. A person's being convicted need not be simply negative; it can have a positive moral and interpersonal goal toward which one is challenged. Furthermore, a person's being convicted toward loving others can increase over time. This increase would prompt one's becoming *increasingly* loving toward others, even toward one's enemies. This is central to Paul's two prayers noted previously, and it agrees with the primary love commands from Jesus (Mark 12:30–31; cf. John 21:15–19).

One's being convicted and led by God toward *agapē* for all people cannot be reduced to a belief. A belief need not include an intrusion from volitional pressure on an agent toward *agapē* that appears not to be of the agent's own doing. Such uncoercive pressure toward enemy love goes against one's natural tendencies and those of one's peers. It involves experience of a will, rather than a mere belief. The experienced will in question is an intentional power beyond any belief, and its self-manifestation can give experiential evidence to a person. A belief could arise for one without one's being experientially engaged by a divine self-manifestation in the uncoercive manner suggested. So, one's being convicted by God does not reduce to a belief. The increasing of one's being convicted to love others as God does would be central to one's awareness in conscience of being led by God in an *intentional* manner.

Divine conviction of a person toward loving others would not end with one recipient of that person's love. It would extend eventually to *all* available recipients of this love. It would be an ongoing process moving a person, uncoercively, *toward a goal*, thus making it intentional and person guided, not haphazard or nonpersonal. In being convicted, a person thus would have evidence of an *intentional agent* (rather than a mere physical process) motivating that person's being convicted toward loving others. This would take one beyond mere efficient causation to an experience of the intention or purpose of

15. See Forsyth, *Holy Father and the Living Christ*; Bradley and Forsyth, *Man and His Work*, 113–38.

a loving agent in action. Absence of moral defect in the agent would indicate a morally perfect agent at work, perhaps even an agent worthy of worship.[16]

The ultimate goal sought by a morally perfect God would be divine-human fellowship, or *koinōnia*, for the sake of what is best for all concerned. This goal would be crucial to a lasting flourishing community for all concerned, under divine guidance. It would include an I-Thou acquaintance with God irreducible to an I-It relationship. In this respect, the *koinōnia* relationship sought by God would be *interpersonal* and hence irreducible to any relation to a nonintentional object. It thus would differ from typical scientific knowledge of an object and any merely *de dicto* knowledge that something is the case. We may think of it as *filial* knowing, whereby a parent draws a child into a morally robust relationship of benevolent fellowship under parental authority.

God could hide divine self-manifestation from people opposed or indifferent to it, in order to avoid their being further alienated from God. A redemptive God would wait for the opportune time for such an intervention in human experience. So, God need not make evidence of God's reality publicly available to all inquirers. Many advocates of natural theology, among other people, assume otherwise, and thereby beg a key question about the divine giving of self-evidence.[17]

If one's experiential evidence of seemingly being convicted and led by God into morally robust *koinōnia* faces no defeater, that evidence will underwrite well-grounded, epistemically reasonable belief in God for one. The fact that some other people hold beliefs in conflict with one's belief in God will not be a defeater for one, because a conflicting belief does not automatically yield evidence for one against one's belief. A defeater will arise for one only if one's evidence supports that defeater, and that typically will be a function ultimately of what one's overall experience indicates regarding what is the case. Evidence is a truth- or factuality-indicator of some sort, and mere conflicting beliefs fall short of that status.[18] So, one cannot undermine a person's well-grounded belief in God just by an appeal to the conflicting beliefs held by some other people. The position on offer is a version of evidentialism, which thus contrasts with what is called "reformed epistemology."[19]

---

16. For further discussion of being convicted and led by God, in connection with human conscience, see Moser, *God Relationship*, 313–23; Moser, "Convictional Knowledge"; Moser, "Divine Hiddenness"; see also Forsyth, *Principle of Authority*; N. Robinson, *Christ and Conscience*, 76–80.

17. For relevant discussion of divine hiding, see Moser, *God Relationship*, 161–90; in connection with divine theodicy, see Moser, "Theodicy, Christology, and Divine Hiding."

18. For details, see Moser, *Knowledge and Evidence*.

19. For problems with the latter view, see Moser, "Doxastic Foundations."

The relevant belief in God can be *de re*, relating directly to God, with minimal *de dicto* content. This is important because it allows one to be convicted and led by God without one's having a conceptual understanding of God as God. It also allows that different people led by God could have different understandings of God and even know God by different names. This kind of diversity would not undermine or otherwise threaten the well-groundedness of belief in God. As long as the *de re* experiential base is in place, in the absence of defeaters, one's belief in God can be epistemically reasonable for one.

We can offer a new argument from moral experience for God's reality on the basis of a distinctive kind of *agapē*-conviction in conscience. This is not a "moral argument for God's existence" on the basis of mere "objective moral facts," because it gives a central role to *intentional agency* in moral experience of conviction.

1. Necessarily, if a person is directly acquainted, in the moral conviction of conscience, with a guiding character of perfect moral goodness toward perfect *agapē*, then this results from the morally authoritative power of an intentional agent of perfect moral goodness.
2. I am directly acquainted, in the moral conviction of conscience, with the guiding character mentioned in premise 1.
3. Therefore, an intentional agent of perfect moral goodness exists.
4. Necessarily, if an intentional agent of perfect moral goodness exists and is worthy of worship, then God exists.
5. The guiding character of the perfectly good intentional agent of premise 2 is worthy of worship.
6. Therefore, God exists.

The argument does not assume that it is a logically or conceptually necessary truth that God exists.

Premises 2 and 5 get their evidential support on abductive, explanatory grounds. Regarding premise 2, the best available explanation for me, without undefeated defeat, of my relevant moral conviction of conscience is that an intentional agent of perfect moral goodness is guiding me (if at times with my resistance). Regarding premise 5, the best available explanation for me, without undefeated defeat, of premise 2 is that a God worthy of worship exemplifies the guiding character of perfect moral goodness.[20]

20. We need not require omnipotence, omniscience, immutability, or (timeless) eternality of an intentional agent worthy of worship, contrary to a long-standing tradition among monotheists; for relevant discussion, see Moser, "Attributes of God."

Suppose that the character of the intentional agent of perfect moral goodness is best explained as having perfect moral goodness *inherently*, without depending on another agent. In that case, we have a prime candidate for a God worthy of worship. Any created being who is perfectly morally good would depend on the Creator for his or her being so, and thus would not have perfect moral goodness inherently. If one can have evidence for an intentional agent who has perfect moral goodness inherently, one can have evidence for a God worthy of worship. Such evidence could come, for instance, from grounded testimony from the agent in question, and it could come in the absence of undefeated defeat by other evidence. In addition, such evidence could arise in one's history of experience regarding the intentional agent of perfect moral goodness. It need not arise in a single moment.

My evidence bearing on premises 2 and 5 can be current in my experience, and it can be historical as a supplement to my experiential evidence. This is illustrated by two statements by Paul. First, it can be a matter of our current experience, or at least a best available explanation thereof, that "when we cry, 'Abba! Father!' it is [God] bearing witness with our spirit that we are children of God" (Rom. 8:15–16 NRSVue). God would have the option of bearing witness *de re*, in self-manifestation of moral character; and *de dicto*, with propositional content relayed to a person. A salient result could be the renewing, or regenerating, of a person in the moral image or character of God.[21] Second, we can factor in historical considerations about God's redemptive actions in history, such as this: "God proves his love [*agapē*] for us in that while we still were sinners Christ died for us" (Rom. 5:8 NRSVue). We cannot use the historical event of Christ's crucifixion alone to confirm God's existence, but it can contribute to one's relevant evidence in conjunction with the more interpersonal evidence of premise 2. So, given the argument at hand, there is no need to disregard historical evidence, including evidence that develops over time.

The argument on offer concerns *my* experience, from *my* first-person perspective. It may or may not bear on the experience of another person. So, we should not suggest that it has universal rational cogency. A person will need to have the relevant experience of intentional guidance for the argument to be rationally compelling for himself or herself. This consideration does not undermine or otherwise challenge the argument. It simply identifies that rational cogency can vary among persons relative to their actual experiences. Evidence typically has that feature and thus contrasts with truth. If God

---

21. See Forsyth, *Person and Place of Jesus Christ*, 195–210; Hubbard, *New Creation in Paul's Letters*.

seeks to relate to a person on an individual basis (which does not entail *only* an individual basis), we should not bar a role for nonpublic, nonuniversal evidence. We thus should not in principle reject reasonable agnosticism for people lacking needed evidence.

My experiential evidence can be unaccompanied by defeaters, which can arise directly or indirectly. A *direct* defeater of initial evidence consists of additional evidence (not to be confused with mere beliefs) that challenges *the support* of the initial evidence for a statement in question. For instance, my initial visual evidence indicates that there is a bent stick submerged halfway in a basin of water. The support offered by this evidence can be defeated by my additional visual evidence indicating that my initial visual evidence fails, when joined with the additional evidence, to indicate that there is a bent stick in the water. In contrast, an *indirect* defeater of evidence consists of evidence that challenges *the truth (claim) indicated* by that evidence. For instance, my visual evidence indicating that there is a table before me can be defeated by my additional visual and tactile evidence indicating that only a holographic image of a table is before me.

Regarding premise 2, I *could* have a defeater provided by my experience (for instance, an indication of a hallucination or a dream). As a matter of fact, however, I do not have one, inside or outside the sciences, and that fact is evidentially important. We should not disregard that fact or obscure it with mere possibilities of what could be the case.[22] A skeptical challenge for me would need to supply a defeater of my evidence that has a basis in evidence available to me. It could not be a mere belief of another person; defeaters do not arise in such an easy, evidence-free manner. I do not suggest, however, that my best available explanation bearing on premises 2 and 5 yields a satisfactory explanation of our world at large. For instance, we do not have a satisfactory explanation of unjust suffering in the world at large. In addition, I doubt that we reasonably should expect to have such an explanation.[23] So, I am not appealing to abduction as supporting a satisfactory theistic worldview. That appeal would be to overreach our actual evidence and to divert attention from the key evidence for God's reality in moral experience.

Is the argument 1–6 (above) an example of natural theology? I doubt that much depends on the answer, given that talk of what is "natural" is often slippery and variable. One's answer will depend on whether one's understanding

22. For relevant discussion, see Moser, *God Relationship*, 256–330; Wiebe, *God and Other Spirits*.

23. For the bearing of this consideration on Christian philosophy and theodicy, see Moser, "Theodicy, Christology, and Divine Hiding"; Moser, "Christian Philosophy and Christ Crucified."

of "worthiness of worship" in premise 5 fits with what is "natural." I will not digress to the matter, because I doubt that it has vital importance. The key evidence for God's reality, in any case, does not consist in an argument. Instead, it resides in divine self-evidencing in self-manifestation to humans, at the times chosen by God. In this respect, the evidence is interpersonal, and irreducibly so. It thus is not abstract and speculative in the manner familiar to philosophical approaches to God. Our engaging evidence for God's reality cannot be a spectator sport for us. It bears on our response to an offer of moral conviction toward God's morally perfect character. It thus bears on who we are, and resolve to be, as morally responsible agents before God.

Value in Natural Theology?

Having deflated the evidential value of representative arguments of natural theology, we should ask whether natural theology has any value. I have argued that it does not have conclusive or even confirmatory value relative to the existence of a God worthy of worship. I also have suggested that it does not serve as an effective preliminary or initial step toward reasonable commitment to a God worthy of worship. Even so, I grant that some natural theology can have more modest value, namely, *interrogatory value* in prompting questions about God and evidence for God. Its claims and arguments can suggest questions that illuminate God's character and inclinations. For instance, an argument of natural theology can invite us to ask what kind of evidence we should expect from God: nonpersonal or interpersonal, public or private, experiential or speculative.

The interrogatory value of natural theology is largely conceptual and intellectual. It typically does not take us to an existential challenge, such as that found in moral conviction in conscience. In that respect, it is morally thin. In addition, it is not directly redemptive as a challenge nudging one to reconciliation with God, including ongoing fellowship with God. We have a sharp contrast from the I-Thou evidence of God outlined above and in the New Testament writings of Paul and John. That evidence yields a vital lesson: to the extent that we neglect or resist *agapē*-conviction in conscience, we neglect or resist evidence of God's reality. More tragically, we thereby neglect or resist *God*.

One can be confused or misled about the evidence of God's reality, and many people are. Even so, we are morally responsible before God for how we respond to the challenge of *agapē*-conviction in conscience. Do we ignore it, suppress it, trivialize it, examine it, or value it? The relevant evidence does not make the decision for us; nor does anything else. *We* decide in the face of our challenges in conscience, and some of these challenges can signal the face of God. Even if some deliverances of conscience are misleading, God still can seek acquaintance with humans via *agapē*-conviction in conscience. God's moral character can emerge there and challenge us to renewal before God. This would be redemptive evidence, the kind of evidence suited to a God worthy of worship. The remaining question is whether we are willing to seek such evidence and, if found, give it the divine authority it merits. This is an ongoing challenge for all people, whether theists, atheists, or agnostics. Indeed, it is of primary importance for human life, inside and outside philosophy and theology.

Contemporary Response

CHARLES TALIAFERRO

W e see in Paul Moser's chapter a clash between natural theology (*theologia naturalis*) and the I-Thou encounter involving God's disclosure and loving moral guidance (*testimonium internum spiritus sancti*). He grants that natural theology can play an interrogative role, raising questions about God, but it is not effective in leading us to the God who is worthy of worship. Moser writes with passion and zeal, with critical acumen and constructive skill.

I begin this response on the ontological argument, with some observations on how it may function in our moral reflections, and then offer some positive remarks on other theistic arguments. I then offer some reflections on worship. I conclude with some speculative remarks on different ways of knowing each other and God.

On the ontological argument: on the version I defend, I introduce the Anselmian concept of God as maximally excellent. Inquiry begins with asking what sort of being would be maximally or unsurpassably excellent. Such a being would have the greatest compossible set of properties. I believe that most (or many) of us would identify those properties as omnipotence, omniscience, goodness (or perhaps Moser's notion of perfect moral goodness), and existing necessarily (noncontingently). A great deal of work needs to go into clarifying these properties (or attributes), arguing for their coherence and compatibility. For example, some critics have proposed that omnipotence is incoherent or incompatible with omniscience. I believe that these critics can be answered and that a string case can be made for the coherence of these divine attributes. The next stage of the argument is to take note that an ostensibly necessary being either exists necessarily or is impossible. For example, the proposition 1 + 1 = 2 cannot just be contingently true; it is either necessarily true or impossible (necessarily not possible). The next stage is to argue that this maximally excellent being is possible. If the being (or the existence of such a maximally excellent being) is possible, it is not impossible. If it is not impossible, it is possible, and therefore the maximally excellent being necessarily exists.

Consider some objections:

Necessarily existing is not a property. Reply: it certainly seems to be. Some states of affairs seem to necessarily exist (1 + 1 = 2). And we seem well suited to judge when states of affairs are impossible (1 + 1 = 3). As a Platonist, I believe there are good reasons to think there are uncountably many necessarily existing abstract objects.

The argument can be reversed by arguing that it is possible that the maximally excellent being does not exist, and therefore it is impossible that this being exists. I believe this is a serious objection but unsuccessful. It is one thing to not conceive of the maximally excellent being existing, but it is another matter to actually conceive of such a being and contend that it is an actual possibility that such a being does not exist. Arguably, this would amount to seeing that such a being is impossible. We can identify reasons why 1 + 1 = 3 is impossible (it violates the law of identity); what is it that makes the maximally excellent being impossible? Is there an incoherence among the great-making properties? This can (and is) argued over, and I suggest that the case for coherence is stronger than a case for incoherence.[1]

Can't the ontological argument be used to make a case for the existence of a maximally excellent island to be an evident absurdity? I have two replies. The first is the usual reply that the concept of a maximally perfect island is incoherent. The second is more dramatic: if we allow (for the sake of argument) that there might be a maximally perfect island, what sort of attributes would it have? Wouldn't it be omniscient? What about omnipotence? Goodness? Necessary existence? Such an "island" would turn out to be a metaphor for the maximally excellent being (just as God has been described as a fountain, a mighty fortress, a lion, and so on).

Why should we trust our intuitions about what is possible or necessary or impossible? I think we do indeed trust such judgments and that our awareness of ourselves in the world would utterly fail if we could not trust such judgments. Any judgment that you are reading a book right now relies on the supposition that such an act is possible and not impossible. Elsewhere I

---

1. The most systematic case for coherence is Swinburne, *Coherence of Theism*.

have defended a principle according to which, if some state of affairs seems to you to be conceivable, imaginable, consistently describable as obtaining, then (in the absence of independent reasons for thinking the state of affairs is impossible) it is reasonable for you to believe the state of affairs is possible.[2]

Objections and replies can be given further attention elsewhere, but consider here Moser's specific objection that the ontological argument is a static kind and does not leave room for the elusiveness of the evidence for God. Actually, it can make room for elusive evidence. If the best evidence for God comes in the form of an I-Thou encounter, that is evidence that God is actual. Any evidence that God is actual is evidence that God is possible and that the critics of the ontological argument who argue that God is impossible are mistaken.

What use might the ontological argument have for our other beliefs, for example, our beliefs about the Bible? If we believe (as I do) that God is maximally excellent and that this God is revealed in and through the Bible, then we have reason to interpret parts of the Bible as flawed by human limitations when it portrays God as not morally excellent. I suggest that if you have reason to think God is maximally excellent and that homosexual relations can be as healthy and good as heterosexual relations, you have reason to think that the biblical prohibitions of homosexuality are not truly divinely revealed precepts or that they should be interpreted as condemning specific, errant relations (e.g., condemning homosexual temple prostitution).

On the other theistic arguments in natural theology, I follow Richard Swinburne (except when he rejects the ontological argument) in contending that a strong, plausible case can be (and has been) made for the explanatory and descriptive primacy of theism over its closest competition, secular naturalism. What about God being worthy of worship? If natural theology does not provide grounds for acknowledging that God is worthy of worship, has it failed in some way, or is it deficient?

Let's back up. What is worship? I believe that worship involves reverence, praise, adoration, perhaps awe, maybe joy or delight in what or who is worshiped. In the case of a personal reality, it may involve recognizing either the primacy or the sole holder of honor as deserving of one's devotion, allegiance, and, in the case of the God of the Abrahamic faiths, obedience. There is an abundance of terms other than "worship" and its cognates that have been used in Christian spirituality about the soul's relationship to God: "purgation," "illumination," "the unitive way," "abiding or dwelling in God." Sometimes it seems that worship and praise are not the primary dimension of our relationship to God. Perhaps confession and repentance, with a supplication for

2. See, e.g., Taliaferro, "Sensibilia and Possibilia."

forgiveness and expiation, are at the forefront at times in Christian spirituality. Petitionary prayer may sometimes take primacy over worship. Maybe there are layers and layers of spiritual dimensions of the soul's relation to God, from bridal mysticism (see Bernard of Clairvaux's sermons on the Song of Songs) to the celebration of friendship, as found in *Spiritual Friendship* by St. Aelred of Rievaulx. And, of course, there are corporeal acts of seeking justice and the relief of suffering.

The above observations are not intended to counter anything Moser has claimed. I am only seeking to amplify the many dimensions in the Christian understanding of worship and the other ways in which persons are invited to live out their lives in the presence of God (*coram Deo*).

On our relationship with God and one another: the intimacy and directness of the experience of God in an I-Thou encounter is (in my view) both real and life giving. Not as a counter to Moser, I simply observe here the multiple ways we encounter God and one another. In one of the Episcopal books of prayer, *St. Augustine's Prayer Book*, we pray (for example, I prayed today) for all those who die this day, that God may receive their souls; we also pray for all those who are born today, and all doctors, nurses, and more. Imagine James died today in Paris, Suzzie was born in Madrid, Nichola is a doctor in Brazil, Steffanie is a nurse in Moscow, and Jil is a journalist in Texas. Did I (along with all the others who made such a prayer) just pray for them? I would say yes. The relationship with them is (as it were) long distance, but I claim that it is real and, by the grace of God, meaningful. Now, compare someone who is experiencing God in their life through agape, self-sacrificing love, and someone in a library in graduate school who becomes convinced of an Anselmian ontological argument and offers a prayer of adoration to God. The second person's experience may seem less dramatic and personal, but I suggest that both may be having an authentic, meaningful relationship with the God who created and sustains us and all of creation. Amen.

Catholic Response

FATHER ANDREW PINSENT

P aul Moser's deflationary approach to natural theology begins by defining, or restricting, natural theology to the set of arguments for God's existence. Then he criticizes representative examples of these arguments, constantly coming back to one overarching complaint. This complaint is that none of these arguments can lead someone to conclude the God exists whose inferred existence is worthy of worship. On this account, natural theology is theologically useless even if it works.

In response, I begin by agreeing with the core of Moser's arguments, namely, that the proofs of God's existence leave open many other questions about God, a point that is often obscured by the connotations of the word "God" for those using the proofs. One of my favorite games with students is to ask them where they could find three poetic lines stating that flowers testify to "his love," that the waves "sing of his work," and that he is the origin of all happiness. Typically, they will answer that these lines are from Scripture, or are perhaps from a hymn, after which I reveal that the last line is: "Long live, long live, General Kim Jong-Il!" [1]

The lines come from a translation of an old patriotic song out of North Korea. This song highlights, of course, that the ruler of North Korea, whose regime forbids public worship of the God of revelation, has made himself the object of worship. Moreover, although North Korea is an extreme example, the cult of deification of supreme leaders has proven to be one of the most consistent characteristics of all the communist and many other regimes of

---

1. "Song to General Kim Jong-Il" (Korea, DPR), NationalAnthems.us, accessed August 17, 2023, http://www.nationalanthems.us/forum/YaBB.pl?num=1105481021.

the last hundred years. Such examples offer, at least at first glance, a practical validation of Moser's central thesis: that the existence of some god does not necessarily imply the existence of the God who is worthy of worship.

Nevertheless, I have some disagreements with the details of Moser's arguments. First, he objects to the conclusion of Thomas Aquinas's cosmological argument, namely, the inference of "a first efficient cause, to which everyone gives the name of God."[2] But what, precisely, has Aquinas done wrong? Almost any educated person of the thirteenth century, and many people today, would indeed assign the name "God" to an inferred first cause. Furthermore, it is not foolish, I think, to associate the causation of being in some sense with the causation of goodness and being good. After all, one of the most persistent philosophical accounts of evil, since at least Augustine, is that goodness is equivalent to being, and that evil is a deprivation or perversion of being.[3] A bad apple (whether meant literally or as a metaphor for a bad person) is a corrupted version of something that exists, potentially or actually; and that which causes a thing to be is good, at least insofar as it is a cause of that being. Hence, it is at least plausible to infer that the maximally most potent cause of being should also be maximally good.

Moreover, one does not need to belong to the Judeo-Christian tradition to associate the first cause with goodness. I have had extensive conversations with Father Anthony Barrett, who spent many years living with the Turkana people of northwest Kenya. The Turkana certainly believe in a god, Akuj, meaning the "big" (*epolet*) or important one. Akuj is cool and good, the "coolness" of Akuj being especially valued by a people living close to the equator. Akuj gives life and health, rain and grass, cattle and people, but only "permits" sickness, drought, and death.[4] In this cosmology, only people or "spirits" or certain disordered things make Akuj angry (hot) and push Akuj away, generating evil. Properly speaking, Akuj is understood more in terms of ordering reality well, rather than being a creator ex nihilo, but Akuj is nevertheless the supreme cause in this cosmology, being both good (cool) and causing good (cool). As in the case of those doing natural theology in the Christian tradition, the Turkana people do not divide the supreme cause of being from the supreme cause of goodness, and it would not make sense for them to do so, thereby offering a practical counterexample to Moser's argument that we cannot infer the perfect goodness of the supreme cause of all things.

A review of the case of North Korea above also shows that this case is less supportive of Moser's argument than might at first appear. After all, in the

2. Aquinas, *Summa Theologiae* I.2.3.
3. Pinsent, *History of Evil in the Medieval Age.*
4. A. Barrett, *Sacrifice and Prophecy,* 80.

example above, the song in honor of General Kim Jong-Il ascribes all kinds of good attributes to him, such as being the creator of happiness. More broadly, it would be unthinkable for the North Korean media to blame his father, Kim Il-Sung, the founder of North Korea, or any of his successors for any of the many disasters that have befallen that country. It is not simply that these leaders are regarded as first causes, albeit in a partial or inadequate sense, but they are specifically treated exclusively as causes of goodness and as supremely good. Therefore, even in the case of patently inadequate "gods," the wedge that Moser tries to drive between the existence and goodness of "god," howsoever conceived, does not seem particularly credible, whatever other questions remain unanswered by natural arguments for the existence of God. If one conceives of any god as a source of being, even a patently false or tyrannical god, then it follows that the god is at least a qualified source of good, implying also that the god is at least a qualified good. It also follows that if one conceives of that god as a supreme or first source of being, which is the conclusion of arguments in natural theology for the existence of God, such a god is also supremely good and worthy of worship, if anything is worthy of worship.

My second point of disagreement with Moser is his argument that divine revelation also contradicts natural theology. In particular, he argues that natural theology purports to guarantee the being of God, in conflict with what Moser describes as God's "intermittent hiding and seeking toward humans." Certainly, there are examples of texts in Scripture that seem consistent with the latter claim. For example, 1 Samuel 3:1 states, "The word of the LORD was rare in those days; there was no frequent vision," testifying that there are indeed periods of salvation history during which God is hidden. Deuteronomy 31:17 and 32:20 portray God as hiding or threatening to hide his face from his people, and Isaiah 45:15 describes God as hiding himself. Micah 5:3 also states that God plans to withdraw from or abandon his people for a time, until she who is to give birth has given birth.

Such texts seem, at first, to validate Moser's thesis, that it is a characteristic of the God of revelation to be hidden, at least at times, in apparent conflict with the constancy of the purported inferences of natural theology. The difficulty for this argument, however, is that, to the best of my belief and knowledge, neither the Jewish nor Christian Scriptures really offer any examples of persons who doubt the existence of God due to God's intermittent hiddenness. As an extreme example, consider the case of Job, the righteous man who is permitted to suffer horrendously. From a modern philosophical perspective, it might seem that this situation is a classic or even paradigmatic case of the problem of evil, leading to atheism. Nevertheless, although there is no doubt that Job yearns for an answer for his suffering, he also says, "I know that my Redeemer lives, and at last he will stand upon the earth; and after my skin has been thus destroyed, then from my flesh I shall see God" (Job 19:25–26). In other words, even if Job, while he is suffering, laments the hiddenness of God, there is no evidence that he is contemplating becoming an atheist or even an agnostic.

The underlying issue of what is missing from Moser's argument is the difference between knowing the existence of God and having a covenantal relationship with God, a distinction often highlighted in revealed theology. For example, James 2:19 states that even the demons believe in the existence of God, but such belief is clearly not the same as being in a covenantal relationship with God. On this point one may also cite Aristotle, who affirms the existence of "the God" while denying that it is possible to be friends with God.[5] When the Scriptures refer to the hiddenness of God, or God as hiding his face, the issue is not about the loss of belief in God's existence but, rather, a breaking or suspension or apparent suspension of enjoyment of the covenant with God. In other words, one knows that God exists, but one's relationship with God has been destroyed or suspended. In the case of Job, he wants to confront God to understand his situation (Job 31:35–37), but there is no sense that he has ceased to believe in God's existence. On this account, the loss of the covenant with God, for whatever reason, does not need to imply a loss of belief in the existence of God, a distinction that appears to neutralize any purported conflict with natural theology.

Finally, I have a further and minor disagreement with Moser over the scope of natural theology. As I outline in my chapter, I think we need to avoid reducing natural theology simply to the question of the existence of God. I am reminded of the criticism offered by the soul of George Macdonald to the narrator, presumably C. S. Lewis, in the latter's book *The Great Divorce*,

> There have been men before now who got so interested in proving the existence of God that they came to care nothing for God Himself, . . . as if the good Lord had nothing to do but exist! There have been some who were so occupied in spreading Christianity that they never gave a thought to Christ. Man! Ye see it in smaller matters. Did ye never know a lover of books that with all his first editions and signed copies had lost the power to read them? Or an organizer of charities that had lost all love for the poor? It is the subtlest of all the snares.[6]

In other words, Lewis highlights that anyone who is serious about revealed theology and salvation needs to care about much more than the existence of

5. Aristotle, *Nicomachean Ethics* 8.7.1158b36–1159a5.
6. Lewis, *Great Divorce*, chap. 9.

God. The case of Aquinas illustrates this point. Aquinas covers his five proofs for the existence of God in just a single article in his *Summa Theologiae* (*ST* I.2.3). By contrast, as I have observed in my chapter, Aquinas devotes over a thousand times more effort to questions about human perfection in the context of the covenant with God, namely, the 189 articles of *ST* I-II.55–89 and the 815 articles of *ST* II-II.1–170, covering the virtues, gifts, beatitudes, and fruits. In other words, the huge contemporary attention paid to his five proofs seems to be, at the very least, disproportionate compared to Aquinas's own priorities.

What, then, are the further questions that natural theology can consider? As I highlight in my own chapter, I think that at least some effort should be dedicated to the issue of understanding theological matters as opposed simply to reaching certain theological conclusions expressed as propositions. In addition, one can think of natural theology in a way radically different from grasping theological truths based on the study of nature. As I also point out in my chapter, and as Alister McGrath also argues, one can examine nature from the perspective of a supernatural understanding of revelation. Moreover, the range of issues one can study becomes even greater if one considers the ways in which nature, including human society and knowledge, has been shaped by human beings who purportedly ascribe to Christian revelation. One can consider, for example, the impact of revelation on the philosophy of time and history,[7] the understanding of the human person and individual,[8] the formation of societies,[9] the philosophy of education, jurisprudence,[10] marriage, singleness,[11] gardening, the consumption of food and drink,[12] healthcare, agriculture, and care for the sick and dying.[13]

The extension of natural theology in this way has additional advantages. For example, I agree with Moser insofar as I have tended to find what is ordinarily described as natural theology, namely, proofs for God's existence,

7. See, e.g., Jaki, *Science and Creation*.

8. See, e.g., the theological foundations of the term "person" that are explored in Spaemann, *Persons*.

9. One need not agree with all the bold claims made by Slattery, *Heroism and Genius*. Nevertheless, this book does highlight many important and incontrovertible facts regarding the impact of faith on human society.

10. See, e.g., the compendious Berman, *Law and Revolution*.

11. See, e.g., Huebner and Laes, *Single Life in the Roman and Later Roman World*.

12. Consider the many observations of links between theology and enology in Scruton, *I Drink Therefore I Am*.

13. As an example, I recently spent two extended periods in hospital in the United Kingdom. I was somewhat surprised and gratified to discover that nurses are still called "sister," an echo of the Christian origins of that vocation. Much of this nursing was by nuns, also called "sisters." See, e.g., Tastard, *Nightingale's Nuns and the Crimean War*.

rather pointless and even boring. By contrast, an extended understanding of natural theology can highlight all kinds of interesting and understudied issues. As one of many examples, while studying the impact of faith on table manners, I was intrigued to learn that Cardinal Richelieu was responsible for inventing the table knife, and not just shaping the course of the Thirty Years' War;[14] and that monasteries were responsible for the spread of techniques for the distillation of alcohol, leading, among other matters, to the development of chemistry and the invention of whisky.[15]

Furthermore, beyond acquiring a great deal of fascinating ad hoc knowledge, the extension of natural theology in this way can address Moser's broader concern about its limitations. I fully agree with him that proving God's existence does not, in itself, reveal much about what is meant by the term "God," even if I disagree that proofs of God have no moral implications about God. If, however, natural theology is extended to consider what one might call the roots and fruits of revelation, a huge range of possibilities opens up for learning about God and what is pleasing to God. After all, in a quotation frequently attributed to G. K. Chesterton, a Christian society is one in which "the pint, the pipe and the cross can all fit together."[16] Such apparent incongruities should at least invite careful investigation.

14. Kass, *Hungry Soul*, 143. See also T. Long, "Cardinal Richelieu Makes His Point."
15. Forbes, *Short History of the Art of Distillation*.
16. Dale Ahlquist, president of the G. K. Chesterton Society and one of the few persons in the world who has read the entirety of his corpus, agrees with me that this quotation is almost universally attributed to Chesterton. Nevertheless, despite its plausibility, the quotation cannot actually be found in any of his published work.

Classical Response

ALISTER E. McGRATH

Paul Moser offers us an engaging deflationary account of natural theology, noting some significant difficulties with traditional approaches to this topic, while affirming that the overall enterprise of natural theology nonetheless remains viable and productive. Although at points his analysis is shaped by the restrictive assumption that natural theology is to be understood primarily in terms of "arguments for God's existence," the issues that he raises merit close attention—in particular, his analysis of the shortcomings of various arguments of this kind. Although I do not consider these to be integral to the enterprise of natural theology as I have come to understand this idea, these arguments remain important for contemporary philosophical and theological debate, and it is good to have these concerns articulated and explored.

Moser's critique of Anselm of Canterbury's "ontological argument" is particularly interesting, although as a historical theologian, I take the view that Anselm did not present his reflections on God as an "argument," nor did he speak of it as being "ontological." These are the retrospective categorizations of modern writers, which sit uneasily with Anselm's own working assumptions and stated intentions in the *Proslogion*.

I appreciate Moser's brief engagement with the psychologist William James but wonder if philosophers of religion might be open to a wider engagement on such important questions of intuition, judgment, and belief formation that are grounded in empirical research. Moser's reflections on these categories of arguments for God's existence are chiefly directed toward the professional guild of philosophers of religion. While this is not a problem, it does mean that his analysis does not take account of wider intellectual discussions of human rationality, including the empirical studies of how human beings arrive at conclusions concerning the "naturalness" of belief in God.

A historical example may help to clarify this point. In the early modern period, natural theology arguably reached the zenith of its cultural influence in the interdisciplinary field generally known as "physicotheology."[1] Growing scholarly interest in this field has the potential to enrich theological and philosophical discussion of the reflective empirical human encounter with the natural world, and particularly its theistic implications. As we find the idea explored in the writings of Robert Boyle and others, physicotheology was both empirically grounded and theologically informed. It did not seek to prove God's existence but rather sought to affirm the rationality of a theistic view of the world, on the one hand, and encourage empirical study of that world in the belief that this would enhance human appreciation for the wisdom of God, on the other. For me, natural theology is a particularly appropriate interface between Christian theology and the natural sciences, without in any way excluding engagement with other disciplines, not least philosophy.

Yet more-recent debates need to be brought into this discussion. I wonder if Moser's deflationary account of natural theology might benefit from engaging the discipline of the cognitive science of religion and its important reflections on how human beings intuitively find themselves inclined to some form of natural theology.[2] These themes are properly and productively engaged by the philosopher Helen de Cruz (Danforth Chair in the Humanities at Saint Louis University and presently managing editor of the journal *Faith and Philosophy*), in relation to both the "natural" character of natural theology and the reliability of human intuitions, which have the potential to illuminate and enrich our understanding of natural theology.[3] The question of whether (and why) we can trust our intuitions is clearly significant in arguments for the existence of God (think, for example, of C. S. Lewis's appeal to intuition at multiple points in his apologetic writings). I suspect that this might prove to be a philosophically fertile area of discussion. De Cruz's engagement with cognitive science brings home the point that, by its very nature, natural theology is an interdisciplinary enterprise, which may be

1. There is considerable scholarly interest in this topic, which has yet to feed into wider theological and philosophical reflection; see, e.g., Blair and von Greyerz, *Physico-Theology*; and Greenham, "Clarifying Divine Discourse in Early Modern Science."
2. For the origins of this movement, see particularly J. Barrett, *Why Would Anyone Believe in God?*
3. See, e.g., de Cruz, *Natural History of Natural Theology*. Her work with Johan de Smedt is also important to any discussion of "natural" perceptions; see, e.g., de Cruz and de Smedt, "Intuitions and Arguments."

defined in certain ways by certain intellectual guilds, yet is best understood as a deep and wide intellectual landscape, open to exploration, using different conceptual tool kits.

Although Moser and I diverge at some points, he makes some important observations concerning certain approaches to natural philosophy that I completely endorse. The most significant of these concerns the disparity between arguments that lead to belief in "a creator of the universe" and those that lead to "a God worthy of worship." This is an important point and can be helpfully illustrated and developed with reference to the history of natural theology. Consider, for example, William Paley's *Natural Theology* (1802), which exercised considerable influence in England during the first half of the nineteenth century.[4] Paley's arguments for the existence of God as Creator are based on envisioning nature as a complex machine, comparable to a watch, whose intrinsic complexity makes it implausible to think that it could have arisen by any means other than what Paley terms "contrivance"—that is, deliberate design and construction.[5]

Two fundamental criticisms were made of this approach during the nineteenth century, both of which echo Moser's important concerns. First, machines were widely seen as ugly; who would want to worship their creators?[6] Second, such a God lacks the transcendent majesty that warrants worship and adoration. This view, set out with particular force by John Henry Newman, tended to see natural theology as an obstacle, rather than as a gateway, to religious belief, since it pointed to a God who had little connection with contemporary human needs and aspirations.[7] It is a fair point, and Moser is right in noting that such concerns "deflate" the evidential value of the arguments of natural theology.

This helps us understand Moser's interest in "I-Thou evidence for God," which shifts the focus from intellectual assent to the existence of God and onward to a potentially transformative and existentially significant relationship with God. Moser develops this approach in dialogue with William James, a perceptive critic of rational arguments for God, which he believed did little more than "corroborate our preexistent partialities."[8] I agree with Moser here and wonder if he might have developed this point further, particularly in dialogue with James. I have in mind James's remarkable reflections on the

4. Fyfe, "Reception of William Paley's *Natural Theology*."
5. McGrath, "Chance and Providence in the Thought of William Paley."
6. A view that was forcibly expressed by the Scottish paleontologist Hugh Miller; see Brooke, "Like Minds."
7. Fletcher, "Newman and Natural Theology."
8. James, *Varieties of Religious Experience*, 428–29.

changes in the way in which we perceive nature that arise from adopting a theistic perspective: "At a single stroke, [theism] changes the dead blank *it* of the world into a living *thou*, with whom the whole man may have dealings."[9] This line of reflection might well have positive outcomes for identifying "evidence suited to a God worthy of worship."

Moser's reflections offer us a welcome stimulus to think further on the options that remain open to us in considering the rationality of religious belief in general, while opening up the relational and existential aspects of natural theology. As he rightly points out, traditional forms of natural theology are "largely conceptual and intellectual" and do not offer us the kind of "existential challenge" that can lead to new relationship with God. While Moser's recognition of the importance of "*agapē*-conviction" takes us some distance from traditional notions of natural theology, it helps us realize that there is more for us to discover about natural theology and its relevance to meaningful human existence. I look forward to further explorations of such second-person approaches to natural theology in the future.

9. James, *Will to Believe*, 127.

Barthian Response

JOHN C. McDOWELL

In the Fourth Gospel, Pontius Pilate is portrayed as sneeringly responding to Jesus's mention of "truth": "What is truth?" (John 18:38 NRSVue). Pilate's question is deliberately designed to rhetorically evade any challenge to his authority, an authority that represents locally the *absolute power* of Rome herself, the "victor's" power to ultimately determine what is "true." While this political assertion is anything but epistemically relativistic, it is clear that the Gospel portrays two clashing perspectives on where authority, and therefore truthfulness and trustworthiness, lies. Using the governor's question as a launchpad, Hans-Georg Gadamer reflects on the way interpretation or understanding is conditioned or mediated. He declares, "We are of necessity caught within the limits of our hermeneutical situation when we inquire into truth."[1]

Over recent decades, philosophy of religion has reflected on the truth-telling quality, and therefore epistemic trustworthiness, of what it generalizingly calls "religious experience" as a condition for rationally inferring the existence of God. Among common difficulties with a certain form of that philosophical approach, it appears to be distinctly cavalier to the significance of concrete contexts and conditions for speaking of "experiences" that are (to use a rather nebulous and deeply contested term) "religious," and from there to acclaim the veridical nature of the supposed experience as validly contributing to providing rational support for beliefs in God's existence.

First, there is a flattening of phenomenologically describable differences into a homogenized "experience." This strategy had been common in the once intellectually fashionable religious pluralism that is now, however,

---

1. Gadamer, "What Is Truth?," 40.

generally regarded as impoverishing matters through its inability to attend to the concrete, and even to recognize its own intellectual situatedness and discursiveness. Yet, recently, Kai-Man Kwan has announced, "It seems to be a rational strategy to try to reconcile their reports as much as possible. For example, a common core can be identified. . . . I believe the 'contradiction' is not as stark as it is commonly made out to be."[2] Here, thick ethnographies would be concerned that just such a claim functions more as an assertion imposing a commonality than as a phenomenology of actual experiences. Accordingly, working from Michel Foucault, Grace Jantzen reasons that "there is no such thing as an abstract 'essence' of mysticism [or any other kind of "religious experience"] which could be discovered by a theologian pondering in her study or praying in a church. Rather, what counts as mysticism will reflect (and also help to constitute) the institutions of power in which it occurs."[3]

Second, the approach is theologically clumsy in its handling of the supposed "object" of "religious experience." William Alston may appear to be making a profound point when he recognizes that cataphatic theological approaches are far from universal. "On the one hand, many people . . . take it to be unproblematically true that God is loving, powerful, wise, good, and so on, not to mention active in various ways. And theology is filled with such characterizations. On the other hand, some strains in the traditions emphasize the mystery, ineffability, incomprehensibility of God to such an extent that none of our concepts can be strictly true of him."[4] In the process of being schooled in what Nicholas of Cusa calls "learned ignorance," the Christian tradition, at least, has had a considerably more complicated understanding of how God-talk functions than Alston's descriptive/denial binary would suggest. The way Alston frames the issue is the product of massive shifts in modernity over what God-talk is. According to Nicholas Lash, talk of divine attributes had been, for the tradition,

> not descriptive but grammatical. . . . And because we do not know God's nature, they served as protocols against idolatry, reminders that anything whose nature we *do* know, anything that we can imagine, consider, or come across as an individual object among the other objects that there are, is not God and is not to be worshipped. . . . In the tradition which runs from seventeenth-century deism to contemporary philosophy of religion in the empiricist tradition, however, the

---

2. Kwan, "Argument from Religious Experience," 264–65, referring to C. Davis, *Evidential Force of Religious Experience.*

3. Jantzen, *Power, Gender and Christian Mysticism,* 14.

4. Alston, "Mysticism and Perceptual Awareness of God," 212.

divine attributes are (in marked contrast) taken to be specifying characteristics, identifying properties, of an individual entity, a being called "God."[5]

Paul Moser's chapter is, at least, not prone to some of these common complaints leveled against arguments from "religious experience." For instance, it is clear about its privileged particularism when using claims that are grounded in the Christian Scriptures, thereby implicitly subverting the rather vacuous talk of "mystical experiences" that requires homogenizing "religious experiences." As numerous commentators observe, the Christian "mystical" traditions, for example, emerge freighted with, and from within, the *irreducibly* rich content of Christian traditions or frameworks of interpretation and what Charles Taylor calls the social imaginary.[6] Among other things, the irony is that the Christian "mystical traditions" are as much theological warnings against the identifiability of any experience as an experience of God, and they press toward a deep sense of the very *inexperienceability* of God as utterly incomprehensible or *supersensible*. Pseudo-Dionysius, from whom Thomas Aquinas learned much, uncompromisingly declares that God is "the Superunknowable," since, if all acts of knowledge are of beings, that which is beyond being utterly transcends all knowledge.[7] In fact, God is even beyond being ineffable and unknowable since these are categories that creatures use to speak about the limits of their acts of cognition. Jantzen puts the matter starkly in pronouncing that "any competent undergraduate can quite easily show that what philosophers say or assume mysticism is like bears little resemblance to the actual historic mystics of western Christendom."[8] Of course, Moser's approach itself raises questions about how those relate to claims attesting religious experience within other traditions, but his particularist approach does at least prevent his claims from being vulnerable to critical observations that experiences and practice-embedded beliefs differ *substantively*. The focus on the Christian tradition and its foundational stories does permit a better sense of the contextual production of interiority, of the social construction or mediatedness of experiences, than tends to be the case among those who construct an argument for the existence of God from religious experience.

Nonetheless, important issues emerge at this point. Why take these *Christian* texts and the traditions of "experience" within which they are performed as normative for the case he makes? For what reason should one trust the

---

5. Lash, *Easter in Ordinary*, 104.
6. See C. Taylor, *Modern Social Imaginaries*.
7. Pseudo-Dionysius, *The Divine Names* 1.1.588A, 593B.
8. Jantzen, *Power, Gender and Christian Mysticism*, xiv. Alston admits awareness of the difficulty (Alston, "Mysticism and Perceptual Awareness of God," 209).

reliability of their interpretations of interiority, of the self as encountered by
God? After all, those who encountered Jesus did not all experience him and
his significance in the same way: not only Pilate, but also his own disciples,
especially Judas. The apostolic writings are replete with differences, contesta-
tions, and varieties of understanding among the primitive Jesus communities.
These issues require comment, and therefore some considerable intellectual
work would need to be done to satisfy a range of conditions that would support the practice of reading these claims as trustworthy, as being experiences
of the reality of *God's* presence. Additionally, what would be required for these
claims to become rationally compelling to someone inhabiting a different,
and competing, interpretive tradition?

Richard Swinburne's principles of credulity and testimony do not help
here. They sound like someone claiming an unusual experience who enjoins
"trust me" when one knows well that people testify to all manner of (conflicting) experiences and are not particularly adept at interpreting the content of
their experiences without the conditions provided by a range of interpretive
frameworks. Lash warns of generalizing about terms such as "experience"
since "there is no such thing, and hence there is no such thing as pure or raw
experience."[9] Elsewhere Moser, along with Chad Meister, argues that "one
can have an experience of something that is not a sensory object."[10] But what
is it that makes this an "experience"? Several philosophers of religion conceive
of religious experience as analogous to sensible experience. Without this,
religious experience becomes a special (transcendental) case of experience,
something sui generis, a kind of aesthetic sublime. The difficulty is that a
materiality provides the grounds and contexts for inference and reflection on
even nonmaterial experiences (such as that of love—after all, there are lovers
and beloveds). The conditions for experience of worldly matters are, at least in
theory, universal and open for public testing, whereas the so-called experience
of God is not.[11] T. J. Mawson deals with a potential counterclaim regarding
testimonies to color from sighted people alongside nonsighted people. Only if
a blind person were "to hear numerous but conflicting testimonies about the
world of color, [would] he or she . . . be reasonable in suspending judgement.
. . . But, as a matter of fact, in our society, . . . numerous . . . testimon[ies]
of sighted people [are] largely consistent."[12] Perhaps the notion of changed

---

9. Lash, *Easter in Ordinary*, 12.
10. Moser and Meister, "Introduction," 1.
11. In fact, T. J. Mawson argues that claims to the experience of God that work from testimonies of those who believe to have experienced God overlook the subversive "evidence" of
those who believe themselves to have *not* experienced God (*Belief in God*, 169).
12. Mawson, *Belief in God*, 173–74.

lives, signifying the transformative presence of a God worthy to be worshiped, might be the *material* response. If so, then it would be an evasion of potential parallel transformations within other interpretive contexts. What about the lives that appear to be morally vicious? The case would involve a selective partiality that would have David Hume spinning in his grave, given his criticism of the discrimination involved in teleological claims made by theistic argument.

This is, however, only the beginning of my puzzlement with Moser's chapter. The context for its claims is proclaimed to be the provision of a "deflationary perspective." Moser's work attempts to let out the air from theists' ballooning arguments for the existence of God that imagine themselves to rationally ascend from the known to the unknown. Yet this is rhetoric that can distract from the fact that many theists have admitted for some time now that the arguments, even in a cumulative inferential strategy of argument, are limited in their rational persuasiveness. Moser claims that trying "to get there with *super*natural means (say, divine self-manifestation to humans)" renders "the presumed underlay of natural theology . . . evidentially superfluous and dispensable." The notion of "underlay" suggests that he is criticizing foundationalist approaches to natural theology that function as prolegomena through which a believer *must* pass in order to claim that her belief is rationally held. Given that many now regard rationality as tradition conditioned, for whom is argument "superfluous and dispensable"? Perhaps for the one having the experience, and the community whose language it is that the experience emerges from and stays within, although that person may, at some point, question the veracity of her interpretation of the experience. What argument does, at its best, is hold a claim up to public accountability—that is, to its responsibility to test that it is not the product of misdirecting desires. Moreover, it is a communicative act that does something other than simply *assert*, "It's my experience, so trust it and me," and therefore holds off, as well as it can, the potential for ideological false consciousness. In this vein, Lash claims, "Argument is a form of conversation."[13] Moser rhetorically asks, "What do we value more? Knowing God or knowing an argument regarding God's existence?" This is a distinctly odd choice. After all, if Moser's God is experienceable, then one can report various things, or argue (since a case can be made) from the effects of God. Paul's approach in 1 Corinthians 15, for instance, makes a case for the corporeality of the eschatological event of Jesus's having been raised. The issue for Moser seems to be that of arguing from persons and nonpersons: "A misplaced focus on nonpersonal evidence

13. Lash, *Easter in Ordinary*, 6.

in arguments can hinder our awareness of evidence in interpersonal self-manifestation." This simply does not work with persons, since their effects, their traces, say much about them and their acts, and the Christian traditions have long held that the incomprehensible God can be known only from God's effects, from the (personal) stories of holy living as well as the createdness of all things.

Moser, though, does not want to relinquish argument at all, despite what is claimed about deflating "natural theology"; here he argues for a chastened apologetics that "attends to the right kind of evidence," by which he means "the kind of experiential evidence." There are, however, truly enormous questions over how a person's experience of that which appears *directly* can function in a public setting, or veridically, without simply manifesting persuasion by arbitrary assertion. According to Alston, "There *are* tests for the accuracy of particular reports of mystical [or other 'religious'] perception."[14] Nevertheless, these are tests appropriate within particular sets of practices, beliefs, and expectations, and they do not travel well when they have to play their language games away from home. Judging by the paucity of philosophical interest among those who are not already committed to a theistic perspective, or even culturally in Western churches, it seems as though they are losing their matches quite comprehensibly and scoring few goals in the process. While there are publicly intelligible tests for experiences of things in the world, what would count as a rationally appropriate test for claims to experience God, "than which nothing greater can be conceived" (Anselm)? Richard Gale recognizes the force of this difficulty: "There is no religious experience analogue to this concept of objective existence, there being no analogous dimensions to space and time in which God, along with the perceiver, is housed and which can be invoked to make sense of God existing when not actually perceived and being the common object of different religious experiences. Because of this big disanalogy, God is categorically unsuited to serve as the object of a veridical perception, whether sensory or *nonsensory*."[15] In fact, there is no agreement among Christian communities and their theological intelligentsia as to what, if anything, could function as a public test of the veracity of anyone's claim to be experiencing God. If this makes things difficult, to return to Lash, that is precisely the theologian's job. "The theologian does not *invent* either the complexity and illegibility of our history or the pain and confusion of contemporary circumstance. . . . Part of the theologian's responsibility is to help discipline the propensity of the pious imagination

14. Alston, "Mysticism and Perceptual Awareness of God," 216.
15. Gale, *On the Nature and Existence of God*, 327; cf. Martin, "Religious Experience," 121–23.

to simplify facts, texts, demands, and requirements that are resistant to any such simplification. . . . Serious theological reflection, in other words, is and should be made to be, *hard work*."[16] The theological task involves, as much as anything, the disruption of the established simplistic certainties held by the theologically educated just as strongly as by the theologically uneducated.

In addition, what does it mean to speak of a "God worthy of worship"? "We should expect evidence," Moser and Meister claim, "for a God inherently worthy of worship to be morally significant in a way that represents God's perfect moral character."[17] If it should become definitively clear that Jesus's bones have been resting in a tomb somewhere near Jerusalem, then a radical reconfiguration of Christian claims, practices, and interpretation of one's theo-ethical experiences would need to occur. Likewise, if a compelling case should somehow be made that the world is self-grounded and conditioned, then the very appeal to "experience" would appear irredeemably subjective. Accordingly, Douglas Geivett argues, "To the extent that background beliefs do condition one's understanding of an of-God experience, it will matter whether those background beliefs enjoy an appropriate degree of justification by independent means. . . . In such cases belief in God must already have some positive epistemic standing."[18]

It is worth pressing the very notion of "worthiness." Is a God who reveals God's Self to only *some*, for some reason, worthy of worship? Fyodor Dostoyevsky's Ivan Karamazov offers a haunting refusal to believe that this is so, and hence he hands back his ticket to heaven. Is a God who spends time revealing God's Self *to be worshiped* actually worthy of worship when there is inequity, unjust suffering, trauma, and catastrophe in that God's world? Thorny questions of suffering and injustice cannot be cavalierly skated over as they so often are among bourgeois academic philosophers of religion. Without wanting to open Pandora's box, the question is whether an appeal to the evaluative criteria of "worthiness," as a counter to the practice of rational inquiry and reflective argument, can be handled in something other than a distinctly glib and superficial fashion. How does arguing from perceived experience render a God worthy of worship any more fruitfully? Much atheism is, after all, a response to the gods confessed that are perceived to be curbs on real worldly flourishing. Here is where the question of selectivity again appears in the case being made. Many *from within overlapping traditions* claim to have different understandings of the *moral* significance of

16. Lash, *Easter in Ordinary*, 290–91.
17. Moser and Meister, "Introduction," 6.
18. Geivett, "Evidential Value of Religious Experience," 195.

their experiences. Where one person experiences a call to inclusively love all
things in self-dispossession, another person experiences reasons to engage
in colonizing and other-dominating forms of behavior, self-interest, and so
on. Finally, while the question about interpretive context of experience has
already been raised, another matter arises on broadly similar grounds. How
can the interpretation of an experience test itself? This is not so much a matter of how to specify *public* criteria as much as the more subjective capacity
for self-examination, for which the Johannine writer calls: "Test the spirits"
(1 John 4:1) warns the Jesus communities to ensure practices of brutally honest self-evaluative iconoclasis. Yet, again, there is simply no common mind
on how "experienced" Christians should deal with, and make judgments
on, *any* moral matter—from the generation and distribution of capital, to
whether war is ever justified and if so what kind of conflict is theo-ethically
legitimate, to how immigrants should be treated, to how to live within a
global environment requiring maintenance for future generations, to what
role women should play in public society and ecclesial communities, to how
to reason about and address issues of poverty, and so on. Terry Eagleton
goes as far as declaring that "religion is as powerless as culture to emanci-
pate the dispossessed. For the most part, it has not the slightest interest in
doing so."[19]

   That religious experience cannot be explained away does not get the
act of providing a credible witness very far off the ground. Considerably
more would need to be done for the philosopher to take it further into the
sphere of advocacy. Certainly, defeating intellectually complacent defeaters,
as Moser's deflationary perspective is inclined to do, remains a task worth
pursuing, at least if done with appropriate and honest attention to details
and seemingly intractable difficulties. The danger is that an appeal to "my"
(or our) experience(s) may practically function more as a form of affective
soothing of rational doubts than as a challenge to believers to engage in the
most intensive forms of self-interrogation as they iconoclastically test every
spirit. According to Ludwig Wittgenstein, "Nothing we do can be defended
absolutely and finally."[20] The capacity to appeal to "my (private) experience"
can be a real recipe for rational evasion and therefore of unaccountability to
what Martin Buber calls appropriate "holy insecurity." Working from Buber
here, Lash worries about the "Gnosticism" of "the fascination of religious
experience for those who hope to find, *in* such experience, some relief from
the Cartesian anxiety, some point of fixed certainty and unshakeable re-

19. Eagleton, *Reason, Faith, and Revolution*, 165.
20. Wittgenstein, *Culture and Value*, 16.

assurance in our unstable and most insecure world. . . . All Gnosticism is egocentric, and egocentricity subverts relationship."[21] More needs to be done, then, to dissuade those who reason that the approach, to use H. H. Price's language, "now looks more like a therapeutic one and less like an investigation or exploration."[22]

21. Lash, *Easter in Ordinary*, 183.
22. Price, "Faith and Belief," 23.

A Deflationary Reply

PAUL K. MOSER

The familiar arguments of natural theology, as I have argued in this volume, fail to deliver a God worthy of worship and thus fall short of the prominent biblical God of Abraham, Isaac, Jacob, and Jesus. The previous exchanges have not yielded an argument that challenges this short-coming in the familiar arguments in question. This is an important lesson, especially for inquirers favoring those familiar arguments.

Alister McGrath evidently agrees with my main misgiving about the familiar arguments of natural theology. He writes: "Although Moser and I diverge at some points, he makes some important observations concerning certain approaches to natural philosophy that I completely endorse. The most significant of these concerns the disparity between arguments that lead to belief in 'a creator of the universe' and those that lead to 'a God worthy of worship.' This is an important point and can be helpfully illustrated and developed with reference to the history of natural theology." Here is a good suggestion, and I regret that space limitations preclude additional illustrations from the history of natural theology.

McGrath makes note of William James's "remarkable reflections on the changes in the way in which we perceive nature that arise from adopting a theistic perspective: 'At a single stroke, [theism] changes the dead blank *it* of the world into a living *thou*, with whom the whole man may have dealings.'"[1] This line of reflection might well have positive outcomes for identifying "evidence suited to a God worthy of worship." In any case, McGrath evidently shares

1. James, *Will to Believe*, 127.

my concern that "traditional forms of natural theology are 'largely conceptual and intellectual' and do not offer us the kind of 'existential challenge' that can lead to new relationship with God." He adds: "While Moser's recognition of the importance of '*agapē*-conviction' takes us some distance from traditional notions of natural theology, it helps us realize that there is more for us to discover about natural theology and its relevance to meaningful human existence." McGrath thus uses a broad notion of "natural theology"; I have no objection to doing so as long as we avoid reliance on the dubious familiar arguments I have challenged in this volume.

McGrath comments: "I wonder if Moser's deflationary account of natural theology might benefit from engaging the discipline of the cognitive science of religion and its important reflections on how human beings intuitively find themselves inclined to some form of natural theology. . . . I suspect that this might prove to be a philosophically fertile area of discussion." I have misgivings, however, about the suggestion of some who advocate the cognitive science of religion that humans are naturally "inclined to some form of natural theology." I think it is relevant here that most humans seem not to be theists at all, particularly if we attend to people of agnostic, Buddhist, Confucian, and Taoist persuasions. In any case, I doubt that humans "naturally" believe that God exists or that some kind of "natural theology" is correct. Our empirical evidence regarding theistic belief appears to support such doubt.

Andrew Pinsent expresses some agreement with my line of argument: "I begin by agreeing with the core of Moser's arguments, namely, that the proofs of God's existence leave open many other questions about God, a point that is often obscured by the connotations of the word 'God' for those using the proofs. . . . Such examples offer, at least at first glance, a practical validation of Moser's central thesis: that the existence of some god does not necessarily imply the existence of the God who is worthy of worship."

Pinsent reports "some disagreements with the details of Moser's arguments. [Moser] objects to the conclusion of Thomas Aquinas's cosmological argument, namely, the inference of 'a first efficient cause, to which everyone gives the name God.' But what, precisely, has Aquinas done wrong? Almost any educated person of the thirteenth century, and many people today, would indeed assign the name 'God' to an inferred first cause." Aquinas, I submit, has given inadequate attention to an inferred first cause in relation to a God who is worthy of worship by virtue of perfect goodness. This deficiency is not corrected by the suggestion that most educated people of the thirteenth century, along with many contemporary people, would assume that an inferred first cause is God. Such people, I suggest, suffer from the deficiency I have attributed to Aquinas.

Pinsent adds:

> It is not foolish, I think, to associate the causation of being in some sense to the
> causation of goodness and being good. . . . Even in the case of patently inad-
> equate "gods," the wedge that Moser tries to drive between the existence and
> goodness of "god," howsoever conceived, does not seem particularly credible,
> whatever other questions remain unanswered by natural arguments for the ex-
> istence of God. If one conceives of any god as a source of being, even a patently
> false or tyrannical god, then it follows that the god is at least a qualified source
> of good, implying also that the god is at least a qualified good.

We can grant, if only for the sake of argument, that if a god is a source of
being overall, then that god is "at least a qualified source of good." A qualified source of good, however, is not perfectly good and hence is not worthy
of worship. So, we fall short here of the God of Abraham, Isaac, Jacob, and
Jesus.

Pinsent continues: "It also follows that if one conceives of that god as a
supreme or first source of being, which is the conclusion of arguments in
natural theology for the existence of God, such a god is also supremely good
and worthy of worship, if anything is worthy of worship." This does not
actually follow. A god can be a "supreme or first source of being" but suffer
from moral deficiency of some sort. An agent's being a first, supreme, or
primary cause of the universe does not guarantee that agent's perfect moral
goodness. It is logically consistent to ascribe a moral defect, such as a feature
of selfishness, to such a first cause. As a result, Pinsent's conditional statement
is false. It therefore does not underwrite an agent worthy of worship. So,
Pinsent fails to deliver a God worthy of worship from a first-cause argument
of natural theology.

Pinsent continues: "My second point of disagreement with Moser is his argument that divine revelation also contradicts natural theology. In particular,
he argues that natural theology purports to guarantee the being of God, in
conflict with what Moser describes as God's 'intermittent hiding and seeking toward humans.'" He acknowledges what appear to be some supporting
biblical texts for my approach to divine hiding: for instance, 1 Samuel 3:1;
Deuteronomy 31:17; 32:20; Isaiah 45:15; and Micah 5:3. Even so, he adds:
"The difficulty for this argument, however, is that, to the best of my belief and
knowledge, neither the Jewish nor Christian Scriptures really offer any examples of persons who doubt the existence of God due to God's intermittent
hiddenness." I suspect such examples occur in a number of biblical passages,
such as Psalm 42:3: "People say to me continually, 'Where is your God?'"

(NRSVue). We may plausibly take that as doubt about God's existence on the basis of God's seeming absence for some people. I suspect something similar is at work in some teachings of Jesus and Paul about hiddenness regarding God (Matt. 11:25–30; 2 Cor. 4:4).[2] In any case, many people have endorsed agnosticism or atheism in the light of divine hiddenness.

Finally, Pinsent remarks: "I think we need to avoid reducing natural theology simply to the question of the existence of God. . . . For example, I agree with Moser insofar as I have tended to find what is ordinarily described as natural theology, namely, proofs for God's existence, rather pointless and even boring. By contrast, an extended understanding of natural theology can highlight all kinds of interesting and understudied issues." I have no problem with the previous sentence, particularly if it makes reference to religious experience. I hold that divine self-disclosure is best understood in terms of morally challenging religious experience.[3]

Charles Taliaferro reports that his previous "observations are not intended to counter anything Moser has claimed. I am only seeking to amplify the many dimensions in the Christian understanding of worship and the other ways in which persons are invited to live out their lives in the presence of God (*coram Deo*)." My position is compatible with the latter aim, and I have no objection to it.

Taliaferro finds value in an ontological argument regarding God. He takes exception to "Moser's specific objection that the ontological argument is . . . static and does not leave room for the elusiveness of the evidence for God." He adds: "Actually, it can make room for elusive evidence. If the best evidence for God comes in the form of an I-Thou encounter, that is evidence that God is actual. *Any evidence that God is actual is evidence that God is possible and that the critics of the ontological argument who argue that God is impossible are mistaken.*"

I recommend careful attention to a distinction between two claims: God is possible; and God is actual. Showing that God is possible is showing that the idea of God is logically consistent. Critics of the ontological argument can grant that God is possible but deny that God is actual. An inference from the possibility of God to the actuality of God is dubious even if one favors theism and natural theology. Here is the problem: even if a particular concept of God entails an idea of God as existing, perhaps even necessarily existing, the latter idea need not be satisfied by something in reality. It could be a referentially empty idea, even if it is semantically coherent. Critics of the

2. See Moser, *Divine Guidance*, section 3; Moser, "Experiential Dissonance and Divine Hiddenness."

3. For discussion, see Moser, "Divine Self-Disclosure in Filial Values."

ontological argument can use this lesson to shift the explanatory and logical burden to advocates of the argument. I doubt, then, that an ontological argument can deliver a God worthy of worship, even if it gives us a *concept* of a God who (reportedly) exists. We need evidence beyond the latter concept, and I have raised doubt that the familiar arguments of natural theology can satisfy that need.

Taliaferro concludes with an experiential consideration:

> On our relationship with God and one another: the intimacy and directness of the experience of God in an I-Thou encounter is (in my view) both real and life giving. Not as a counter to Moser, I simply observe here the multiple ways we encounter God and one another. In one of the Episcopal books of prayer, *St. Augustine's Prayer Book*, we pray (for example, I prayed today) for all those who die this day, that God may receive their souls. . . . Now, compare someone who is experiencing God in their life through agape, self-sacrificing love, and someone in a library in graduate school who becomes convinced of an Anselmian ontological argument and offers a prayer of adoration to God. The second person's experience may seem less dramatic and personal, but I suggest that both may be having an authentic, meaningful relationship with the God who created and sustains us and all of creation.

I do not deny the meaningful relationships suggested here. I question, however, any needed or evidentially significant role for being "convinced of an Anselmian ontological argument." I do not see any such role for an argument of natural theology in the cases in question.

John McDowell raises the following questions regarding my position on evidence for God: "Why take these *Christian* texts and the traditions of 'experience' within which they are performed as normative for the case he makes? For what reason should one trust the reliability of their interpretations of interiority, of the self as encountered by God? After all, those who encountered Jesus did not all experience him and his significance in the same way. . . . Additionally, what would be required for these claims to become rationally compelling to someone inhabiting a different, and competing, interpretive tradition?"

I have not claimed that some "Christian texts" are "normative" in themselves. Instead, I hold that some texts earn their evidential value for some people by their unsurpassed explanatory worth relative to the overall experience of those people. Abduction (inference to best available explanation) plays a crucial role here, as it does in justification in general. The same applies to "traditions"; I deny that they have normative significance in themselves. As for experiences, however, they call for explanation, regardless of the "traditions" that acknowledge or value them. My appeal to experience, then, does not exclude explaining the experiences acknowledged in various traditions. In addition, I hold that experience-based abduction applies across various interpretive traditions. The experiences I have invoked to be explained are not minimized or even challenged by the occurrence of other experiences or by the reality of interpretive traditions that are not Christian. A challenge will arise only from an opposing explanation (based on experience) that is at least as good as the theistic explanation I have proposed.

McDowell adds: "Elsewhere Moser . . . argues that 'one can have an experience of something that is not a sensory object.' But what is it that makes this an 'experience'?" My answer: a qualitative awareness state or event. Given this answer, a person can experience a range of things that are not sensory objects: logical relations, mathematical relations, moral values and duties, self-consciousness, intentions, God and other personal agents, and so on. It would be implausible, then, to limit experience to sensory objects.

McDowell takes exception to my position that a misplaced focus on non-personal evidence in arguments can hinder our awareness of evidence in interpersonal self-manifestation. He objects: "This simply does not work with persons, since their effects, their traces, say much about them and their acts, and the Christian traditions have long held that the incomprehensible God can be known only from God's effects, from the (personal) stories of holy living as well as the createdness of all things." I mentioned a "misplaced focus" that "can hinder our awareness" of direct evidence of God. This does not contradict knowing God from "God's effects," but I do deny that God can be known *merely* by God's effects. I hold that genuine knowledge of God depends on knowledge of God's unique moral character, and the latter knowledge is not merely knowledge of God's effects. For any alleged effect of God, we have to ask: Is this truly an effect of *God*? If we lack direct knowledge of God, we will be limited (at most) to effects of God, but these effects need an identifiable connection to *God*, and not just to more effects.

McDowell questions the idea of "worthiness" in my characterization of God as "worthy of worship." He asks: "Is a God who reveals God's Self to only *some*, for some reason, worthy of worship? . . . Is a God who spends time revealing God's Self *to be worshiped* actually worthy of worship when there is inequity, unjust suffering, trauma, and catastrophe in that God's world? Thorny questions of suffering and injustice cannot be cavalierly skated over as they so often are among bourgeois academic philosophers of religion." My answer to the previous two questions: Yes, and many biblical narratives confirm this answer. I cannot digress here to the details of a biblical theodicy, but I have provided some of them elsewhere.[4] The book of Job, for instance, makes a case for God's being worthy of worship and trust despite the world's severe suffering and evil and despite Job's inability to identify all of God's purposes in allowing severe suffering and evil. If God seeks people who will trust God in the face of such suffering and evil and promises them due reparation, we should consider how God provides a righteous self-justification of God while being worthy of worship. I contend that a biblical theodicy can serve this purpose. In any case, we should not dismiss God's being worthy of worship without careful attention to a biblical theodicy.

Overall, then, we have not found a compelling case for the familiar arguments of natural theology. They fall short of bringing us to a God worthy of worship, the God of Abraham, Isaac, Jacob, and Jesus. We need, then, a different line of support for commitment to such a God. I suggest that we look to divine self-disclosure in human experience, where God's moral character is at work for the redemption of the world, including us. I cannot think of a more important line of inquiry for humans, regardless of their philosophical or religious persuasions.

4. See Moser, "Biblical Theodicy of Righteous Fulfillment"; Moser, *Divine Guidance*, section 3.

5

A Barthian View

JOHN C. McDOWELL

Preface

Demands for rational intelligibility and persuasiveness do not tend to bother diviners, astrologers, voodoo priests, and the like, or at least not terribly much. There is, in contrast, something quite different about the logic of Christian claims, and this has substantially produced theological reflections since the early days of the primitive Jesus communities. Christians have long retained internal motivations for finding persuasive ways of communicating with others, and these motivations have resulted in a refusal to reduce the faith to a private language. Christianity has not, consequently, been formed in some gnostic cult in which esoteric "truths" are available and relevant to only its members. There is instead a real pressure on Christian discourse that pushes it toward making claims that have a global relevance. For instance, Christians, in some way or another, confess not merely a hope that they have as individuals (1 Pet. 3:15) but also a hope that speaks of the *telos* (end or purpose) of all things as creatures of God. There is, of course, the evangelistic mandate (Matt. 28:19–20). Yet, without some criteria for testing the truthfulness of its claims, efforts to be persuasive when communicating the gospel are reduced to various methods of coercion (self-indulgent emotionalism, political enforcement, and so on). This entails that there is some sense of accountability, even if specifying what form that takes may not be self-evident or agreed upon.

There is something else, though. In a paper titled "Theological Integrity," Rowan Williams asks whether Christian theology can trust that "it is really talking about what it *says* it is talking about."[1] Speech, even theological talk, can conceal agendas shaped by interests different from what is claimed (in which case, it is not *really* talking about what it says it is talking about). This process results in stepping "back from the risks of *conversation*." What Williams has in mind here is a discourse that presents itself as *finished*, complete in and of itself, and that immunizes itself against "the possibility of correction."[2] Rational accountability, then, requires practices of deep attention that take shape in self-testing, so that Christian claims to faith's veracity may avoid being a form of false consciousness, pious delusion, or a mechanism for

1. Williams, *On Christian Theology*, 3.
2. Williams, *On Christian Theology*, 4.

exercising power over others. This self-examination is fundamental to the operations of truthful Christian proclamation since believers are enjoined to "test the spirits" (1 John 4:1). Christians are responsible for testing their God-talk, their worship, their theologically shaped judgments about the good life. This means ensuring, as far as possible, that *God* is the one they are worshiping, even if there are no final or absolute guarantees available that this is so. Just such an iconoclastic temper shapes, in a range of ways, the practice of theologizing. In this regard, theology functions as a form of therapy, weaning us off our idols, "stripping away . . . the veils of self-assurance by which we protect our faces from exposure to the mystery of God."[3] In Karl Barth's terms, it is "criticism and correction of the church's proclamation."[4] In fact, expressions of faith that are fearful of, and resistant to, being exposed to criticism have already slipped into an improper fear. Christians are less fearful of the complex mystery that God is (a mystery incarnated as a rejected and crucified human life), than, more appropriately, fearful of being deluded, being idolatrous. Lurking in this unfitting fear is a discomfort with asking about the nature of Christian language and how it is learned. Consequently, something has gone awry somewhere when theologians develop a reputation for engaging more in a "flight from reality than with strenuous engagement in its obdurate complexity."[5] Williams argues that this flight is a "*political* matter. To make what is said invulnerable by displacing its real subject matter is a strategy for the retention of power."[6] Crucially, "God" would be put to our use, being framed by our own interests and needs.[7]

Depending on the way it is defined, of course, questions around "so-called 'natural theology'" are interesting in this regard (*CD* IV/3.1, 117). "Natural theology" is a term used to depict certain family resemblances and covers

3. Citation from Lash, *Theology on the Way to Emmaus*, 9. Lash explains that in this process, apologetics and theology have not only different *moods* (assertive and interrogative, respectively) but can be seen, even, to have fundamentally different characters (possessive and exposed, respectively) (*Matter of Hope*, 5).

4. K. Barth, *Church Dogmatics* I/1, 280. Hereafter, *Church Dogmatics* will be abbreviated to *CD*.

5. Lash, *Theology on the Way to Emmaus*, 95.

6. Williams, *On Christian Theology*, 4.

7. Years ago, I encountered an "academic" who frequently pronounced that all intellectual opinions matter, and that efforts to deliberate between them are a violent act of a colonizer imposing his or her own voice on those of others. Intriguingly, this amounted to a self-protective device that prevented his own papers from being questioned (or held intellectually accountable), a status he himself in practice denied to those whom he criticized, largely through what is a form of contemptuous rhetoric: name-calling. So, in effect, "All opinions matter, as long as mine matter most, and anyone who disagrees is an idiot!" How can this academic be ascertained to even be engaged in attempting to speak truthfully about any matters concerned with truth at all? How is self-expression here anything but a private language, jealously guarded?

rational deliberation among distinctly complex and multifarious conceptual perspectives and tactical practices. Those resemblances may be describable in terms of efforts in engaging in public conversation that holds theological claims accountable or publicly scrutinizable. For instance, it would be intellectually unjust if non- or anti-theists simply assumed, without any further rational reflection, the veracity of their oppositional claims, thereby ending the possibility of theological conversation when there may be reasons for taking theistic beliefs with some degree of rational seriousness.

The concern that Barth, and what tends to be sheltered under the not entirely helpful and neat category "Barthianism," has is that "so-called natural reason" and its theologizing learns its discursive language in deeply theologically problematic ways.[8] He is notoriously averse to "natural theology"—or better, to a certain version of natural theology.[9] However, in the process, does Barth not deny the very grounds for speaking truthfully and intelligibly about theology, and being seen publicly as attempting to do so?

An Unnatural Theology

In 1937–38 Barth delivered the Gifford Lectures. The Gifford Lectureship Committee's appointment of him to deliver the series was distinctly odd, given his earlier comments on natural theology and his ill-tempered response to Emil Brunner in 1934. After all, in the first part-volume of *Church Dogmatics*, Barth had resolutely announced that the *analogia entis* (that metaphysics of being about which he was disturbed in "natural theology") was "the invention of antichrist" (*CD* I/1, xiii). Though the mood of the resulting lectures delivered at the University of Aberdeen was considerably more measured and less polemical, Barth nevertheless vigorously opened them in a way that remained true to form: "I certainly see—with astonishment—that such a science as Lord Gifford had in mind does exist, but I do not see how it is possible for it to exist. I am convinced that so far as it has existed and still exists, it owes its existence to a radical error. . . . I am not in a position to do justice to the task set me by Lord Gifford's will 'in *direct* affirmation and fulfilment of the testator.'"[10]

---

8. Citation from Torrance, *Ground and Grammar of Theology*, 87.

9. Often the term "Barthianism" gets used loosely as an umbrella term to cover a range of theological works that evidence the imprint of Barth's influence. Explaining why this label is not particularly helpful as a properly descriptive category would require too much of a detailed analysis. It is more useful to encourage readers to engage directly with Barth's extensive writings: reading him is a considerably richer activity than working through a good many of his commentators or those who have developed their theologies to some degree through his influence.

10. K. Barth, *Knowledge of God*, 5.

This example illustrates the magnitude of the task of attempting to understand where his account may be helpful for articulating how claims to Christian knowing work. Yet it hardly needs to be said that a good deal hangs on how the term "natural theology" is defined, and how that is aligned with what it is that Barth is criticizing. In one reading of the matter, if "natural theology" has to do with the conditions for rational or truthful engagement with those who do not share one's beliefs in the createdness and purposiveness of things, and if Barth rejects it, then Barth seemingly is advocating a theological approach that secludes theology within its own private language game and is thereby securing theology within its self-contained world.[11] Even if Barth's theological work exhibits an internal coherence of its own, it would fail to cohere with a range of phenomena in the world that are discussed outside that (now viciously impregnable) circle. This reading would be a little like observing how consistent J. R. R. Tolkien's description of Middle Earth is while recognizing that it is not a description of reality or the world we observe around us. If this is what Barth is doing, then the theological ramifications would be pronounced. What kind of theology claims to follow the God of the crucified Christ when it exerts a power to speak undisturbed by critical questioning? What kind of theology attempts to witness to the creator of all things, when all things cannot be spoken of meaningfully as "creatures"? After all, "what we need is a metaphysics that thinks of matter itself as invariably and necessarily communicative."[12] How can theology be an ambassador for the gospel of reconciliation when it has to shout at, or resort to simple self-assertion over against, those to whom it addresses its proclamation? Clark Pinnock, for instance, once argued that for Barth, "The theologian and the atheist are engaged in a shouting match: one says, 'Religion is man's invention!,' the other 'No, it's not!' Barth offers us no help in resolving the question of who is right."[13]

Theology's Following of Its Subject Matter

Barth explains that he is unable to follow the trajectory of natural theology precisely because he, "as a Reformed theologian," is subjected to a fundamentally different "ordinance." Admittedly, this would not appear to be a good start for any "natural theologian" who seeks resources in Barth for speaking well about things (everything). Nonetheless, it is important to recognize what is going on in this. Crucially, Barth announces that Reformed

11. See Alston, *Perceiving God*, 289.
12. Williams, *Edge of Words*, xi.
13. Pinnock, "Karl Barth and Christian Apologetics," 70.

theology's positive task "lives independently [of natural theology] by its positive content."[14] Here Barth highlights two things.

First, the business of theologians is to follow the logic of God's presenting God's Self. In Hans Frei's language, this is a form of "Christian self-description" that does not correlate with universal "human, cultural quests for ultimate meaning."[15] It is vital to notice from the outset, then, that Barth simply does not begin with faith or expound it as the subject matter of theology. To do so would be what is often referred to as "fideism" or "subjectivism." "Theology becomes, if it is to be 'scientific' and rational, a faithful and obedient *Nachdenken* (literally, 'after thinking'). In other words, it has to be a thankful, realistic, and a posteriori reflection upon and explication of the divine object of faith's speaking, and that, of course for Barth, is in and through Christ."[16] This move Barth famously articulates through the Anselmian slogans, *fides quaerens intellectum* (faith seeking understanding) and *credo ut intelligam* (I believe in order to understand), later arguing, with respect to the former, that this is "what distinguishes faith from blind assent."[17] Such a process, for Barth, could never be irrational since it is rather the proper location of a well-functioning reason.[18]

Second, "natural theology" is a theological mistake, but only because of the theological commitments that it has. This means that Barth's critique of natural theology is compelled by, or is the flip side of, what he positively affirms as theologically appropriate. As Christopher Morse argues, theology involves engagement in the "task of faithful disbelief."[19] Barth's critique nowhere

---

14. K. Barth, *Knowledge of God*, 9. There is a burgeoning discussion among Barth scholars as to the impact of Immanuel Kant's epistemology on Barth. Often inattentive critics simply equate Barth's rejection of the possibility of natural theology with Kant's account of the limitations of pure reason. Even some slightly more astute commentators claim that Barth follows Kant epistemologically but that he revises Kant's reduction of "religion" to ethics by objectifying revelation, so as to make revelation the epistemic "foundation" (in other words, coming closer to positioning revelation in Kant's first critique, the *Critique of Pure Reason*, so that God is knowable according to God's making God's Self phenomenally observable). However, as D. Stephen Long observes, "If Barth's revision is that God makes himself phenomenal, his theology is at best a form of Gnosticism" (*Saving Karl Barth*, 119). Barth theologically rejects an a priori philosophical agnosticism for theology's use (see CD I/2, 29–30, 244–45; II/1, 183). Occasionally, one reads commentators who suggest that Barth revised Kant, but the claim comes in such a way that it is difficult to see what, in fact, is actually meaningful about even continuing to speak about Barth as in any way "Kantian." This is a complex area, so I will not comment on it other than to continue by offering an intentionally un-Kantian reading of Barth.
15. Frei, "Eberhard Busch's Biography of Karl Barth," 103.
16. K. Barth, *Göttingen Dogmatics*, 3, 8, 11.
17. K. Barth, *Evangelical Theology*, 44.
18. McDowell, "Unnaturalness of Natural Theology," 251–52.
19. Morse, *Not Every Spirit*, 14.

features, then, as a theme in its own right. Technically, he does not even *reject* natural theology. Rather, he denies its very theological *legitimacy*.

The first commandment of the Decalogue is axiomatic. By this is meant that it sets theology's task. It functions as "the presupposition of all theology," which is grounded in a knowledge of God "on the basis of revelation."[20] Of course, this kind of claim needs to be considered as to whether it insulates theology as *God*-talk from examination and critique, perhaps replacing the foundations of rational first principles with that of a rationally arbitrary belief in God as a basic belief. Even so, such an examination would be hard-pressed in at least two ways. In the first place, it itself would have to begin from somewhere, and the issue is whether that place is any more rationally demonstrable than the conditions for belief in God as axiomatic. In the second place, God is not the name of a thing that can be spoken of, examined, affirmed, or rejected in the way that those interrogative practices relate to things in the world. As Williams argues, "The challenge in speaking about God is the challenge of referring appropriately to what is not an object among others or a definable substance that can be 'isolated' and examined."[21] True, the belief in God can be tested in its own way, and later we will have to explicate the logic of Barth's approach that produces criteria for the critical interrogation of the church's proclamation.

Barth's is a theological claim about how God-talk functions as a *response* to God's self-articulation that faithfully follows its self-explicated logic. This self-communication is what Barth understands by "revelation." It is crucial, here, to recognize that the concept has a particular role. Commonly the notion has been used methodologically as a way of referring to God's communication and how it becomes known, thus becoming largely an epistemic matter. In this regard, Scripture (special revelation) and the nonhuman creation (general revelation) can be referred to as "revelation." John Webster, however, complains that this problematic use of the term emerges in modernity with "the collapse of the cultural metaphysic in which classical Christianity had developed."[22] Webster helps draw attention to the shifts in the way theological language is used. Christian thinking comes to inhabit a conditioning framework that alters the content of the very concepts of theology itself. Theism's dogmatically underdeveloped "language about revelation became a way of talking, not about the life-giving and loving presence of the God and Father of . . . Jesus Christ in the Spirit's power among the worshiping and witnessing assembly, but instead of an arcane process whereby persons acquire knowledge through

20. K. Barth, "First Commandment," 64; *CD* I/2, 306.
21. Williams, *Edge of Words*, 17.
22. Webster, *Holy Scripture*, 11.

opaque, non-natural operations."[23] Whether Webster is correct in regarding this as a mistake or not, at least one can encourage readers to recognize that "revelation" is reserved largely as a synonym for "God" in Barth's work. It is a term that names the means of our knowing (an epistemic or noetic category) less than talking about *God* as a self-presencing or communicative agent.[24] Accordingly, Barth spends considerable time explicating the trinitarian logic of the revelatory event in terms of the Revealer, revelation, and revealedness, with each being attributed to a particular mode of God's triune being-in-becoming.

Given the dogmatic job that the concept of revelation holds in his thinking, it cannot properly make sense to speak of any creature of God as being "revelation." So, when Barth announces that Scripture or the nonhuman creation, or in fact any other creaturely being or activity, is not revelation, the theo-linguistic context must be understood. They are not revelation per se. How can they be when the term means God's being-in-act? We will have cause to return to this matter later when we consider the *means* of revelation (the creaturely ways in and through which God speaks).

One frequent worry is that this *act* or *event* of revelation can come only as an insertion, an interruption from outside, an immediateness that is sometimes referred to as "occasionalism." This is often linked to concerns about Barth's account of divine freedom, that a "free" God is an arbitrary one: free in any given moment or on any specific occasion to determine how and where to reveal God's Self. Barth considerably clarifies matters in *CD* II/2, though, in his development of a dogmatics of election. Here he reflects that God elects God's own *Self* to be God for the creature. There is no God hiding behind God's revelation of God, God's making God's Self present to the creature. Revelation is nothing less than God in God's eternally free commitment to that which God creates. In this context, talk of God's freedom is talk of divine *self-sufficiency* or *unconditionedness*, which consequently acts *graciously*. God does not choose from a neutral stance, as if freedom is reducible to choosing between options. Rather, God elects or determines to be *for another* in the manner that expresses *ad extra* who God eternally is in God's own life. "He does not will to be God without us; . . . He creates us rather to share with us and therefore with our being and life and act"

23. Webster, *Holy Scripture*, 12.

24. There have been efforts to claim that Barth's concerns are largely epistemological when he speaks of revelation and natural theology (e.g., Johnson, *Karl Barth and the* Analogia Entis, 168). Frequently, this takes the unconvincing form of suggesting a deep connection between Barth and Kant, and a lifelong influence of the Prussian philosopher on the thought of the Swiss theologian.

(*CD* IV/1, 7). Barth simply rejects as theologically inappropriate the notion of a pure will that often lurks in theologies of divine freedom. Instead, God is as God wills, and God wills what God is: being and act cannot be separated. God *is* in God's act, and God is in God's *act*. God's freedom, then, is bound to the tautologous claim regarding divine self-sufficiency that "God is God."

Among other things, this means that *all* things are creatures, products of God's self-election to be God for the creature. All things, then, have their being as gifts of God's grace. They are formed and conditioned by this theological context. Consequently, creatures cannot be independent from God in the sense of being autonomous and utterly self-defining. They do have their own integrity, their freedom to be who they are, but that integrity to be free is not an expression of some neutral state. Rather, they necessarily have their shape and form as creatures of the God who freely loves. In this way, the created order has a *covenantal shape*. Human beings are the result of God's creative activity to be graciously committed to the creature, and they have their purposefulness in living faithfully in gratitude to the source and goal of their very existence.

What is more, this election, this covenanting act of God, takes a specific form: the self-election of God in Jesus Christ. There are all kinds of technical debates among Barth scholars as to what this entails. For now, though, it is sufficient to iterate that the theme in Barth's theology has a number of consequences. For instance, it theologically grounds the claim that Jesus Christ is *the* revelation of God. Thomas F. Torrance attributes this to the doctrine of the Son's being *homoousios* (of one substance) with the Father in the Creed of Nicaea of 325 and the Nicene Creed of 381.[25] In other words, the One who is one with the Father (and the Spirit) becomes incarnate as Jesus Christ: consequently, Jesus Christ is nothing less than the very presence of God enfleshed. Moreover, election means not only that Jesus Christ is *God* enfleshed but also that Jesus Christ is *the* creature, the human being through whom all of creation has its reality, form, and purpose. He is the shape of the Reality in whom all things become real (see John 1; Col. 1). By this is not meant some kind of vague "cosmic Christology," that Jesus is relevant somehow to consideration of the cosmos. It is more concrete than that. He is the created order's very Alpha and Omega. Furthermore, Jesus Christ is not the marker of *the* creature in a way that replaces creatures, substituting for them as a competitor or as the one among the many. Rather, Christology involves an inclusivity in that all creatures are formed by, and have their lives

25. See Torrance, "Introduction."

within, God's way in Jesus Christ. Thus Christ is both the divine gift and the human response in whom all creatures are bound up. In this way, Barth's is an intensively *Christocentric*, or Christ-shaped, theology.

"What this means for human beings, among other things, is that they cannot be other than what they are under the conditions of the purposefulness of divine creativity (for Barth, of course, that purposefulness is what the doctrine of election grounds). To be human is not to be engaged in an enterprise of self-construction, or in the natural realization of the gusts of *Geist*. Rather, it is to find oneself having been grounded in, and formed by, the gift of God's election of Jesus Christ as '*the* elect One.'"[26] In other words, election results in knowing oneself to be determined by *God's* electing choice. I hesitate to use the term "ek-centric" of Barth's account of human being as if he decenters what the human is. Instead, being human in and through Christ, the only real human being, entails that humans have their being not ek-centrically but rather in being who one is, in and through one's Christ-formedness (through faithful engagement with the One in whom God and human are presenced, or presented, to each other).[27] The creature, then, can have no independence from, or autonomy over against, Jesus Christ (see *CD* II/1, 166). Autonomy, in fact, when it is not a way of speaking of the ordering of freedom to be who one is in Christ, is a sinful act. It is the disobedience that unwittingly, and bizarrely, is self-destructive in that it attempts to contradict and resist God's covenantal purposes.[28]

The Possibility That Is God's Readiness for the Creature

God is irreducibly who God is in God's self-revelation in Jesus Christ. Christ is the incarnated presence of God and the true creature, or the electing God and elected human being. He is the objective actuality of God's own Self. Barth nonetheless provides an account of what he calls the *possibility* of revelation (*CD* I/2, §13 subsection 2) and the *readiness* of God for God's loving the creature in freedom (*CD* II/1, §26 subsection 1). The language, though, is theological, a way of speaking of God within the *ordo essendi* (order of being). By asking about "the possibility on the basis of which God is known" (*CD* II/1, 63), which can emerge only from the *actuality* of knowledge of God, the subsection is a way of impressing further that God's revelation is *free*.

26. McDowell, "Being and Becoming in Gratuity," 242, citing K. Barth, *Knowledge of God*, 75, my emphasis.
27. Barth's is, according to Eberhard Busch, an account of revelation that opens "the new grounding of human subjectivity" (Busch, *Great Passion*, 78).
28. See McDowell, "Much Ado about Nothing."

By this freedom is meant a freedom that is positively nonarbitrary, a being free *for* others that, as its flip side, rejects any notion that God's being for the creature can be conditioned by anything outside of God's Self. Revelation is an objective actuality, "given in a quite definite way," precisely because it is a freely chosen eternal possibility for God (*CD* II/1, 64). "This decision [to be known *ad extra*] was made from eternity and in eternity by the fact that God is who He is" (*CD* II/1, 67). God loves the creature because God is God's own readiness for humanity. Consequently, nothing can set the terms for God's self-revelation, nothing can call it into being, nothing can necessitate it or shape and determine it. (In the event of God's self-election, how logically could there even be *anything* that could be considered as setting the terms for God's act anyway?) "Therefore even the knowability of God among us and for us, which lies at the foundation of the fulfilment of our real knowledge of God, is first and properly God's own possibility" (*CD* II/1, 67). In this theological ontology of gift, there is a significant problem with any proposal regarding any intrinsic capacity or feature possessed by the creature (mind, substance, relationality, intuitiveness, capacity for words or revelation, and so on) that can be said to have a capacity for knowing or relating to God. One can only begin, theologically, with an account not of humanity's readiness for God but of the absolutely prior creating, reconciling, and redeeming God's readiness for the creature that the creature's disposition is *consequent* upon, *responsive* to, and a *following after*. Nonetheless, within this theo-logic, there is a necessary way of speaking precisely of humanity's readiness for God, a readiness that comes as gift. "This cannot be an independent readiness" (*CD* II/1, 129). Barth approvingly does even talk of a capacity or point of contact (*Anknüpfungspunkt*) between God and the human: only thereby comes a christological reference. In other words, it relates to God's elective prevenience to be for the creature eternally in Jesus Christ.

The Means of Revelation

God's self-revelation is the presence of the self-electing God in the Holy Spirit to be the God of the elect human. Jesus Christ thus grounds an important claim about the means or manner of the event of revelation. God's self-revelation does not simply *appear*. It does not insert itself into the created order as a singular and unrepeatable *moment*. It is, rather, an event that is *mediated*, irreducibly so, in fact. This is not, as mentioned above, because the creaturely medium through which God reveals God's Self determines or necessitates God's revealing. Rather, it is because the creature is made to be *fitting*. It is fitted out, that is, to be the means of revelation. In other words, the theological description continually has to be chastened by recalling the prevenience or priority of God's being-in-act.

Church Dogmatics (I/1, §4) offers an account of the means of revelation, the means through which God communicates God's presence to the creature. It does so in an image of concentric circles that articulates the threefoldness of the Word of God. The circles of Scripture and, enclosing it, the church's proclamation—both have at their core the humanity of the Word incarnate: they witness back to Christ, just as God in Christ continues to communicate God's Self outwardly through the Scriptures, and the Scriptures likewise in the church's proclamation. These words testify appropriately to the Word, and their faithfulness is measured by that Word. In this regard, Barth speaks of Scripture in a way that causes misunderstanding among those who locate "revelation" talk within an epistemic context—the Scriptures *become* revelation. At the earliest stage of Barth's dogmatic writing, his actualistic rhetoric triggers the question of what it is about the Scriptures that enables them to become revelation through the free activity of the self-revealing God. Barth would vigorously gesture to the content of the Scriptures: they witness to God's activity in Jesus Christ, as anticipated by the prophets and recalled by the apostles.[29] In fact, he not only speaks of the *indispensable* role of the Scriptures in the Christian life but also defines theology in terms of testing the proclamation of the church against "the revelation which is attested in Holy Scripture" (*CD* I/1, 283). To speak of the Scriptures becoming revelation is, in Barth's account in *CD* I/1, to point to the way the self-revealing God of Jesus Christ, through the revealingness of the Spirit, makes that which the Scriptures witness to contemporaneous with faithful readers. Because of their role in the self-revealing purposes of God, through an act of rhetorical metonymy, Barth can even speak of the Scriptures *as* revelation.[30]

It is in this context that Barth's later talk of extra-ecclesial and nonhuman means of revelation (*CD* IV/3.1) should be read, not as suggesting that he has changed his mind, but rather as a more formal expansion of the trajectory of his earlier thinking and practice.[31] After all, in *CD* I/1 he has enjoined listening to God every place where God may be heard and has catchily mentioned a vast array of means. These are as disparate as "Russian communism, a flute concerto, a blossoming shrub or a dead dog, . . . a pagan or an atheist" (*CD* I/1, 55). Moreover, the series of lectures published as *Protestant Theology in the Nineteenth Century* constructively engages with significant German

---

29. A particularly careless handling of this would be to imagine that Barth posits or requires a theological commitment to the necessity of error within the scriptural materials.

30. Cf. Watson, "The Bible"; Oakes, "Revelation and Scripture," 251.

31. See, e.g., Brunner, "New Barth."

philosophers. In fact, as Hans Urs von Balthasar helpfully recognizes, "There is hardly an important thinker to whom Barth has not devoted a detailed *excursus* in his *Dogmatics*."[32] Finally, among many other things, Barth has spoken exuberantly of Mozart's music as articulating a joyousness over creation (*CD* III/3, 297–99).[33] Barth's use of Mozart, then, was not *merely* aesthetic, as if it could be trivialized simply as a matter of mere taste or personal quirk.[34] It is "a type of music for which 'beautiful' is not a fitting epithet: music which for the true Christian is not mere entertainment, enjoyment or edification but food and drink; music full of comfort and counsel for his needs" (*CD* III/3, 297–98). Theodore Gill records an incident when leaving Barth's study. When Gill noticed the side-by-side portraits of Calvin and Mozart, Barth announced something over which Gill puzzles: "My special revelation [looking at Calvin]. And my general revelation [smiling at Mozart]."[35] In fact, as late as 1958, while continuing to deny natural theology, Barth even went as far as declaring that "the golden sounds and melodies of Mozart's music have been from early times spoken to me not as gospel but as parables of the realm of God's free grace as revealed in the gospel."[36]

In the light of this theologically informed practice of conversation and engagement (including the interrogative mood of self-examination), it is unsurprising that Barth exhorts the theologian to "eavesdrop in the world at large" (*CD* IV/4, 116) so as to pay *appropriate attention* to it. By this is meant listening "with the required openness to the world."[37] The openness involves, among other things, listening to the world's own voice without overlaying it with one's own. In fact, when God's voice is heard through these extra-ecclesial words (when their truthfulness is perceived), they can reorient one's knowledge of God and thereby aid one to read the Scriptures better. Not insignificantly, then, Barth observes that the theologian, just as much as the historian, or nonacademic in any and every area of life, is an entirely historically and materially *situated* knower. Accordingly, he recognizes the role of presuppositions in the act of interpretation and lays them open to being tested and reconfigured whenever necessary, urging the readers to become aware of what they are doing in the process so that their apprehensions are made serviceable, meaning that they "acquire . . . fitness through . . . encounter with

---

32. Von Balthasar, *Theology of Karl Barth*, 36–37.

33. Cf. McDowell, "Theology as Conversational Event," 495–96.

34. It is true that Barth mused that the angels sang Bach carefully in public but Mozart at home for fun (K. Barth, *Wolfgang Amadeus Mozart*, 23).

35. Gill, "Barth and Mozart," 405.

36. K. Barth, *How I Changed My Mind*, 71–72. Cf. K. Barth, *Wolfgang Amadeus Mozart*, 33–34.

37. K. Barth, *Evangelical Theology*, 150. Cf. von Balthasar, *Theology of Karl Barth*, 157.

and pursuit of the scriptural word" (*CD* I/2, 730). The crucial issue is not whether one comes to the reading of Scripture with presuppositions, with a philosophy of some sort or other. That is beyond dispute. "Where the question of legitimacy arises is in regard to the How of this use" (*CD* I/2, 730).

In this vein, the likes of William Placher and David Ford advocate approaches that they term as formally or procedurally "pluralistic": "Christians ought to speak with their own voice and not worry about finding philosophical 'foundations' for their claims," but they nonetheless learn from others such as philosophers on appropriate occasions when they "wrestle [well] with analogous problems."[38] Hans Frei, for his part, articulates a sense of Barth's "ad hoc apologetics." By this he means that Barth "was about the business of [critical] conceptual redescription" and self-examination, but in such a way that, in an ad hoc fashion, he "makes use of third-order free, unsystematic, and constant reference to conceptual patterns of a non-Christian, nontheological kind."[39]

Again, however, a couple of dogmatic cautions need to be put in place. First, the truthfulness or testimonial analogousness of any phenomenon to God derives from the prior action of God. This means that Barth can speak of God's making analogies. He explains what he means: it is "an analogy to be created by God's grace, the analogy of grace and faith to which we say Yes as to the inaccessible which is made accessible to us in incomprehensible reality" (*CD* II/1, 85). The flip side, and second dogmatic caution, is that no phenomenon, *in and of itself* (whether by any feature of its "nature" or existence), is perceived to be analogous to God. "So-called 'natural theology,'" then, "is quite impossible within the Church, and indeed . . . cannot even be discussed in principle" (*CD* IV/3.1, 117; II/1, 85).

The fullest articulation of this theology of attention to "the polyphony of creation as the external basis of the covenant" can be found in *CD* IV/3.1, §69 subsection 2 (*CD* IV/3.1, 159), respectively. As the incarnate fullness of God and creature, the irreducibly particular Jesus Christ "is the one and only light of life," which "means that he is the light of life in all its fullness, in perfect adequacy; and negatively, it means that there is no other light of life outside or alongside his, outside or alongside the light which he is" (*CD* IV/3.1, 86). Here Barth does not deny that there are other lights. Far from it. In fact, he insists that the church "not only may but must accept the fact that there are such words and that it must hear them too, notwithstanding its life by this one

38. Placher, *Unapologetic Theology*, 13; cf. Ford, *Christian Wisdom*, 345.
39. Frei, *Types of Christian Theology*, 43; cf. Thiemann, *Constructing a Public Theology*, 82: "Barth did not eschew philosophy; he simply used it eclectically in service of the Christian faith."

Word and its commission to preach it" (*CD* IV/3.1, 114–15). Why is this? In the creative and reconciling work of God in Christ, "all men and all creation derive from His cross, from the reconciliation accomplished in Him, and are ordained to be the theatre of His glory and therefore the recipients and bearers of His Word" (*CD* IV/3.1, 117). Indeed, reconciliation does not *replace* creation but is its renewing within the eternal purposes of God. Accordingly, Barth insists on the integrity of the creaturely witness, an integrity granted to them by the gracious work of God (*CD* IV/3.1, 164).

Barth grounds these distinctive words, or "parables of the kingdom" (*CD* IV/3.1, 114), in light of the Word that is Christ. This means that they have a "relative validity," a derivative status, functioning as testimonies to the light of that Word (*CD* IV/3.1, 147). Accordingly, these "words . . . [cannot] say anything different from this one Word" (*CD* IV/3.1, 115). A formal criterion for distinguishing these words from other, darkening, words is their "agreement with the witness of Scripture" (*CD* IV/3.1, 126; cf. 111). Scripture, then, functions as the measure over "whether or not, and with what fidelity, they are witnesses of this one Word" (*CD* IV/3.1, 98). Barth continues to oppose all talk of creatures' intrinsic *capacity* to operate as the means of revelation. The Word's self-illumination in and through these little "lights of . . . creation" remains "quite beyond any capacity of their own" (*CD* IV/3.1, 152, 111). More specifically, these lights or words only enlighten or speak insofar as the Light or Word can be perceived to be illuminating in and through these secular parables of truth, to some degree (*CD* IV/3.1, 123). All this not only provides the conditions for understanding the status of these extra-ecclesial words as witnesses that "express the one and total truth from a particular angle" but also frames the inability of natural theology to describe their origins and their testimonial function (*CD* IV/3.1, 123).

So, there is a *comprehensiveness* about Barth's work of attempting to propose a coherent theological witness to God's self-articulation, and that requires a comprehensive range of potential critical conversations. In this way, and only slightly tongue in cheek, Stanley Hauerwas proclaims, "Karl Barth is the great natural theologian of the Gifford lectures."[40] Theology, then, is always a provisional activity, never permitted to finalize its claims since the critical conversations it can have cannot come to a close in a world that remains eschatologically unconsummated. Accordingly, theology can never run out of things to talk about.

Crucially, for Barth, this comprehensiveness is grounded christologically. In that regard, Christology provides an inclusivistic sensibility (albeit par-

---

40. Hauerwas, *With the Grain of the Universe*, 20.

ticularistically concrete, since it has to do with the theological significance of Jesus Christ), not an exclusivistic one.[41] The language would certainly trouble Barth (given his reduction of the referent of "sacrament" to Jesus Christ), but there would be a way in which he himself, and many inspired by him on the question of natural theology, could echo Denys Turner's declaration that "the world's being created . . . is itself quasi-sacramental and . . . reason is a sort of human participation in that 'sacramentality' of the world."[42]

What Barth offers is a theological grounding for well-ordered reading postures, a disciplined training in learning how to see the world correctly.[43] In Lash's terms, theology "is not a distinct discipline, but an interpretative framework within which our secular activity is carried out."[44] Ingolf Dalferth puts the matter like this: "Barth's theology is not only an exemplary piece of constructive dogmatics but [also] a sustained hermeneutical enterprise which does not deny the secularity of the world but reinterprets it theologically in the light of the presence of Christ and the world of meaning which it carries with it."[45] The criterion for reading is the knowledge of God in Jesus Christ (how, given his theo-logical commitments, could it be anything other?), just as much as the test for the faithfulness of scriptural reading and ecclesial proc-lamation is christological as well. In this regard, practices of reading can be appropriately held to account by the attentiveness to God's speaking in and through extra-ecclesial elements. Here, in these self-critical tactics, is where Alasdair MacIntyre locates the health of a, and indeed any, tradition.[46] The difference is that "nature," if by that one means the nonhuman creation, is distinctly vague as a witness. What happens when one observes young spiders committing matricide, or the colonizing progress of a virus? John Calvin, after all, even declared that the testimony of the eucharistic elements is vague and potentially misleading, which is why they require the added word of procla-mation to provide their interpretive context. In fact, his reading of Romans 1, early in the *Institutes of the Christian Religion*, suggests that while he wants to protect the claim that God is just (because human beings are, somehow, responsible for their sinfulness) through an account of the *sensus divinitatis*, it is nonetheless eminently clear that he regards this consciousness as more liable to mislead, to distort true religion, and to manifest itself idolatrously.[47]

---

41. Cf. Hunsinger, *How to Read Karl Barth*, 235.
42. Turner, *Faith, Reason and the Existence of God*, 25.
43. Cf. Hauerwas, "Demands of a Truthful Story," 65–66.
44. Lash, *His Presence in the World*, 36; cf. CD I/1, 5.
45. Dalferth, *Theology and Philosophy*, 121.
46. MacIntyre, *Whose Justice?*, 398–99.
47. See Welker, *Creation and Reality*, 23, 27. Barth occasionally suggests that a residual natural theology is indeed in the Reformers. However, he draws on their theologies of grace

In fact, Barth even regards each and every means through which God reveals God's Self to be vague and difficult to read (*CD* II/1, 55–56). In the Gospels, for instance, observers of Jesus react in markedly different ways to him and his claims. This is certainly the way that Barth himself depicts Romans 1. In the first place, he explains that the passage is part of the articulation of the *kerygma* and is therefore an expression of revelation (*CD* I/2, 306). In the second place, the argument of the material is precisely that the so-called natural knowledge led to idolatry.[48] Consequently, "Paul says nothing at all about the heathen maintaining a remnant of the 'natural' knowledge of God in spite of this defection. . . . Now that revelation has come, and its light has fallen on heathendom, heathen religion is shown to be the very opposite of revelation: a false religion of unbelief" (*CD* I/2, 307). In this sense, then, God's revelation provides the context for perceiving the exposure of "religion" as idolatrous (*CD* I/2, 314).

While Barth retains the language of "revelation" for God's self-communication, much of what he describes here can indeed be aligned with a *certain kind* of appeal to general revelation among premodern Reformed theologians. General revelation, as a category used at its best, functions as a way of claiming that, in some sense, all things bear witness to their Creator and have their ground and *telos* in the God of Jesus Christ.[49] Their fittingness to be witnesses, or means by which God reveals God's Self, is the consequence of the elective activity of the eventful God. Here Barth talks about an *analogia fidei* (analogy of faith, or what faith is able to perceive of God's self-revelatory condescension). Of course, what can be offered by such a claim regarding analogy does remain more than a little vague. As Torrance recognizes, "Nature by itself speaks only ambiguously of God,"[50] and Barth's account draws attention to a range of difficulties in "reading" the nonhuman creation.

There are certainly options for reflecting a way that describes a range of learnings that fall under the *ordo cognoscendi* (order of knowing). Barth does

---

in order to *internally* repair that. Their theologies are centered on grace and the givingness of the free God, and he applies the radicality of that to their accounts of the knowledge of God (see K. Barth, "First Commandment," 73; Torrance, *Ground and Grammar of Theology*, 146–47). Even so, Keith Johnson goes too far when claiming that "the doctrine most central to the knowledge of God is not creation but justification" (Johnson, *Karl Barth and the Analogia Entis*, 108). By the time of *CD* II/2 and III/1, there is no contrast between the doctrines of creation and reconciliation, and even Johnson's geometric imagery here itself becomes inappropriately ossifying. What is central, if anything, is Jesus Christ as the electing God and elect human.

48. Cf. K. Barth, *Shorter Commentary on Romans*, 15–16.
49. See Welker, *Creation and Reality*, 23.
50. Torrance, *Space, Time and Incarnation*, 59.

not himself provide that kind of reflection. The closest one comes to seeing how this works is through sketching out the actual conversational practices he engages in and tracing some of the dimensions of his talk of the "secular parables of truth." But his hesitancy to be any more specific is owed in large measure to the continued concern with reading just phenomena. What can look parabolic at one moment can prove to be unfitting, distorted, and even dangerously damaging at another. It is deeply contestable as well in a way that the presence of God in Christ is not disputed for the Christian community. Moreover, the parabolic is intensively contextual, being particular to concrete times and places, and cannot therefore be ossified into a lasting witness. Other thinkers, however, while retaining a substantial critical hesitancy in their own account in this regard, nonetheless reflect on this matter more positively. Rowan Williams, for example, regards it as a necessary task to identify the parabolic in the world as far as possible.[51] Torrance, for his part, develops an account of theological science that supposedly, but not altogether successfully, identifies points of overlap between theology and the natural sciences.[52] What Barth does do well and more specifically, however, is to identify phenomena that more clearly demonstrate distortions of the parabolic. These he calls "the lordless powers," conditioning and disciplining systems within which human living takes its shape and which results in the diminishment of human beings.[53]

Natural Theology as a Theo-grammatical Mistake

Up until now, this chapter has dealt with natural theology largely by suggestion, allusion, and implication. While it has been a lengthy journey, it has been necessary to follow the prolonged and winding pathway. The route comes finally to the point when the rationale for Barth's theological denial of the legitimacy of natural theology can begin to be understood.

Theological grammar is orderly, and that very orderliness pays attention to the ways in which the disordering of theo-grammar occurs. Natural theology

---

51. Williams, *On Christian Theology*, 42.

52. Torrance proposes "that there is a deep interrelation between theology and science" (*Ground and Grammar of Theology*, 75). Yet, Torrance's work in this area tends to be a conversationally reductive one. He largely *uses* the natural sciences for theological *illustrative* effect, adopting certain scientific terms in the articulation of theology. Moreover, there is a worry that Torrance continues to describe revelation in terms that suggest he remains caught in an interventionistic framing, likely learned from theologically trying to repair Kant while largely assuming his epistemic categories, thereby also suggesting too readily a sense of the passivity of the knower in the noetic process. See McDowell, "Torrance on Revelation."

53. K. Barth, *Christian Life*, §78.2.

belongs to an entirely different theo-grammatical order, one that theology actually has to declare to be not only an impoverishment but also utterly distorting. It is like imagining that, during an American football game, cricket bats can be taken to the ball to score a goal or that the striker can pick up the ball and run with it when it is in play. What those depict are not different ways of getting to the same end result but inaccurate ways of imagining how the game of football can be played. Accordingly, argues Eberhard Busch, the "differing approaches" of so-called natural theology and Barth's account of revelation "point to a *different* God."[54]

The notion of a natural theology features surprisingly little in Barth's massive corpus. For one thing, he regards it as being an expression of "a mortal attack on the Christian doctrine of God," and therefore "it cannot even be discussed" by Christian dogmatics (*CD* II/1, 85). But, and this is crucial to recognize, he is considerably more interested in understanding and contesting the conditions for the disturbing subjection of God-talk to the "experiences" of the individual subject.[55] On this issue, the anti-theist Ludwig Feuerbach serves in crucial ways as the climax of the way of Friedrich Schleiermacher and his theological heirs (*CD* I/2, 290). Such a theological reduction to an anthropology of the experiential subject is what Barth came to view as having undergirded the projection of the German self onto "God" in the *Kriegstheologie* of Kaiser Wilhelm's imperialistic aggression (1888–1918) and Barth's theological teachers who supported it. (This concern is intensified with Barth's concern later over the National Socialists' appeal to "blood and soil" [*Blut und Boden*] and the Germanic sense of being a people.) As George Hunsinger argues, "Neither natural theology nor cultural phenomena like nationhood could be allowed to compete with or compromise scripture."[56] From there, a further genealogical hunch projects the problem into theologies that predate that—particularly, and problematically as a reading, the approach of Aquinas. Encounters with the work of the Roman Catholic Eric Przywara convinced Barth that the problem is that of a theological metaphysics that promotes a sense of the univocity between God and creature. After all, according to David Burrell, "Without a clear philosophical means of distinguishing God from the world, the tendency about all discourse of divinity is to deliver a God who is the 'biggest thing around.'"[57] This kind of test is what Barth senses as being failed by the *analogia entis* (analogy

54. Busch, *Great Passion*, 61, 69.
55. Cf. K. Barth, "First Commandment," 78; McCormack, "Karl Barth's Version of an 'Analogy of Being,'" 107.
56. Hunsinger, *Evangelical, Catholic, and Reformed*, 90.
57. Burrell, *Faith and Freedom*, 4–5.

of being). It is this category that, quite often for a particular period of time, does the heavy lifting for Barth's critical delegitimizing of natural theology. According to Barth, "We possess no analogy on the basis of which the nature and being of God as the Lord can be accessible to us" (*CD* II/1, 75). The reasoning here has something of a Humean feel about it, but the grounding is quite different from David Hume's notion of the limitations of rational claims as such. For Barth, reason functions only as the *ratio* of the creature that follows the divine *Ratio*.[58] With a polemical rhetorical flourish, Barth denounces this kind of account of the *analogia entis* "as the invention of Antichrist" (*CD* I/1, xiii). Even so, with the right kinds of hesitations from the likes particularly of Gottlieb Söhngen demonstrating that the *analogia entis* is about *analogy* (analogy is as much about unlikeness as likeness) and not univocity (univocity predicates an evident likeness at the level of being), Barth even admits by *CD* II/1 that his (rather troublingly generalizing) critique of Roman Catholicism in this area may well be mitigated.

Alvin Plantinga and Nicholas Wolterstorff assert that Barth is unclear, nevertheless, as to where the challenge to religious believing has made a mistake.[59] Yet, Barth clearly offers a range of critical claims regarding "religion" and "natural theology," grounded in the *analogia entis* in some way or other, as idolatrous. By this he means that natural theology generates a "god" that is no God, a Being among beings, a "god" not confessed by the Christian traditions that have followed the trajectory of the self-revealing God. Several specific critical claims appear in Barth's work.

The first substantial reason for rejecting the possibility of a natural theology is that it involves an effort to work toward "god" via an autonomous rationality. This stands in marked contrast with the "finding" that occurs in following where God reveals God's Self to be. In this way, it is *abstract*. By this is meant that it abstracts itself from the *concrete* particularity of the self-giving of God. Any sense of natural theology's functioning as an *independent* rational exercise, then, displaces God's prior activity of self-identifying. Natural theology involves the impossibility of "guaranteeing the knowability of God apart from grace" (*CD* II/1, 85). Simply put, there can be no vantage point from which to look into the possibility of revelation from outside its gift-givenness-givingness. As John Cobb declares, "Every natural theology reflects some fundamental perspective on the world. None is the pure result of neutral, objective reason."[60] In contrast, if the term "natural theology" has

58. For a fuller account of this theme, see K. Barth, *Anselm*.
59. Plantinga and Wolterstorff, *Faith and Rationality*, 7.
60. Cobb, *Christian Natural Theology*, 175.

any meaning when it is properly located and repaired, it is only as it "works within revelation. Nature is then a theological concept. . . . Because God has spoken, there is no realm of pure nature."[61]

Second, natural theology, operating independently of God's revelatory self-givingness, arrives at an *idol*, "a false god" (*CD* II/1, 86), rather than the reality of the God who acts. Barth's assessment here redevelops his earlier critique of "religion" as a human invention (and he primarily has Christianity in his sights, not non-Christian traditions as such). The *analogia entis* violates the reality that God is by introducing "a foreign god into the sphere of the Church" (*CD* II/1, 84). Barth is certainly not as polite as D. Z. Phillips, but Phillips's talk about a God who provides a philosophical *explanation* of physical occurrences as being confused is something of what Barth is after.[62] Phillips attempts to encourage philosophers to stop thinking about whether God can or cannot be demonstrated, about the rational grounds for belief in the existence or nonexistence of God, and instead to ask whether the subject matter they are interested in is "itself appropriate for such a question."[63] Barth certainly pulls no rhetorical punches when proclaiming that the process of reasoning apart from revelation derives "from an attempt to unite Yahweh with Baal, the triune God of Holy Scripture with the concept of being of Aristotelian and Stoic philosophy" (*CD* II/1, 84). After all, Williams explains, "A God discovered in that way is a God who waits to be discovered. . . . This is a God who has to be thought of as essentially silent, passively there to be uncovered by our enquiries."[64] Such an idle god is no "God." Barth instead urges his readers "to cling solely to the god who has revealed himself in Jesus Christ."[65] This is the God who cannot in any way be possessed, cannot be captured, cannot be used for human interests. As Busch explains, "In 1914. . . he heard his liberal teachers contend 'seriously that war was a *revelation* of God.'"[66] Yet *Deus non in genere est* (God is not a kind, a particular instance of a species), Barth often claimed.[67] Simply put, "the God of the Gospel, therefore, is neither a thing, an item, an object like others, nor an idea, a principle, a truth, or a sum of truths."[68] With the purpose of witnessing to the eternal richness of God, Barth develops an image of "a bird in flight, in

---

61. Long, *Saving Karl Barth*, 124.
62. See Phillips, *Religion without Explanation*.
63. Phillips, *Religion without Explanation*, 4.
64. Williams, *Edge of Words*, 1.
65. K. Barth, "First Commandment," 77.
66. Busch, *Great Passion*, 59, citing K. Barth, *Predigten 1914*, 523.
67. See Busch, *Great Passion*, 69.
68. K. Barth, *Evangelical Theology*, 15. "He is not a known thing in a series of things" (K. Barth, *Epistle to the Romans*, 82).

contrast to a caged bird."[69] This statement comes near the very beginning of his *Evangelical Theology* lectures. He proceeds to describe theology as "an eminently *critical* science, for it is continually exposed to judgment and never relieved of the crisis in which it is placed by its object, or rather to say, by its living subject."[70] In a succeeding lecture in the series, Barth explains that this means theology can never stand still, it cannot freeze its gaze, it cannot come to an end.

It is becoming somewhat clear now that Barth's contesting the legitimacy of natural theology, to adapt the words of Placher, is not "directed against the Christian tradition, but against what modernity did to it."[71] This becomes even clearer with the third main objection one can derive from his scattered remarks on the matter. "So-called 'natural theology'" attempts to be independent of the divine revealer *and the concrete human knower* in Jesus Christ (*CD* IV/3.1, 117). This too is a theological impossibility that occurs only because it is constructed from a theological mistake. Here, the very operations of human knowing are abstracted from their ground and reality in the elected human for all, Jesus Christ.[72] That means that Barth unpacks, to use von Balthasar's description, "what man is by nature in the light of revelation. . . . Man's humanness depends on his being already related to God."[73]

The implication of this is that, among other things, "we Christians are once for all dispensed from attempting, by starting from ourselves, to understand what exists, or to reach the cause of things and with or without God to reach a general view."[74] Accordingly, Barth uses the term "nature" on occasion to depict the self-consciousness that is theologically impossible, a form of false consciousness (cf. *CD* II/1, 112). Moreover, for reasons made clear earlier, Barth cannot entertain any notion assuming that God and creature can be seen "together on a ground common to both and therefore neutral" (*CD* II/1, 81). Not only is this idolatrous with regard to its conception of God, but it also is anthropologically distorted. In fact, in a not-inconsequential turn, Barth explains that papering over this type of anthropology with Christian

69. K. Barth, *Evangelical Theology*, 15.
70. K. Barth, *Evangelical Theology*, 16.
71. Placher, *Domestication of Transcendence*, 2.
72. Still useful resources on Barth's opposition to a range of modern anthropologies are Kerr, "Cartesianism according to Karl Barth"; and Kerr, *Immortal Longings*, chap. 2.
73. Von Balthasar, *Theology of Karl Barth*, 126–27. It would be a feat of considerable conceptual acrobatics to claim that Barth in any meaningful way *assumes as legitimate* modernity's epistemic "turn to the subject." It is entirely insufficient to flip that subjectivity around by identifying it with God's subjectivity, as if the doctrine of election can allow for a confession of God as unrelated and unhistorical (which is what the unsituated individuatedness of modern subjectivity requires) and as pure self-knower.
74. K. Barth, *Dogmatics in Outline*, 60.

imagery and concepts does anything but solve the problem: "When we do not leave out Jesus Christ, but refer to Him, it is still an illusion" (*CD* II/1, 165). If anything, it merely masks the nature of it as a problem.[75] In this context Barth comments about the distortion of perception, or that God cannot be known from reflecting on phenomena because of sin. Sin distorts. But this, and the nature of the distortion itself, can be known only as it comes to light in God's gracious reconciliation.[76]

In the fourth place, by way of something of a supplemental criticism, comes the question as to whether natural theology has advanced human knowledge. If it should prove to be rationally successful, then, Barth admits, he would have to take it seriously. The problem is that it has proven not to have been rationally compelling at all (*CD* II/1, 89).

On Not Ending with a Conclusion

"Natural theology" is something of an amorphous phrase that covers an array of quite methodologically disparate and even conflicting approaches. Much depends on the language game the term "nature" is used in. As Eberhard Jüngel complains, "The debate about analogy has usually been carried on within recent Evangelical [viz., Protestant] theology with an astonishing lack of understanding and horrifying carelessness."[77] Within a deistic/theistic approach, it tends to be used to refer to the natural rational capacity of reason to discern theo-significance in phenomenality, whereas within many Protestant theological accounts the term tends to depict sinful nature in a nature-grace scheme.

While it may appear to be (deceptively) easy to criticize a range of options such as those often referred to as "foundationalism" or "evidentialism," it is considerably more challenging to provide a positive description of how the knowing of God occurs. Certainly, something very odd happens when theology attempts to secure itself against the ravages of an exposed and vulnerable life. If human lives are complex and contingent upon circumstance, then why should one imagine that one's belief claims can be any less so? If theology articulates how the world looks from a certain place, what is there

---

75. Barth sees many distinguishable forms of what he calls "ignorance of God" (K. Barth, *Christian Life*, 127).

76. One commentator on Barth's conflict with Brunner perceives a fatal flaw in Barth's approach: "It proceeds as if *no* intrinsic relationship between God and humans exists after the Fall" (Johnson, "Natural Revelation in Creation and Covenant," 142). This is simply a mistake. One can be in a relationship but utterly misperceive it. Moreover, a relationship can be a negative one of distancing. The commentator's language unhelpfully frames the issue in far too loose a way.

77. Jüngel, *God as Mystery of the World*, 281.

to determine why things should be regarded from that place rather than any other, or to determine that certain places for observing constitute a *mistake*, or to recommend that place as a fitting place for the observations? With regard to Barth, Hauerwas has a point in claiming that the Swiss theologian "did not try to 'explain' the truth of what Christians believe about God and God's creation."[78] There is no *apologetic* form of Barth's discourse that would, or properly could, answer the question of why the Christian witness to God's presence in and to all things in Jesus Christ is, or at least can be, compelling. The dogmatic salve or therapy he provides is not one that justifies the truthfulness of Christian speech over against other accounts but instead one of expansively witnessing to the character of the revelatory presence of God's self-communicative action. That said, his account is meaningful only insofar as it can be seen to cohere adequately with the way things are; where there may be tensions (for instance, questions over the veracity of the witness to the resurrection of Jesus), then a rethinking would be required.

Nonetheless, Barth's theology, at least, does provide a set of parameters: theology cannot speak of anything other than what it claims it speaks about, on the grounds that it has been enabled to speak; and the doctrine of election sets the terms for the doctrine of creation. Moreover, Barth's is not a total perspective that asserts the veracity of its reading in a way that refuses to be responsive to, and corrected by, others. Rather, he offers a theological articulation that compels the theologian to listen for God's voice attentively wherever it may be heard. That is why Barth displays a form of intense and self-critical modesty that, in principle, exposes the theologian who refuses to dispense with self-protective tactics. In his self-critical theological description, his adamant assertion that theology is not answerable to any ground beyond itself, Barth nonetheless does cast an eye back to the intelligibility of accounts of rationality that themselves display such a kind of comprehensiveness that results in dictating the terms of theology. In fact, the question of whether such a model of universal rationality is even believable in the contemporary academy is not a minor matter. Even so, how far this account is persuasive certainly remains a contested question, of course. But then we may have to come full circle and ask what kind of shared account can be meaningfully provided for the conditions of rational theological knowing, and how disagreement over the matter may even begin to be resolved intelligibly.

---

78. Hauerwas, *With the Grain of the Universe*, 146.

Contemporary Response

CHARLES TALIAFERRO

D uring a job interview for a philosophy of religion position at Princeton Theological Seminary, one professor said to me: "You must *really* hate [name withheld]."

"Why?" I asked.

The reply: "He's a Barthian."

For the record, I do not hate Barthians, and I seek to avoid *odium theologicum* (theological hatred) at all costs. I think John McDowell offers us a compelling portrait of the theology of Karl Barth. In this response, I propose that while "contemporary natural theology" may be carried out in ways that are impoverished, distorting, and even idolatrous, thus distracting persons from the divine self-disclosure in the life, teaching, crucifixion, and resurrection of Jesus of Nazareth, this is far from obvious. Natural theology can instead give us reasons for taking seriously Christian revelation claims. I develop my response, addressing relevant issues directly and without exegesis on how to interpret Barth. If the Swiss Calvinist might accept all my proposals, great. And if my observations are wide of the mark, I defer to McDowell as the expert.

Imagine that tomorrow you come to accept that it is rational for you to believe there is a maximally perfect being based on the ontological argument. Imagine you are also a practicing Christian and convinced of the reality of the living Christ. How would your accepting the ontological argument distort your faith or concept of God? Even more bizarrely, how would it lead you to idolatry? I remember the day I became convinced that a theistic version of the ontological argument is sound and valid; it was in the fall of 1978 in Robbins

Library, Emerson Hall (Harvard). I can report that it did not lead me to be lax
in attending the Episcopal monastery to which I am still attached. Agreed, if
you come to believe in *Spinoza's* version of the ontological argument, there
will be a rupture in your life of faith (Spinoza was a nontheist who denied
that we have free will, and so on, though he had an exceptionally high view
of Jesus, which led some of his critics to think he was a radical Protestant).
But it is hard to see how accepting one of Anselm's arguments would lead
one astray as a Christian. As it happens, while Barth thought that Anselm's
ontological arguments were not good theistic arguments, Barth proposed that
Anselm's thinking (forged by religious experience) can shed light on what it
is for a person of faith to seek understanding.

Imagine that next week you continue to explore natural theology. You
come to think there is good reason, based on versions of the cosmological
and teleological arguments, that theism is more reasonable than its closest
competitor, some version of naturalism. Would you be tempted to lay aside
the God disclosed in the Gospels and worship instead the God of theistic
philosophy? Would you cease to exercise Christian humility and take great
(vain) pride on your becoming convinced of a theistic argument? Both seem
to me highly doubtful. Perhaps both outcomes are imaginable (I mean, they
can't be ruled out on conceptual grounds), but I do not see either as even
remotely likely.

In McDowell's chapter are references to the language used about God.
Without plumbing the depths of Barth's claims, consider an ordinary case.
Last month, I sought to comfort a friend whose husband had died. I said
something like this: "God knows your sorrow. We may take some solace that
Russ is now in the hands of a God of limitless love and power." Now, it is
rather straightforward that reference to God's hands is not literal but a matter
of analogy, a metaphor or a figure of speech to refer to being in someone's
power. But I think it is natural (and not impious) to think that many of the
other terms are either univocal or analogous to the way we use these words to
describe one another. Take "knows": I suggest that *the way God knows* you
and the world is different from the way we know ourselves and the world, but
"knows" used of God and us is most reasonably thought of as either univocal
or analogical. Do we thereby somehow treat "God" anthropomorphically?
That seems dubious, not least because to think that any reference to anything
(a dog or dolphin) knowing something is to treat it improperly as human.
Various thinkers insist that God (whatever God is) should not be thought
of as one thing among others. Some even go so far as to claim that because
God is not a *thing*, we should refrain from saying that God exists. I do not
share this stance (though I do not *hate* it). "Thing" can be used as a referent

for contingent, material objects, but if by "thing" one means something far broader, for example, a possible object of thought, then I suggest there are two categories: things and nothing. Assuming that Christians do not think of God as nothing, I believe there is an ordinary, religiously, and philosophically respectful way of thinking of God as a thing. Even saying the Lord's Prayer would make little sense if you thought of God as nothing or no-thing. Side note: the idea that *God is greater than which can be conceived* is not equivalent to the idea that *one can form no conception of God*.

If I were to write that *natural theology can be a friend to Barthians*, this might seem as welcome as when my dentist told me before oral surgery that the drill is my friend. Be that as it may, natural theology can be of assistance in addressing a recent objection to relying on one's sense (experience) of God's presence. McDowell begins his chapter with reference to voodoo and diviners. In recent philosophy of religion literature, it is argued that having a sense of God's presence is one of many senses (having a sense of ghosts, spirits, aliens, demons and angels, and so on) that are known to be false (they generate "false positives"; that is, they positively generate beliefs known to be false). Therefore, one should not trust the sense of God's presence. One way to address this argument (sometimes called the X argument, in which X refers to a large class of putative senses of X, most of which are known to be false) is by appealing to good work in natural theology that shows theism to be an intelligible, plausible worldview. There is no convincing equivalently plausible worldview supporting the sense that your house is haunted or that aliens have been in your neighborhood, and so on. Natural theology can be of service in replying to the X argument. Natural theology is not a theological mistake equivalent to playing a sport not according to the rules of the game. It can rather provide reasons for playing the game, though I personally would prefer a different metaphor for theology and religion than a game.

I end on what, in my mind, is a positive note. Barth has much to say to philosophers. But I read him more as a homilist or as preaching or exhorting or maybe even prophesying than writing the way my philosophical role models write, from C. S. Lewis to Eleonore Stump. Please do not misunderstand: as a Christian philosopher, I actually have an exceedingly high view of prophecy, exhortation, and preaching (good preaching is far from the pejorative adjective "preachy"). Reading Barth's *Epistle to the Romans*—which I read as an exhortation, rather than a philosophical discourse—when I was in graduate school was a much-needed, life-changing experience. And speaking of preaching, let us not forget that for all his acts—miracles of healing, feeding the hungry, raising the dead, and his own suffering and resurrection—Jesus was and is now (through Scripture and the sacraments) still preaching to us today.

Catholic Response

FATHER ANDREW PINSENT

begin by highlighting how much I appreciate John McDowell's chapter for its clarity and insight, an especially fine contribution to a collection of excellent chapters. In my view, McDowell acts as an outstanding window and guide into Karl Barth's approach to natural theology. As a consequence, my comments in what follows are principally about Barth's approach as described in this chapter rather than McDowell's own work in presenting this approach so superlatively.

McDowell rightly begins by setting out the meaning of natural theology or "so-called 'natural theology,'" as the term is described by Barth in *Church Dogmatics* (IV/3.1, 117). On this account, "'Natural theology' is a term used to depict certain family resemblances and covers rational deliberation among distinctly complex and multifarious conceptual perspectives and tactical practices. Those resemblances may be describable in terms of efforts in engaging in public conversation that holds theological claims accountable or publicly scrutinizable." From this description, it is clear that natural theology is meant to cover a much larger field of exploration than proofs for God's existence, or other theological truths in the absence of revelation. Indeed, the claim above that natural theology involves holding "theological claims accountable or publicly scrutinizable" can presumably include the subjection of revelation to the demands of human reason, as well as the impact of revelation on the natural world. At first glance, this approach therefore aligns well with the broader account of natural theology proposed by some other authors of this volume, encompassing nature transformed by revelation as well as nature in the absence of revelation.

Nevertheless, as McDowell shows, Barth is suspicious of natural theology. On one hand, one cannot legitimately study the theology of the pure created world prior to revelation since "creatures cannot be independent from God in the sense of being autonomous and utterly self-defining." These plausible words exclude natural theology in the traditional sense, but they conceal an ambiguity. Across a vast theological spectrum, no Christian would argue that creatures are entirely "autonomous and utterly self-defining." Nevertheless, across much of the same spectrum, Christians have been careful to distinguish the mode of relation to God in the order of creation from the mode of relation to God in the order of grace. This distinction is why Christians refer to themselves as being born again in baptism, distinguishing natural birth from the supernatural birth into the life of grace. By contrast, across a wide range of issues, including baptism, Barth downplays or denies this distinction, illustrating how the principles behind his rejection of natural theology also shape his account of revelation.

On the other hand, natural theology in an expanded sense also seems problematic for Barth. As McDowell writes, "The business of theologians is to follow the logic of God's presenting God's Self," which he further explicates in the following quotation: "Theology becomes, if it is to be 'scientific' and rational, a faithful and obedient *Nachdenken* (literally, 'after thinking'). In other words, it has to be a thankful, realistic, and a posteriori reflection upon and explication of the divine object of faith's speaking, and that, of course for Barth, is in and through Christ."[1] As McDowell comments, this approach is not (or at least, I would add, is not meant to be) a simple "fideism" or "subjectivism." Nevertheless, on a Barthian approach as described above, it seems that theology should keep close to the explicit gospel as it is delivered or, more precisely, "faith's speaking," presumably referring to the words of the New Testament. Such an approach might appear commendably simple, but there is little place for the more remote consequences of the gospel. Examples include saints, councils, liturgies, canon law, or the principles of Christian government and society. Indeed, Barth's emphasis on "faith's speaking" also seems to offer little place to the silent and nonverbal celebration and communication of the faith, for example, in Christian art and architecture. One can refer to all these matters as the fruits of the faith, and their omission circumscribes severely any prospects for natural theology in a broad sense, with its theme of the created world glorified by grace.

What, then, is concerning about Barth's approach, which upholds revelation itself even if it excludes its a priori natural roots and the a posteriori

1. K. Barth, *Göttingen Dogmatics*, 3, 8, 11.

fruits? My concern goes back to the core teaching of the Christian faith about the incarnation. The very word "incarnation" comes, via Norman French, from the late Latin *incarnationem*, from *in-*, "in," plus *caro* (genitive *carnis*), meaning "flesh."[2] Applied to Jesus Christ, the word "incarnation" therefore denotes the Word of God being made flesh, an act that requires two prerequisites, the Word of God and the flesh, consistent with the teaching of the Council of Chalcedon (451), that Jesus Christ is one person, two natures, divine and human. According to a vivid image from St. Catherine of Siena, Jesus Christ is therefore a bridge between heaven and earth.[3] One end of the bridge is, of course, the divine nature of Jesus Christ as the Second Person of the Most Holy Trinity. The other end is the human nature of Jesus Christ, drawn from the Blessed Virgin Mary, who also represents the involvement of the natural world in the incarnation. Hence, with the one person of Jesus Christ, God has given us a perfect bridge by which created human beings, gifted with the life of grace in union with the Holy Spirit, can cross into heaven.

Since Barth, however, has delegitimized natural theology, what, then, happens to the bridge of the incarnation? The lesson of the centuries leading up to Chalcedon is that some movements were condemned for denying the divinity of Christ, but others were condemned for denying the unity of Christ or the human nature of Christ. In other words, all those movements that were ultimately condemned as heretical were condemned principally for denying one or other aspect of the bridge of the incarnation, by attacking either one or another of the ends of the bridge or the span itself. In the case of Barth, although he does not attack the divinity of Christ, that divinity has to inhere in *something* to enable the bridge to be a bridge, and to manifest its fruits to enable its truth to be known and understood as the source of salvation. By undermining natural theology, Barth, I fear, has also undermined the natural end of the bridge, to the point that it ceases to function as a bridge. Admittedly, he upholds revelation itself. My concern, however, is that "bare revelation," stripped of its roots and fruits in natural theology, will tend to wither and ultimately be discarded, under the pressure, for example, of biblical criticism unmoored from a broader theological tradition.

At this point, some readers might think that I think my criticism against Barth might play out in the history of the Reformation as the practical outworking of his theological principles, and they would be correct. Indeed, the Reformation is a theme of McDowell's chapter, insofar as he states that Barth situates his opposition to natural theology in the fact that he is a *Reformed*

---

2. "Incarnation," *Online Etymology Dictionary*, accessed October 8, 2022, https://www.etymonline.com/word/incarnation.

3. Catherine of Siena, *Dialogue of St. Catherine of Siena*, 32.

theologian. To a great extent, those who initiated the Reformation were, at least in part, disgusted by the abuses and intellectual decay of the late medieval Catholic Church. Confronted by the disfigured face of the bride of Christ (Rev. 21:2, 9–10; Eph. 5:22–33; cf. 2 Cor. 11:2–4), they sought a new and purified faith, unhindered by what they saw as the accretions of natural theology and the vast edifice of scholastic works that had attempted to give concrete expression to the fruits of faith. This spirit is articulated in the famous slogan "Scripture alone!" and in many actions of the Reformers and their successors, such as Martin Luther burning the books of canon law, and the iconoclastic destruction of much medieval art. People have to judge for themselves if the Reformation has given or ever could give rise to a purer and more successful Christianity, given that the history is ongoing: all I can point out here is that there have been many sobering critiques.[4]

To conclude, what, then, can be learned from McDowell's chapter? Given that Barth links his opposition to natural theology to being a Reformed theologian, it seems that the recovery of natural theology is intimately linked to the recovery of catholicity in theology, by those who are already Roman Catholic or who are, to a greater or lesser extent, fellow travelers, such as Orthodox Christians or many other individual non-Catholics, such as C. S. Lewis.

On this reading, I also think that natural theology needs, and has been given, a patroness. As noted above, the Blessed Virgin Mary can act as a symbol of the natural world, anchoring one end of the bridge of the incarnation that is Jesus Christ. On a Catholic reading, this natural world, as represented by the Virgin Mary, has always been free by grace of the stain of original sin.[5] She is never without grace, but that is how our human nature was meant to be. Hence Mary represents the subject matter of natural theology understood in a broad and perfect sense: the exemplar of the pure created world open to revelation as well as the glorified created world that is the fruit of revelation.

---

4. See, e.g., Gregory, *Unintended Reformation*; Newman, *Certain Difficulties Felt by Anglicans*.
5. Pope Pius IX, *Ineffabilis Deus*, 1854 (cited in Denzinger, *Sources of Catholic Dogma*, 413–14).

Classical Response

ALISTER E. McGRATH

John McDowell offers us a clear and useful account of Karl Barth's views on natural theology, which will serve as an excellent introduction to the field. Barth was the first theologian I read in any depth as I made the painful transition from the natural sciences to Christian theology back in the 1970s. I used the funds unexpectedly arising from winning an Oxford University prize to buy his *Church Dogmatics* and spent many months exploring its depths, emerging a wiser person—though not always, I have to say, as a result of Barth's own ideas. I sometimes found that his generous engagement with others pointed me toward theological strategies and approaches that turned out to be more interesting and persuasive than those of Barth himself.

Barth is a theological landmark, and I found engaging him rewarding, formative, and encouraging. Although the extent and quality of his engagement with the natural sciences is somewhat disappointing, his critical assessment of the deficiencies of Heinrich Scholz's approach to theological method was acute and persuasive[1] and clearly laid the groundwork for a theologically productive engagement with the natural sciences. It was not difficult to see how this could be developed further: one of my great intellectual pleasures was discovering T. F. Torrance's *Theological Science* (1969) while I was doing theological research at Cambridge University.[2] I found Torrance's use of Barth in developing his distinctive views on the relation of theology and the natural sciences to be masterful.

---

1. For my own views on this, see McGrath, "Theologie als Mathesis Universalis?"
2. For my reflections, see McGrath, "Manifesto for Intellectual Engagement."

Barth's views on natural theology are well known, and I enjoyed McDowell's lucid presentation of its core themes. In responding to McDowell, I open up a few issues for further discussion. Barth's views on natural theology are expressed most sharply in his 1934 debate with Emil Brunner. As McDowell notes, Barth's response to Brunner's critical assessment of his views on nature and grace, which included reflections on natural theology, was "ill-tempered." Yet this debate surely needs more discussion. In 2014, I published a monograph on the development of Brunner's theology, including a substantial engagement with the 1934 debate with Barth,[3] which persuaded me of the importance of this debate in connection with any contemporary articulation or critique of a natural theology. I return to this point later in this response.

In his judicious analysis of Barth's position, McDowell makes the important point that Barth's hostility toward natural theology might actually be directed against a "certain version of 'natural theology.'" This is an important concession. Recent discussions of natural theology have stressed that it is not a "natural kind," as if there is some self-evidently correct definition of this enterprise.[4] It is clearly an actor's category, which demands that we ascertain how the many actors participating in this discussion understand the concept. While historians might disagree over precisely how many different definitions of natural theology have been used over time, there is no doubt that the term is now used to designate a wide range of such understandings. The discipline of the philosophy of religion, for example, would certainly endorse the broad definitions of natural theology offered by Richard Swinburne or William Alston; yet this is a convention, a habit of thought, a form of ideographical shorthand, which is not binding on anyone else.[5]

My fundamental point is that Barth engages with a specific and limited approach (or range of approaches) to natural theology; his criticisms of the theological legitimacy of this understanding cannot be extrapolated to the *totality* of the wide range of understandings of natural theology evident in Christian history—in other words, to "natural theology" *tout simple*. To avoid any misunderstanding at this important point, let me make it clear that I share Barth's concerns about constructing a self-serving concept of God, or trying to find God under conditions and circumstances of our own choosing, rather than being attentive and respectful toward the specific historical

3. McGrath, *Emil Brunner*.
4. McGrath, "Natürliche Theologie."
5. Swinburne's "ramified" natural theology is of considerable interest and importance, not least on account of the importance he attaches to the correlation with Christian specifics, rather than theistic commonalities. See the excellent discussion in Holder, *Ramified Natural Theology in Science and Religion*.

forms of God's self-disclosure. Although Barth makes important criticisms of a certain range of the spectrum of possible natural theologies, he does not invalidate the general category. His contribution, in my view, enables us to develop a responsible natural theology, which takes into account the legitimate concerns he expresses.

A second point concerns the range and diversity of the Reformed theological tradition.[6] McDowell rightly notes that Barth declares himself to be "unable to follow the trajectory of natural theology precisely because he, 'as a Reformed theologian,' is subjected to a fundamentally different 'ordinance.'" Yet I think this needs further discussion. I do not think there are good grounds for suggesting that the Reformed theological tradition is *intrinsically* hostile to natural theology as such, although I can certainly see good reasons for asserting its hostility toward a concept of God derived purely from human reason or rational reflection on the natural world. Yet Reformed theology in the sixteenth and seventeenth centuries was intellectually hospitable toward forms of natural theology holding that the beauty and ordering of the natural world *pointed toward* the Christian God—but did not *define, constitute, or prove the existence* of such a God.[7] In defending the idea of a natural knowledge of God, John Calvin was proposing this not as an alternative to the God of the Christian revelation but as a gateway for discovering this God through the intelligent and reflective reading of Scripture.[8]

It is certainly possible to argue that the Reformed theological tradition moved toward adopting a harder rationalist form of natural theology in the late seventeenth and eighteenth centuries, as the rise of the Age of Reason across Europe made it increasingly important to affirm the rational basis for Christian belief.[9] There is a debate to be had about whether this eighteenth-century development represents a temporary apologetic tactic or a permanent theological divergence from the roots of the Reformed tradition; yet earlier Reformed approaches to natural theology cannot be dismissed with such ease.

The Barth-Brunner debate of 1934, it has always seemed to me, is really a discussion about the theological identity of the Reformed tradition, within which Barth and Brunner both locate themselves. The Reformed tradition was not theologically monolithic in Barth's day, nor is it so today.[10] Barth is entitled to interpret his Reformed theological identity as precluding natural theology,

---

6. See, e.g., the diversity evident within Willis-Watkins and Welker, *Toward the Future of Reformed Theology*.

7. There is a large body of literature: see, e.g., Sudduth, *Reformed Objection to Natural Theology*, 9–41; Wallace, *Shapers of English Calvinism*, 167–204.

8. Léchot, "Calvin et la connaissance naturelle de Dieu."

9. For a good example, see Klauber, "Turrettini (1671–1737) on Natural Theology."

10. See Kim, "Identity of Reformed Theology."

as he understands it; this cannot, however, be allowed to stand as a *normative* judgment for this rich and complex tradition as a whole. Nevertheless, Barth's judgment has been influential within the Reformed tradition, so that many who would locate themselves within this tradition remain suspicious of what they term "natural theology."[11] Yet Barth cannot be allowed to define what natural theology *has been* or *should be* and thus shut down a conversation of considerable theological and cultural significance.

Barth has much to say to us concerning natural theology, and I welcome his critical voice in any discussion about the nature, focus, and limits of natural theology, just as I welcome McDowell's lucid and engaging account of his landmark contribution to our debate in this volume.

---

11. Kock, *Natürliche Theologie*, 392–412.

Deflationary Response

PAUL K. MOSER

John McDowell offers a summary and a defense of Karl Barth's influential approach to natural theology. His interpretation of Barth agrees for the most part with my own, but I recommend that we have serious misgivings about the cogency of Barth's approach. It comes across as a dogmatic statement of systematic theology that fails to engage the main concern behind natural theology: the concern to identify a rationale for theological commitment that avoids begging relevant questions as much as possible in interpersonal inquiry.

Barth's Claims

McDowell cites the following from Barth: "So-called 'natural theology' is quite impossible within the Church, and indeed, . . . cannot even be discussed in principle" (*CD* IV/3.1, 117; II/1, 85). Perhaps Barth intends this striking claim to be a conversation stopper. In any case, contrary to Barth, we *can* discuss natural theology, even "in principle" and "within the church." We are discussing natural theology now, even "in principle," and we could have this discussion "within the church" if we wished. We have a sign here of how Barth often indulges in ungrounded sweeping claims, with his easy rhetoric getting the best of him. We miss an opportunity to learn something important about theology, however, if we yield to Barth's unduly dismissive attitude toward natural theology.

Philosophers and theologians often mean different things by the locution "natural theology," as is common for terms involved in controversial topics.

241

People define "natural theology" as they wish, of course, but we humans typically do not theorize in isolation. We have people around us, as did Barth, who promote natural theology of different kinds, and we should ask if these people have a common purpose in their quest for such theology. We thus should consider what moves them to pursue natural theology. This lesson results from a principle of charity in interpretation.

We can identify a common purpose, at least for many of the people in question: they aim to formulate a rationale for their theological beliefs that avoids begging relevant questions as much as possible. Specifically, they want to avoid a kind of arbitrariness, relative to evidential support, that invites a charge of "irrational," "ungrounded," "unconvincing," or "merely dogmatic" against their theological beliefs. They are aware, as we should be, that there is an abundance of diverse and competing *conceptions of God* and *claims about God* in circulation. They naturally wonder whether anything can reasonably ground, on the basis of evidence, a particular conception of God and a corresponding set of theological claims in a way that recommends acceptance over available competitors. That concern is fitting and above reproach, from a cognitive point of view.

The relevant inquirers about natural theology are not all, or even largely, anti-theistic. In addition, they do not all wield a narrow conception of evidence at odds with the God of Christian theism. I happen to be among those inquirers, despite my being unconvinced by the traditional arguments of natural theology and their contemporary variations. (As my chapter in this book indicates, I find them to be either seriously question-begging or deficient in yielding a God worthy of worship, such as the proposed God and Father of Jesus.) It is an open question, then, whether the inquirers at issue must or will, as Barth suggests, arrive at a "false god." We need to have the cognitive modesty to look and see, with due patience and care. Begging key questions against our interlocutors about natural theology will not benefit us or our theological beliefs, from a cognitive point of view.

Barth apparently holds that attention to natural theology somehow challenges an important Creator-creature distinction with a presumption of human "autonomy." McDowell thus cites his remark that "the creature, then, can have no independence from, or autonomy over against, Jesus Christ (see *CD* II/1, 166)." This remark is unhelpful and potentially misleading because it fails to distinguish different kinds of autonomy. If God is Creator, then *ontic* autonomy for humans is at least questionable regarding the causal origins for humans. *Epistemic* autonomy for humans, however, is a more complicated matter, because God, if real, would decide the parameters for human knowledge of God, and this topic, regarding what God has decided, is controversial.

Some inquirers find no problem with God's giving humans a certain degree of autonomy in discovering evidence of God's reality and in formulating notions and standards for evidence for divine reality. It gains nothing to beg the key questions in this area of controversy. Barth's theology, in any case, is not the only game in town, nor has it ever been. We must be candid, then, about the epistemic relevance of competing theological views and their proposed bases of evidence. We should not, and do not, do theology in a theological vacuum filled only by Barth. Responsible theology does not proceed in Barth's dogmatic manner.

McDowell offers the following quotation from Barth: "Theology becomes, if it is to be 'scientific' and rational, a faithful and obedient *Nachdenken* (literally, 'after thinking'). In other words, it has to be a thankful, realistic, and *a posteriori* reflection upon and explication of the divine object of faith's speaking, and that, of course for Barth, is in and through Christ."[1] Even if Barth is right here, we still need to ask *which Nachdenken*, if any, captures (some of) the reality about God. There are many variations on *Nachdenken* in circulation, and they do not all capture, or otherwise represent, the reality about God. As one New Testament writer notes: "Do not believe every spirit, but test the spirits to see whether they are from God, for many false prophets have gone out into the world" (1 John 4:1 NRSVue). Similarly, from the apostle Paul: "Test everything; hold fast to what is good; abstain from every form of evil" (1 Thess. 5:21–22 NRSVue). Test we must, but we as self-reflective inquirers need to explain how the testing is to proceed for the sake of its *trustworthiness*. Barth is altogether unhelpful here, and therefore his dismissal of natural theology fails to convince or to advance the discussion of natural theology.

McDowell proposes a major limitation on Barth: "The dogmatic salve or therapy he provides is not one that justifies the truthfulness of Christian speech over against other accounts but instead one of expansively witnessing to the character of the revelatory presence of God's self-communicative action." Such witnessing is *arguably* an option, but the suggested contrast with justification or evidence is cognitively dangerous in its neglect of needed evidential support for witnessing. Many fair-minded inquirers, including many exploring natural theology, want to know, in keeping with 1 John 4:1 and 1 Thessalonians 5:21–22, whether the witnessing in question is actually "from God" rather than from a "false prophet." That is, they want to know whether the theological witness on offer by Barth and others is true rather than false, and they want evidential support in this regard. Barth fails us here, in his

1. K. Barth, *Göttingen Dogmatics*, 3, 8, 11.

neglect of 1 John 4:1 and related New Testament injunctions. The dominant biblical position is that testing for the real God is acceptable, and even advisable, so long as the testing is not biased against God or God's perfect moral character. Suitably grounded faith in God depends on such testing, as the injunction of 1 John 4:1 suggests.

McDowell explains Barth's dogmatic thinking as follows:

> The first commandment of the Decalogue is axiomatic. By this is meant that it sets theology's task. It functions as "the presupposition of all theology," which is grounded in a knowledge of God "on the basis of revelation."[2] Of course, this kind of claim needs to be considered as to whether it insulates theology as *God*-talk from examination and critique, perhaps replacing the foundations of rational first principles with that of a rationally arbitrary belief in God as a basic belief. Even so, such an examination would be hard-pressed. . . . It itself would have to begin from somewhere, and the issue is whether that place is any more rationally demonstrable than the conditions for belief in God as axiomatic.

The suggestion is that, according to Barth, belief in God is "axiomatic" because it functions as "the presupposition of all theology." Contrary to McDowell, however, it is false that "the issue is whether [some alternative starting] place is any more rationally demonstrable than the conditions for belief in God as axiomatic." The issue is about evidential support for a theological position, not whether we have a "rationally demonstrable" argument for it. Evidence (such as from religious experience of a certain sort) need not be a "rationally demonstrable" argument. Evidence can confer epistemic support without conferring a rational demonstration.

If belief in God is taken as an "axiomatic" starting point, with no need or acknowledgment of evidential support, we have a case of dubious question-begging against many people concerned with natural theology. Such people naturally ask, "*Which* God merits the axiomatic role in question?" Is the God of the terrorist Islamic state ISIS (Daesh) an equally good candidate in comparison with the Christian God? If so, what, if anything, recommends Barth's God over the violent God of ISIS? We also can ask, What, if anything, recommends Barth's theism over an endorsement of either agnosticism or atheism? Inquirers about natural theology raise such questions, for good reasons. They properly aim to avoid cognitive arbitrariness and mere dogmatism in their theological commitments.

We cannot exonerate Barth with the following observation by McDowell: "Barth's is a theological claim about how God-talk functions as a *response*

2. K. Barth, "First Commandment," 64; *CD* I/2, 306.

to God's self-articulation that faithfully follows its self-explicated logic. This self-communication is what Barth understands by 'revelation.'" Even if God-talk functions in that manner, it still can go awry; and it often does go awry, given the conflicting versions of God-talk in circulation. It cannot be the case that *all* of the versions of God-talk are correct. So, how are we to separate the wheat from the chaff, the accurate from the inaccurate, as commanded in 1 John 4? An appeal to our favorite view of God (or of belief in God) as "axiomatic" will not meet fitting challenges; nor will our saying that our favorite "God-talk functions as a *response* to God's self-articulation." A deeper account is needed, and much of natural theology looks for that deeper account, regardless of its ultimate success.

McDowell aims to support Barth's dismissal of natural theology as follows: "Theological grammar is orderly, and that very orderliness pays attention to the ways in which the disordering of theo-grammar occurs. Natural theology belongs to an entirely different theo-grammatical order, one that theology actually has to declare to be not only an impoverishment but also utterly distorting." Such a dismissal is too quick to be convincing. Whatever we say about "theological grammar," we should acknowledge that it is diverse among theological inquirers. The theological grammar of the members of ISIS, for instance, differs markedly from that of, say, the apostle Paul or the Methodist John Wesley. This is particularly clear if such grammar includes norms for using theological terms. The assumption that a singular theological grammar exists and is "orderly" simply begs a key question regarding the nature of theological discourse. Our empirical evidence concerning such discourse supports diversity rather than singularity here. As a result, we need to face questions about competing theological grammars and relevant supporting evidence. Barth fails us in this area of inquiry.

McDowell claims that "the first substantial reason for rejecting the possibility of a natural theology is that it involves an effort to work toward 'god' via an autonomous rationality. This stands in marked contrast with the 'finding' that occurs in following where God reveals God's Self to be." This claim rests on a false charge regarding natural theology. A natural theology can coherently recommend "following where God reveals God's Self to be." What it cannot consistently recommend is that we take belief in God as "axiomatic." As suggested, it pursues a needed evidential rationale for belief in God. That rationale could provide an evidential basis for "following where God reveals God's Self to be." In doing so, it would avoid the mere dogmatism suggested by Barth. It then would underwrite a recommendation of a particular kind of "following where God reveals God's Self to be," in contrast with competing approaches. Neither Barth nor McDowell has reasonably excluded this live option.

We have already taken exception to the sweeping claim of Barth and Mc-Dowell that "natural theology, operating independently of God's revelatory self-givingness, arrives at an *idol*, 'a false god' (*CD* II/1, 86), rather than the reality of the God who acts." Such a claim calls for a careful case, based on actual evidence, regarding the results of natural theology; but neither Barth nor McDowell has offered such a case. Instead, we have dismissive claims regarding natural theology. A natural theology can, at least in principle, make a coherent case for "God's revelatory self-givingness," on the basis of evidence (such as that of religious experience), and then recommend that we follow this evidence. Such evidence could support, at least in principle, a conclusion of "the reality of the God who acts"; in doing so, it could avoid supporting ontic autonomy for human inquirers. It also could support, at least in principle, that all evidence for God comes ultimately from God, and it therefore could avoid an assumption of "operating independently of God's revelatory self-givingness." We have been given no good reason to think otherwise.

McDowell endorses Barth's following exception to natural theology: "We Christians are once for all dispensed from attempting, by starting from ourselves, to understand what exists, or to reach the cause of things and with or without God to reach a general view."[3] We have noted that a natural theology does not require ontically "starting from ourselves." It can grant that God as Creator always has a prior role of at least causal influence (not to be confused with causal coercion). Its concern is to identify a cogent evidential basis for theological beliefs, rather than to take them as "axiomatic." To that end, a natural theology can give God an ontic and a causal role in the human effort to "reach a general view." The latter role does not require that an inquirer take belief in God as "axiomatic." God can leave room for inquirers to discover evidence for divine reality as a result of their own examination, without entailing, or their taking, belief in God to be "axiomatic." Neither Barth nor McDowell has foreclosed that live option, and therefore neither has precluded natural theology.

McDowell proposes that "Barth displays a form of intense and self-critical modesty that, in principle, exposes the theologian who refuses to dispense with self-protective tactics. In his self-critical theological description, his adamant assertion that theology is not answerable to any ground beyond itself, Barth nonetheless does cast an eye back to the intelligibility of accounts of rationality that themselves display such a kind of comprehensiveness that

---

3. K. Barth, *Dogmatics in Outline*, 60.

results in dictating the terms of theology." Barth's alleged modesty aside, it is arguable that *God* is not answerable to any authority beyond God, and various parts of the Bible teach as much. It is a separate issue, however, whether we should accept Barth's "adamant assertion that *theology* is not answerable to any ground beyond itself" (emphasis added).

God, of course, is not a theology, and we cannot plausibly claim that our favorite theology, even if Barth's theology, is God. The authority of God is not reducible or automatically transferable to the authority of our theology, however comprehensive the latter is. It is a serious category mistake to conflate the unmatched authority of God with the authority of our theology. Our theology can go wrong, very wrong, in ways that a God worthy of worship does not. So, even if God is self-authenticating, in virtue of supplying evidence of divine reality through self-manifestation, we cannot plausibly say that our theology is self-authenticating or "axiomatic."

If our favorite theology is self-authenticating or "axiomatic," the same privileged status applies to its competitors. That, however, would be a reductio ad absurdum. We need something *beyond* our theology, then, to save our theology, including our hope and belief in God, from disappointing us, cognitively and otherwise. The apostle Paul recognized this vital truth, even if Barth did not.

Correction from the Apostle Paul

Writing to the Roman Christians, Paul appeals to a basis for distinguishing grounded hope and faith in God from the "disappointment" of ungrounded, wishful thinking: "Hope [in God] does not disappoint us, because God's love [*agapē*] has been poured into our hearts through the Holy Spirit which has been given to us" (Rom. 5:5). Paul has in mind at least *evidential* disappointment that arises from ungrounded hope, the kind of hope that fails to rise above wishful thinking. His thinking here bears on faith in God, too, as is suggested by his mention of such faith in Romans 5:1.

Paul acknowledges that something must be said, and invoked, to counter a claim of the disappointment of hope and faith in God. He invokes a distinctive religious experience: "God's love has been poured into our hearts." This love, in Paul's thinking, is evidence of God's reality and presence. It is the self-manifestation of God's unique character of righteous love. That self-manifestation is not a belief or a theology, let alone an axiomatic belief or theology; it is, as understood by Paul, a feature of a religious experience, and it can serve as evidential support for theological commitment.

Paul's thinking enables us to avoid taking belief or hope in God to be "axiomatic." His appeal to religious experience allows us to ask a vital question: What best explains the experience of the kind of love Paul has in mind? Is it best explained by a claim that God has in fact intervened? If so, we can begin to compare and assess some competing theological claims on the basis of evidence.[4] Barth overreacted negatively to religious experience in response to Friedrich Schleiermacher, but Paul points us in a different direction. This may not be standard "natural theology" in Paul, but it points to a key role for experiential evidence in theology. Paul saves us from cognitive disappointment in this regard, but Barth, alas, does not. I therefore recommend Paul over Barth.

4. I have developed this kind of epistemological approach in Moser, *God Relationship*; and Moser, *Understanding Religious Experience*. For its relevance to Jesus, see Moser, *Divine Goodness of Jesus*.

A Barthian Reply

JOHN C. McDOWELL

Walter Benjamin once admitted, "Writers are really people who write books not because they are poor, but because they are dissatisfied with the books which they could buy but do not like."[1] While a volume of reflections such as this one can lean toward what Theodor Adorno calls "reproductive thinking," each contributor is certainly enabled to articulate and possibly advocate a perspective that is dependent on, and shaped by, a certain dissatisfaction with the other perspectives.[2] This, of course, is standard in most collections that incorporate a range of outlooks. What is more intellectually interesting than that, however, is the opportunity to respond to each chapter. This better facilitates the testing of both the rational warrants of each other's claims and the responsibility of our attention to detail in our readings of texts and handling of arguments. In this performance of peer accountability, the responses can begin to reflect on, and elucidate, the very nature and status of the disagreements between the contributions as an act of "clarifying and purifying the conversation."[3]

It would be intellectually frivolous at this point, though, to reduce the disagreements to different conclusions that veer away from otherwise agreed premises, so that by showing the workings of our formula we can simply decide on whether someone offering a dissimilar conclusion has appropriately

---

1. Benjamin, *Illuminations*, 61.
2. In Adorno and Horkheimer, *Towards a New Manifesto*, 4–5. This is a reminder and a clarification, since Paul Moser's response to my chapter conflates my voice and that of Karl Barth, suggesting, among other things, that my analysis "endorses" that of the Swiss theologian.
3. Lash, *Easter in Ordinary*, 13.

followed the logic where it should lead. Several of the disagreements actively involve conflicts that are considerably more substantial than that. The differences seep deeper into the very materials that compose the fabric of our perspectives. This is the product of markedly different histories of learning, and the consequent shape of the habituation of the skills of identifying materials adjudged most appropriate for working with them. After all, there is no agreement regarding either the role of "evidence" with respect to "natural theology" so-called, or what would properly constitute "evidence." Similarly, a theologically odd shift has occurred when the difference between God and creature becomes ontologically definable within the parameters of being existent, as if only "things" are the opposite of "nothings." "God does not form part of our common experience," Henri de Lubac argues.[4] "God is not a fact any more than . . . an 'object.'"

According to Hannah Arendt, "All thought arises out of experience, but no experience yields any meaning or even coherence without undergoing the operations of imagining and thinking."[5] Consequently, rational frameworks themselves "determine what would even count as evidence; one's ultimate stance affects the significance of every possible 'fact.'"[6] Charles Taliaferro's puzzle with Barth misses the mark when he asks how it is that utilizing Anselm's ontological argument, for instance, leads to idolatry. Perhaps my chapter's description was too elusive, but I indicated that Barth is providing a theological framework for reading, for perceiving (all) things well, so that his viewpoint has to critically reflect on the substantive disagreement with other perspectives. What he has in mind, then, is not any particular series of tactics as such, any particular argument or another that can take shape remoto christo (apart from Christ). If Barth is skeptical of the persuasiveness of any actual argument that claims logical validity and justificatory warrant, understanding what is going on requires one to pay attention to the context and specificity of the critique. Barth sets his critical sights intensively on the rational framework that he refers to as the analogia entis. Intelligible speaking about the createdness of materiality, Barth avers in his dogmatics of creation, is a statement of faith. This does not mean that it is nonrational, since Barth does not fall into the trap of contrasting "faith" and "reason" as noetic strategies. Instead, the claim indicates that the vestigiality of things is not straightforwardly evident. After all, whatever else it may be, it is not rational nonsense to say that talk of the existence of things does not require the predication of any first cause.

4. De Lubac, Discovery of God, 46.
5. Arendt, Life of the Mind, 87.
6. Hughes, "Proofs and Arguments," 4.

Given the appeal to *argument* in his critique, and his concern with the meta-physical assumptions of what he perceives as being theologically problematic claims, it would be premature to dismiss Barth as simply overreacting without one spending considerably more time critically interrogating his rationale and the reality of "competing rationalities."[7] To adapt a claim made by Alasdair MacIntyre, rather than for one to dismiss Barth in this way, rational attention is needed to provide "a more accurate and informed definition of disagreement rather than . . . [hastily seek] progress toward its resolution."[8] Equally, as one is engaged in theological argument regarding the content of the Christian theology in the *ordo essendi* (order of being), it is rationally problematic to speak of Barth's "dogmatism," as Paul Moser does; or of Barth as simply a "homilist," in Taliaferro's case.[9] Besides, using Anselm here is not the best example since it was the metaphysics of what Barth construed as the *analogia entis* (of a certain kind) that is at issue and that he traces to Thomas Aquinas rather than Anselm (even if his reading of Thomas in this has been properly problematized over recent years).

That the disagreements are substantive should not come as a surprise. Philosophers and theologians have long recognized the multiplicity of frame-works or traditions that provide the conditions for interpretation, under-standing, and one's own hermeneutical improvisations that emerge from "contingent processes of socialization."[10] For instance, political philosopher Arendt, reflecting on the pressure of Immanuel Kant's epistemology, claims, "The world appears in the mode of it-seems-to-me, depending on particular perspectives determined by location in the world as well as by particular organs of perception."[11] From among the guild of theologians, Edward Schil-lebeeckx declares, "Such [theistic] apologetic procedures overlook that the fundamental orientation of the life of a person is based on a whole cultural history."[12] That certain rational frameworks dominate certain university de-partments, intellectual institutions, or even the disciplines themselves is not an encouragement to critical complacency of the sort that ossifies this and that universally imposes itself on a range of contextually different approaches

7. MacIntyre, *Whose Justice?*, 3.
8. MacIntyre, *Whose Justice?*, 3.
9. I suspect that Taliaferro may have projected the trouble many critics have had with reading the theo-rhetoric of the second edition of Barth's *Romans* commentary onto his succeeding corpus. In any case, to reduce the intellectual options to "exhortation . . . [and] philosophi-cal discourse" requires a better appreciation of the kind of intellectual work being done as dogmatic theology or fundamental theology. As Lash argues, "Theological investigation is, in itself, neither preaching nor prayer" (*Easter in Ordinary*, 292).
10. Benhabib, *Situating the Self*, 5.
11. Arendt, *Life of the Mind*, 38.
12. Schillebeeckx, *Church*, 81.

unduly. Discussions of "natural theology" have themselves been the product of concrete and particular intellectual contexts, so that to read these texts without these conditions or histories of practice is a distinctly odd hermeneutical handling of texts and can support an evasion of the awareness of nature and status of our own reading-contexted specificities. When reasoning about the shifts in traditions of understanding and use of the notion of "natural law," Jean Porter explains, "Ancient claims took on new meanings when they were asserted in the light of new social [and intellectual] conditions, and different strands of thought were drawn together in ways that their originators could not have foreseen, much less intended."[13] Porter's point can offer an important caution against assuming homogeneity of the intellectual traditions of "natural theology." Andrew Pinsent's, Alister McGrath's, and my own chapters regard an array of types of "natural theologies" as providing something of an umbrella term under which a range of intellectual perspectives, strategies, and tactics shelter. To return to Porter, the early modern appeal to the natural law constitutes "an innovative reading being framed up in traditional language, and so it is worth underscoring that this is an innovation."[14] Even if the linguistic parameters of these concrete moments overlap with those of others, the temptation to flatten their contextual differences should be stringently resisted. Each text becomes modestly contemporaneous only through the kind of intellectual effort that respects the considerable complexity of the particularities of text and reader. If nothing else, intellectual practices of argument that are contextually attentive can enable each of the contributors to this volume to sharpen their speaking *to*, rather than *past*, each other.

Even if critique begins somewhere and is not indeterminately free from its own situational context, the reason there is considerable suspicion in contemporary theorizing of modern epistemological traditions' talk of "truth" and "truth-telling" is because of the ways in which appeals to "reason" can evade questions about their contingency by assuming foundations on metaphysical props. Forms of idealism, even when they assert themselves to be forms of realism, can sidestep appropriate reflection on the conditions of our learning, and thereby become inattentive to the ways in which reason's perspective can be regulated by interests, desires, and partiality. Accordingly, Adorno warns of "a subjectivity that is ignorant of itself."[15] In this regard, it is important to ask in what ways, if any, "natural theology" can succumb to a circumvention of our historicity, our conditionedness. In popular forms

13. Porter, "Tradition of Civility," 31.
14. Porter, "Tradition of Civility," 43.
15. In Adorno and Horkheimer, *Towards a New Manifesto* 6.

of moral reasoning, something called "nature" is frequently appealed to as a regulating authority for practical reasoning without consensus on what "nature" is, what it is that is morally authoritative, or why appeal to whatever it is and is meant to be produces disagreement as much as shared conclusions. Moreover, there is invariably little awareness here of the fact that the conclusions reached from "nature" as source for making moral judgments tend to reflect the values and assumptions of the one making the appeal. Barth, for his part, was noticeably wary of self-projective appeals to the "natural orders of creation," and he discovered just such conceptualizing in Emil Brunner's *Divine Imperative*. A case from the "natural orders of creation" could well be made for a totalitarian political sovereignty, imperialistic nationalism, the naturalness of aggression and antagonism, and so on. "Language," Nicholas Lash argues, "is an instrument of power."[16]

Without further detailed and substantive interaction, the act of responding to each other can at least encourage accountability to read texts well. Even among those of us whose level of education suggests we should know better, there can be a distinctly cavalier use of texts; interrogating these progresses the clarification and purification of the conversation, even if that is as far as some intellectual conversations can and do progress. To be somewhat pedantic for a moment with Moser, this is not well spoken of as reading with generosity, as if there is a legitimate option to read inhospitably that is here not being selected. An uncharitable reading involves an imposition upon the text that refuses to allow it to speak and be heard in its concrete particularity. This, though, is unfitting to be a *rationally ordered* reading. But this attentiveness is not generous or charitable as such since it does not begin from a fully enclosed position that moves out of itself to the other by *permitting* that other to speak in the moment. As Rowan Williams argues, "We are not in control of the otherness of others; we—whatever our own proper confidence and authority—must learn 'hesitation.'"[17]

With regard to encouraging responsible reading, Moser's suggestion that Barth reductively *dismisses* natural theology requires being directed back especially to the argument constructed in Barth's CD IV/3.1 on "the little lights" of creation. Additionally, Moser's confusion over what talk of the "axiomatic" is doing in Barth's *dogmatic theology*—it is an articulation of the theo-logic of the *ordo essendi* as a self-justificatory assertion within the *ordo cogniscendi* (order of knowing)—needs a more patient reading of the text. The same recommendation is also appropriate for Moser's concern that

16. Lash, *Easter in Ordinary*, 13.
17. Williams, "Teaching the Truth," 37.

Barth is unable to provide conditions for the iconoclastic "testing for the real God." Pinsent asks about "Christian art and architecture" as if this identifies substantive disagreement with Barth. Referring to the theo-logic of Barth's talk of the "secular parables of truth" and the later development of the theme of "the little lights" of creation addresses this. Pinsent's claim appears to be connected to a criticism of the *sola scriptura* that works only if the principle directs diverse Protestant traditions to use Scripture only/alone/solely, and fails to work when that principle functions instead to appeal to the regulative authoritativeness of the Scriptures, through which God's graciousness is understood to refer *everything* to the status of creatureliness. Although I am appropriately sensitive to any accusation that my critical reading of (and even perception of) Barth's claims is misleadingly subtle, conceptually elusive, and imprecise given at least three of the sets of responses to it (Moser's, Taliaferro's, and Pinsent's), I would at this point suggest that these misinterpretations require little further comment.

On another matter of detail, McGrath claims that "Barth's views on natural theology are expressed most sharply in his 1934 debate with Emil Brunner." Certainly, it is a good place to observe that while Barth is indeed fully aware that the Reformed tradition is itself not homogeneous, his own theological improvisation on that tradition provokes him to accuse the likes of John Calvin of not being consistent on the matter with other elements of his theology. Whether or not Barth is being disingenuous here is not my concern (after all, I have not been providing an advocacy for his perspective necessarily). Nonetheless, it is precisely because of this reading of the central concerns of the early Reformed tradition that Barth asserts that it is, or should be, hostile to "natural theology." In many places, especially in the small-print sections of the *Church Dogmatics*, he explains where and why he regards Protestant scholasticism as being unable to move in this theological direction. On the other hand, the rather occasionalistic type of actualistic-sounding rhetoric that Barth tends to deploy against Brunner can be easily misconstrued. His critique takes on a different rhetorical hue once he develops his Christo-ontology of election. My encouragement to McGrath, then, is to move from the Barth of the *Nein!* to that of *CD* II/2, III/1, and IV/3.1. Likewise, the articulation of several of these theological texts provides the resource for addressing Pinsent's concern with apparent Barthian bridge-removals.[18] Here the inclusivist or participatory framework for the discussion of the dialectic (from God to world *and* world to God) functions christologically.

---

18. The bridge metaphor, however, is distinctly limited: if not properly qualified, it can suggest an ontological binarity. On this, see Williams, *On Christian Theology*, chap. 8.

To return to the broader parameters of the topic of natural theology, it can be conceived of as a form of rational activity needing to become aware of its historicity and intellectual contingency. Through this ascetic configuration, it may well be able to do at least three things entailing that it cannot be reduced to either idolatry or a simple intellectual idleness.

First, natural theology can continue to reason about the intelligibility of speaking about the existence of things in terms of createdness and absolute dependency. As Hans Schwarz observes, "In recent times fewer and fewer people seem to feel compelled to think the idea of God, because for an increasing number of people the world makes good sense without ever thinking of God."[19]

Second, the flip side of this is what philosophical rhetoric sometimes refers to as "defeating the defeaters" (the term, however, rhetorically implies that knowledge processes of curiosity and vulnerable dialectics of argument should be configured, instead, as an antagonistic contest). Natural theology perennially has to interrogate the warrants behind strong claims regarding the bruteness of existence. A claim about "sheer thereness" would be no less a learned commitment of the intellectual imagination than a theistic one.[20] Even if "all" people "know God 'naturally,'" that is, by virtue of their nature as creatures, "they do not always recognize" God. So argues de Lubac. "A thousand obstacles, some inward, some external, hinder that recognition."[21] At this point, natural theology can expose what Paul Ricoeur calls "the unintelligibility of the trivial" that comes from "a sham clarity" and thereby removes the obstacles that hinder the asking of the question of contingency (why anything rather than nothing?).[22]

Third, natural theology can reconfigure the kinds of juxtaposing of faith and reason that all too neatly excuse the "faithful" from exercising rational responsibility. After all, it is "wishful thinking," Herbert McCabe argues, that allows "our desires to influence you so that you think a bad argument is a good one."[23] Faith is not a way of knowing that is contextually innocent, devoid of the conditioning by histories of perspectives and contingent forms of learning. The kind of faith that makes a virtue out of evacuating itself of rational reflection comes suspiciously close to suggesting that the object or content of that faith is nothing (not no-thing, as in the apophatic traditions), that faith has nothing to talk about, and that such content demands no responsibility for questioning its coherence, consistency, or integrity. Honest

19. Schwarz, *The God Who Is*, 43.
20. Citation from Arendt, *Life of the Mind*, 87.
21. De Lubac, *Discovery of God*, 75.
22. Ricoeur, "Religion, Atheism, and Faith," 74.
23. McCabe, *Faith within Reason*, 16.

rational reflection requires a critique of the self-securing illusion that shapes religion into offering "consolation" or "shelter," and that idolatrously mitigates the "*ascesis* of desire" within religion's prophetic mode as if it is not to be directed toward the activity of "love of creation."[24]

Natural theology, then, can matter when it is responsible for keeping open the question of the contingency of materiality and the curiosity it provokes for truthful reflection without sheltering within the arbitrary conceptual control provided by individuated intuition, private feeling, and the incurious forms of apologetic sophistry. Perhaps this process can be spoken of, with Pinsent, in terms of "catholicity," at least when that term is appropriately attentive to the rational activity of "finite, embodied and fragile creatures," so that it is purged of the self-securing walling in of ecclesial sovereignty.[25] "Because of the nature of what we speak of, God's liberty, we do not come to an end."[26]

24. Ricoeur, "Religion, Atheism, and Faith," 60, 86, 97.

25. Citation from Benhabib, *Situating the Self*, 5. The image of walled but waning sovereignty is taken from Brown, *Walled States, Waning Sovereignty*.

26. Williams, "Teaching the Truth," 35.

Conclusion

JAMES K. DEW JR. AND RONNIE P. CAMPBELL JR.

At the end of such books as this one, readers are often left asking: "What next?" In what follows, we aim to give the reader just that. Rather than summarizing each of the views and considering places of convergence and divergence, we offer the reader two challenges: the challenge from faith and reason, and the challenge from Christian theology and meaning. These challenges are not meant to be exhaustive, nor are they meant to win the reader to one way or another. Rather, each challenge is presented because it is relevant to the debate on natural theology, giving the reader additional pressure points for further study as she wrestles through her own understanding of natural theology. Shall we now consider each of these in order?

The Challenge from Faith and Reason

In many ways, this debate on natural theology shares affinities with the debate on the relationship between faith and reason. Those familiar with the debate may recall that one of the central issues is the extent of a human being's ability to reason, especially when considering the noetic effects of sin. Right away, we must ask ourselves: to what extent has sin affected our ability to reason about God, his existence, and the divine nature? Moreover, to what extent can we know these things apart from divine self-disclosure and supernatural intervention? For some, the answer is obvious—it is impossible! Sin has too radically impaired our ability to reason, shattering all hope of knowing the truth about God apart from divine self-disclosure and the supernatural working of God in the person's life. Not only has our ability to reason been impaired, but also

257

our hearts and minds have been darkened, and we do not seek the things of God. Some who fall into this camp believe that once God has worked supernaturally in the believer's life, regenerating the person, her ability to reason properly about God has been restored. From within faith, she can then reason and apprehend those truths God has disclosed about his existence, nature, and interactions in the world. From within faith, we then begin to see the world in fresh and new ways. Others, however, are more pessimistic about the extent of our reasoning abilities, even after regeneration. This latter view, which is known as fideism, takes faith as primarily relational and not rational.

On the flip side of the debate between faith and reason, it is believed that although human beings are fallen, they can use their cognitive faculties to reason toward truth and even, perhaps, toward God—though with limitations. Human beings continue to fall prey to the noetic effects of sin. Still, through some mechanism like prevenient grace, God provides the individual with the capacity to believe and trust in him despite their fallenness. As Craig A. Boyd puts it, "God has endowed human beings with rational capacities, and these capacities do not, and cannot, by themselves offer us salvation."[1] Yet, Boyd and others who hold this view believe that sin, though an important theological category, is not primary. Instead, sin is parasitic on the more fundamental category of "nature." In Boyd's view, which he calls the "synthesis view," though sin has corrupted nature and though the effects of sin have damaged it, nature retains continuity with the original state, which "reflects the goodness of God."[2] Such is the case with our ability to reason, which those who hold to this view take to be grounded in the *imago Dei*. Though tainted by sin, our cognitive faculties and ability to reason remain intact.

It takes little effort to see how relevant the debate on faith and reason is to our discussion in this volume on natural theology. Someone who ascribes to fideism would render the task of natural theology impossible. Why is that? It is because sin has affected our ability to reason, especially to know and understand God's nature, existence, and workings apart from special revelation and regeneration. Even within faith, natural theology would have little or no benefit. For others, they recognize that sin impairs our ability to know and understand the things of God; yet, within faith and due to regeneration, the believer's ability to reason has been restored, and thus natural theology may be of some benefit. Perhaps it serves to confirm the truths of faith or even to provide a deeper understanding of God's relationship to the world he created. Finally, for those who hold a view closely aligned with Boyd's,

1. Boyd, "Synthesis of Reason and Faith," 133.
2. Boyd, "Synthesis of Reason and Faith," 135.

natural theology may be of great value. Though sin has affected our ability to reason, and though none can come to God apart from grace, arguments for God's existence may tell us real truths about the nature of God and our world, and they may serve as pointers to the Creator.

The Challenge from Christian Theology and Meaning

We have already touched on the theological category of sin and its effect on our ability to reason about God, and we briefly considered the doctrine of *imago Dei*. We could consider other such theological topics as they bear on natural theology. But in this section, we aim to do something more interesting. In what follows, we seek to explore the intersection between Christian theology, natural theology, and meaning. We will do this by wrestling through the following questions: (1) What value does natural theology have in distinguishing Christian theism from other theistic systems? (2) What value does natural theology have in distinguishing beliefs from within Christian theism? (3) What value does natural theology have in finding significance and meaning in our world? Our purpose here is not to answer one way or another but to provide readers with a way forward as they think and meditate on these questions.

Before we can begin to explore these questions, we must first consider Richard Swinburne's distinction between what he calls "bare" natural theology (BNT) and "ramified" natural theology (RNT). On the one hand, BNT is the attempt at using natural theology to arrive at a generic concept of God, perhaps a God who is Creator, all-powerful, the cause of the universe, an intelligent designer, and a moral agent—the bare bones of what most theists agree on when they think about the concept of God. On the other hand, RNT is a "natural extension" of BNT, seeking to take the natural theologian beyond a generic idea of deity to unique claims of a particular religious system.[3]

Regarding the first question, various attempts have been made to distinguish Christianity from other theistic or religious systems using RNT. Often such attempts zero in on the Bible's miracle claims, Jesus's claim to be divine, or the resurrection. Swinburne's book *Was Jesus God?* is a prime example of such an attempt. In this work, Swinburne wrestles with the question If God exists, why should we suppose that this God is the Christian God? His main aim is to show that if God exists, then those unique doctrines within Christianity, such as the incarnation, the atonement, the resurrection, the church, and the Bible, "are very probably true."[4]

3. Swinburne, "Natural Theology," 533.
4. Swinburne, *Was Jesus God?*, 1.

Others, such as N. T. Wright, Gary Habermas, Mike Licona, William Lane Craig, and Tim and Lydia McGrew focus their efforts on defending miracles and the resurrection of Jesus.[5] For instance, Wright, in his Gifford Lectures, considers his own work as a biblical scholar and historian and labels it an attempt at natural theology. In his lectures, Wright raises an interesting question. Often the Bible is excluded in attempts at natural theology, but why should that be the case? On this, Wright continues:

> But whatever meaning we give to "natural theology" itself, and however we evaluate it, there is something strange in excluding the Bible from "nature." The Bible was, after all, written and edited within the world of space and time, by a large number of individuals situated in "natural" communities and environments. . . . The Bible, after all, purports to offer not just "spiritual" or "theological" teaching but [also] to describe events within the "natural" world, not least the public career of Jesus of Nazareth, a first-century Jew who lived and died within the "natural" course of world history. . . . And this means investigating the actual historical world of Jesus of Nazareth, a turbulent and much-studied world about which real knowledge is available, and which, when studied carefully, includes core beliefs about the overlap of God's world and the human world ("heaven" and "earth") and the regular interplay of the Age to Come with the Present Age. These contextualise Jesus and his kingdom-proclamation in ways remarkably unfamiliar in "historical Jesus" studies through the nineteenth and twentieth centuries.[6]

Here we quote Wright at length, but he raises an important question as it relates to the intersection of Christian theology and natural theology, especially as it bears on arguing for the distinctive features of Christianity against other religious and nonreligious systems: To what extent should we make such a divide between general and special revelation? After all, as Wright has argued, the Bible itself, then, is a book that is not merely spiritual or theological in nature, but also represents what Christians believe to be events that are historical, taking place in real space and time—the "natural world," as Wright puts it.

Finally, regarding this first question, David Baggett and Ronnie Campbell have suggested that certain arguments for God, such as the moral argument, should be marshaled by Christians to point toward a conception of God that is "most worthy of worship, and it is this conception of God, Christians should suggest, who actually exists." On this, they continue, "To the

---

5. Wright, *Resurrection of the Son of God*; Habermas, *Risen Jesus and Future Hope*; Licona, *Resurrection of Jesus*; Craig, *Son Rises*; T. McGrew and L. McGrew, "Argument from Miracles."
6. Wright, *History and Eschatology*, xi–xii.

extent, then, that moral arguments point to a God who is nothing less than omnibenevolent and essentially loving, the evidence points beyond theologies contained in other religions and among Christians themselves that paint God as less than perfectly loving."[7]

What of the second question? Some, like Travis Dumsday, Baggett and Campbell, and others, have argued that RNT not only distinguishes Christianity from other religions but also makes important headway in inner-Christian dialogue.[8] Dumsday believes that RNT is unavoidable and should be practiced by Christians. He provides several examples where this is the case, such as debates on infant baptism versus believer's baptism, or debates on double predestination. Initially, such attempts appeal to Scripture, but such theological issues quickly resort to unavoidable philosophical concerns. Take, for example, double predestination. The problem is not merely debated on scriptural grounds but also includes such issues as God's sovereignty on the one hand and God's justice on the other. For those who argue that such debates should be decided solely by Scripture, Dumsday believes such a claim "falters before some of the broader debates between denominations, such as that over *sola scriptura*."[9] After all, Catholic and Eastern Orthodox theologians and apologists appeal to tradition and the Church as an "authoritative source of doctrine" and believe that there is a genuine "need for a stable, institutional interpreter of Scripture, one which must be guided by God, which in turn points to the need for an authoritative visible Church."[10] Not only does RNT bear on such doctrinal issues, but it also pertains to certain religiously significant supernatural phenomena. According to Dumsday, a range of supernatural phenomena is shared under the umbrella of what C. S. Lewis called "mere Christianity," yet there are distinctive supernatural phenomena often shared by Christians across some denominations (e.g., visions of Jesus and Mary; miracles involving icons, relics, and blessed objects; the real presence in the Eucharist; speaking in tongues) that are dismissed or not shared by others. Dumsday believes that RNT provides a way for settling such disputes. Take, for example, reports of weeping icons. Are such events indicative of supernatural interaction in the world, or can we account for such phenomena through naturalistic explanations? As Dumsday reminds us, "This is not a question that can be answered *a priori* but requires actually delving into the data. And relevance of

---

7. Baggett and Campbell, "Omnibenevolence," 346.
8. Dumsday, "Ramified Natural Theology"; Baggett and Campbell, "Omnibenevolence," 346–52.
9. Dumsday, "Ramified Natural Theology," 330.
10. Dumsday, "Ramified Natural Theology," 330–31.

the data for ramified natural theology indicates clearly the import of such an examination."[11]

Finally, we turn to our last question on the intersection between natural theology, Christian theology, and meaning. Here we urge our reader to consider the nature of the kinds of arguments often presented in natural theology: cosmological, teleological, and moral. Often, these arguments are employed to argue for God's existence. In this volume, we have debated whether that is a viable possibility and what value such attempts have for the believer. But perhaps there is another reason why one might consider the import of natural theology—namely, these arguments tell us or reaffirm something of meaning or significance about the nature of the world itself and God's relationship to it. Here we cannot explore the depth of each of these argument families, but we will only briefly make some suggestions. Take, for example, cosmological arguments: they aim to show that there is an ultimate cause or explanation behind the universe. But certain cosmological arguments point to something more profound—namely, that the universe itself (and all reality that is not God) is radically *contingent*. This further implies that everything within the universe is also radically contingent, owing their existence to that ultimate cause. Likewise, moral arguments go beyond arguing for God's existence to showing that a deeply moral thread runs throughout creation. In other words, the structure of morality in the world is a fundamental feature of reality: *we live in a moral universe*.

Final Reflection

By now, you have read each view. You have seen nuances of each position and witnessed each view's strengths and weaknesses through the back-and-forth of dialogue. Moreover, you have been challenged to consider additional areas that intersect with natural theology. We invite you to continue thinking deeply about this critical debate.

Like all multiview works, this book includes serious dialogue and sometimes deep disagreements. But disagreements should not cause us to dismiss the importance of such a debate, nor should such disagreements keep us from settling into a position. Such disputes should force us to dig deep and wrestle with the issue at hand, even if this means more study. We hope this book did that for you. Our desire for this book is that it becomes a catalyst for further research, leading the reader into a greater understanding and worship of the one true God.

11. Dumsday, "Ramified Natural Theology," 334–35.

Bibliography

Adams, Edward. "Calvin's View of Natural Knowledge of God." *International Journal of Systematic Theology* 3, no. 3 (2001): 280–92.

Adams, Marilyn McCord. *Horrendous Evils and the Goodness of God*. Ithaca, NY: Cornell University Press, 1999.

Adorno, Theodor, and Max Horkheimer. *Towards a New Manifesto*. Translated by Rodney Livingstone. London: Verso, 2011.

Agamben, Giorgio. *Taste*. Translated by Cooper Francis. New York: Seagull Books, 2017.

Alston, William P. "Mysticism and Perceptual Awareness of God." In *The Blackwell Guide to the Philosophy of Religion*, edited by William E. Mann, 198–219. Oxford: Blackwell, 2005.

———. *Perceiving God: The Epistemology of Religious Experience*. Ithaca, NY: Cornell University Press, 1991.

Anderson, Douglas. "The Evolution of Peirce's Concept of Abduction." *Transactions of the Charles S. Peirce Society* 22, no. 2 (1986): 145–64.

Anselm. *Anselm of Canterbury: The Major Works*. Edited by Brian Davies and G. R. Evans. New York: Oxford University Press, 2008.

Apel, Karl-Otto, and Matthias Kettner, eds. *Die eine Vernunft und die vielen Rationalitäten*. Frankfurt am Main: Suhrkamp, 1996.

Aquinas, Thomas. *Summa contra Gentiles*. Translated by the English Dominican Fathers. New York: Benziger Brothers, 1924.

———. *The Summa Theologiae*. Translated by Fathers of the English Dominican Province. 3 vols. New York: Benziger Brothers, 1948.

Arendt, Hannah. *The Life of the Mind*. New York: Harcourt Brace Jovanovich, 1971.

Aristotle. *Metaphysics*. Translated by W. D. Ross. In vol. 2 of *The Complete Works of Aristotle: The Revised Oxford Translation*, edited by Jonathan Barnes, 1552–728. Princeton: Princeton University Press, 1984.

Athanasius. *De incarnatione. St. Athanasius: On the Incarnation (1885)*. Edited by Archibald Robertson. Kessinger's Legacy Reprints. Whitefish, MT: Kessinger, 2010.

Augustine of Hippo. *Augustine: Homilies on the Gospel of John, Homilies on the First Epistle of John, Soliloquies*. Edited by Philip Schaff. Translated by John Gibb and James Innes. Peabody, MA: Hendrickson, 1995.

———. *City of God*. Edited by Vernon Bourke. Translated by Gerald G. Walsh et al. New York: Doubleday, 1958.

———. *Confessions*. Translated by Henry Chadwick. Oxford: Oxford University Press, 1991.

———. *The First Catechetical Instruction*. Translated by Joseph P. Christopher. Ancient Christian Writers 2. Westminster, MD: Newman, 1946.

Baggett, David, and Ronnie Campbell. "Omnibenevolence, Moral Apologetics, and Doubly Ramified Natural Theology." *Philosophia Christi* 15, no. 2 (2013): 337–52.

Baillie, John, ed. *Natural Theology, Comprising "Nature and Grace" by Emil Brunner and the Reply "No!" by Karl Barth*. Translated by Peter Fraenkel. London: Centenary, 1946.

Barr, James. *Biblical Faith and Natural Theology*. Oxford: Clarendon, 1993.

Barrett, Anthony J., Jr. *Sacrifice and Prophecy in Turkana Cosmology*. Nairobi: Pauline Publications Africa, 1998.

———. *Turkana–English Dictionary*. London: Macmillan Education, 1990.

Barrett, Justin L. *Born Believers: The Science of Children's Religious Belief*. New York: Free Press, 2012.

———. *Why Would Anyone Believe in God?* Lanham, MD: AltaMira, 2004.

Barth, Christoph. *God with Us: A Theological Introduction to the Old Testament*. Grand Rapids: Eerdmans, 1991.

Barth, Karl. *Anselm: Fides quaerens intellectum: Anselm's Proof of the Existence of God in the Context of His Theological Scheme*. Translated from 2nd ed. by Ian W. Robertson. London: SCM, 1960.

———. *The Christian Life; Church Dogmatics IV,4 Lecture Fragments*. Translated by Geoffrey W. Bromiley. Edinburgh: T&T Clark, 1981.

———. *Church Dogmatics [CD]*. Edited and translated by Thomas F. Torrance and Geoffrey W. Bromiley. 14 volumes. Edinburgh: T&T Clark, 1956–75.

———. *Dogmatics in Outline*. Translated by G. T. Thomson. London: SCM, 1949.

———. *The Epistle to the Romans*. Translated from 6th ed. by Edwyn C. Hoskyns. Oxford: Oxford University Press, 1968.

———. *Evangelical Theology: An Introduction*. Translated by Grover Foley. London: Collins, 1963.

————. "The First Commandment as an Axiom of Theology." In *The Way of Theology in Karl Barth: Essays and Comments*, edited by H. Martin Rumscheidt, 63–78. Allison Park, PA: Pickwick, 1986.

————. *The Göttingen Dogmatics: Instruction in the Christian Religion*. Vol. 1. Translated by Geoffrey W. Bromiley. Grand Rapids: Eerdmans, 1990.

————. *How I Changed My Mind*. Edited by John Godsey. Edinburgh: Saint Andrew, 1969.

————. *The Knowledge of God and the Service of God according to the Teaching of the Reformation: Recalling the Scottish Confession of 1560*. Translated by J. L. M. Haire and Ian Henderson. The Gifford Lectures, University of Aberdeen, 1937–38. London: Hodder & Stoughton, 1938.

————. *Predigten 1914*. Edited by Ursula Fähler and Jochen Fähler. Zurich: Theologischer Verlag, 1974.

————. *Protestant Theology in the Nineteenth Century: Its Background and History*. Translated by Brian Cozens and John Bowden. London: SCM, 1959.

————. *A Shorter Commentary on Romans*. Translated by D. H. van Daalen. Aldershot, UK; Burlington, VT: Ashgate, 2007.

————. *Wolfgang Amadeus Mozart*. Translated by C. K. Pott. Grand Rapids: Eerdmans, 1986.

Bauerschmidt, Frederick Christian. *Thomas Aquinas: Faith, Reason, and Following Christ*. Oxford: Oxford University Press, 2015.

Belcher, Richard P. *Finding Favour in the Sight of God: A Theology of Wisdom Literature*. Downers Grove, IL: InterVarsity, 2018.

Benhabib, Seyla. *Situating the Self: Gender, Community and Postmodernism in Contemporary Ethics*. Cambridge: Polity, 1992.

Benjamin, Walter. *Illuminations: Essays and Reflections*. Translated by Leon Wieseltier. New York: Schocken Books, 1968.

Berman, Harold J. *Law and Revolution: The Formation of the Western Legal Tradition*. Cambridge, MA: Harvard University Press, 1983.

Bishop, John. "Evidence." In *The Routledge Companion to Theism*, edited by Charles Taliaferro, Victoria S. Harrison, and Stewart Goetz, 161–87. New York: Routledge, 2013.

Blair, Ann, and Kaspar von Greyerz, eds. *Physico-Theology: Religion and Science in Europe, 1650–1750*. Baltimore: Johns Hopkins University Press, 2020.

Blumenberg, Hans. *Die Lesbarkeit der Welt*. Frankfurt: Suhrkamp, 1986.

Bonaventure. *The Journey of the Mind to God*. Edited by Stephen F. Brown. Translated by Philotheus Boehner, OFM. Hackett Classics. Indianapolis: Hackett, 1993.

Bork, Kennard B. "Natural Theology in the Eighteenth Century, as Exemplified in the Writings of Élie Bertrand (1713–1797), a Swiss Naturalist and Protestant Pastor." *Geological Society, London, Special Publications* 310 (2009): 277–88.

Boyd, Craig A. "The Synthesis of Reason and Faith." In *Faith and Reason: Three Views*, edited by Steve Wilkens, 131–74. Downers Grove, IL: InterVarsity, 2014.

Boyle, Robert. "Of the Study of the Book of Nature." In vol. 13 of *The Works of Robert Boyle*, edited by M. Hunter and E. B. Davis, 147–72. 14 vols. London: Pickering & Chatto, 1999–2000.

Bradley, W. L., and P. T. Forsyth. *The Man and His Work*. London: Independent Press, 1952.

Bradshaw, David, and Richard Swinburne, eds. *Natural Theology in the Eastern Orthodox Tradition*. St. Paul: Iota, 2020.

Brooke, John Hedley. "Like Minds: The God of Hugh Miller." In *Hugh Miller and the Controversies of Victorian Science*, edited by Michael Shortland, 171–86. Oxford: Clarendon, 1996.

———. "Science and the Fortunes of Natural Theology: Some Historical Perspectives." *Zygon* 24 (1989): 3–22.

Brown, Wendy. *Walled States, Waning Sovereignty*. New York: Zone Books, 2014.

Brunner, Emil. *The Christian Doctrine of the Church, Faith, and the Consummation*. Translated by David Cairns. Vol. 3 of *Dogmatics*. London: Lutterworth, 1962.

———. "The New Barth: Observations on Karl Barth's *Doctrine of Man*." *Scottish Journal of Theology* 4 (1951): 123–35.

———. "The Risen and Exalted Lord." In *The Christian Doctrine of Creation and Redemption*, translated by Olive Wyon, 363–78. Vol. 2 of *Dogmatics*. Philadelphia: Westminster, 1952.

Buckley, Michael J. *At the Origins of Modern Atheism*. New Haven: Yale University Press, 1987.

Bujanda, J. M. de. "L'influence de Sebond en Espagne au XVIᵉ siècle." *Renaissance and Reformation* 10, no. 2 (1974): 78–84.

Bulgakov, Sergius. *The Bride of the Lamb*. Translated by Boris Jakim. Edinburgh: T&T Clark, 2002.

Burrell, David. *Faith and Freedom: An Interfaith Perspective*. Oxford: Blackwell, 2004.

Busch, Eberhard. *The Great Passion: An Introduction to Karl Barth's Theology*. Translated by Geoffrey W. Bromiley. Grand Rapids: Eerdmans, 2004.

Butler, Joseph. *The Analogy of Religion*. Edited by David McNaughton. Oxford: Oxford University Press, 2021.

Caldecott, Stratford. *Beauty for Truth's Sake: On the Re-enchantment of Education*. Grand Rapids: Brazos, 2009.

Calvin, John. *Institutes of the Christian Religion*. Edited by John T. McNeill. Translated by Ford Lewis Battles. 2 vols. Philadelphia: Westminster, 1960.

Campbell, Douglas A. "Natural Theology in Paul? Reading Romans 1.19–20." *International Journal of Systematic Theology* 1 (1999): 231–52.

Catherine of Siena. *The Dialogue of St. Catherine of Siena: A Conversation with God on Living Your Spiritual Life to the Fullest*. Abridged ed. Charlotte: Tan Books, 1991.

Cicero. *The Nature of the Gods*. Translated by P. G. Walsh. Oxford World's Classics. Oxford: Oxford University Press, 2008.

Clines, David J. A. *Job 38–42*. Word Biblical Commentary. Nashville: Nelson, 2011.

Cobb, John B. *A Christian Natural Theology: Based on the Thought of Alfred North Whitehead*. Philadelphia: Westminster, 1965.

Colish, Marcia. "The Sentence Collection and the Education of Professional Theologians in the Twelfth Century." In *The Intellectual Climate of the Early University*, edited by N. van Deusen, 1–26. Kalamazoo: Western Michigan University, 1997.

Collins, John J. "The Biblical Precedent for Natural Theology." *Journal of the American Academy of Religion* 45, no. 1, Supplement B (1977): 35–67.

———. "Natural Theology and Biblical Tradition: The Case of Hellenistic Judaism." *Catholic Biblical Quarterly* 60 (1998): 1–15.

Collins, Robin. "Naturalism." In *The Routledge Companion to Theism*, edited by Charles Taliaferro, Victoria S. Harrison, and Stewart Goetz, 182–95. New York: Routledge, 2013.

Cone, James H. *God of the Oppressed*. London: SPCK, 1977.

Cottingham, John. "Transcending Science: Humane Models of Religious Understanding." In *New Models of Religious Understanding*, edited by Fiona Ellis, 23–41. Oxford: Oxford University Press, 2018.

Couenhoven, Jesse. *Stricken by Sin, Cured by Christ: Agency, Necessity, and Culpability in Augustinian Theology*. New York: Oxford University Press, 2013.

Craig, William Lane. *The Son Rises: The Historical Evidence for the Resurrection of Jesus*. 1981. Reprint, Eugene, OR: Wipf & Stock, 2001.

Craig, William Lane, and James Porter Moreland, eds. *The Blackwell Companion to Natural Theology*. Malden, MA: Wiley-Blackwell, 2009.

Cullen, Christopher M. *Bonaventure*. Oxford: Oxford University Press, 2006.

Dalferth, Ingolf. *Theology and Philosophy*. Oxford: Blackwell, 1988.

Davis, Caroline. *The Evidential Force of Religious Experience*. Oxford: Clarendon, 1989.

Davis, Philip J., and Reuben Hersh. *The Mathematical Experience*. New ed. New York: Penguin Books, 1990.

Davis, Stephen T. *God, Reason and Theistic Proofs*. Grand Rapids: Eerdmans, 1997.

Davis, William H. *Peirce's Epistemology*. The Hague: Nijhoff, 1972.

Dear, Peter. "Reason and Common Culture in Early Modern Natural Philosophy: Variations on an Epistemic Theme." In *Conflicting Values of Inquiry: Ideologies of Epistemology in Early Modern Europe*, edited by Tamás Demeter, Kathryn Murphy, and Claus Zittel, 10–38. Leiden: Brill, 2014.

de Bolla, Peter. *Art Matters*. Cambridge, MA: Harvard University Press, 2001.

de Cruz, Helen. *A Natural History of Natural Theology: The Cognitive Science of Theology and Philosophy of Religion*. Cambridge, MA: MIT Press, 2015.

de Cruz, Helen, and Johan de Smedt. "Intuitions and Arguments: Cognitive Foundations of Argumentation in Natural Theology." *European Journal for Philosophy of Religion* 9, no. 2 (2017): 57–82.

de Lubac, Henri. *The Discovery of God*. Translated by Alexander Dru. Edinburgh: T&T Clark, 1960.

Denzinger, Henry. *The Sources of Catholic Dogma*. Fitzwilliam, NH: Loreto Publications, 2002.

de Puig, Jaume. *La filosofia de Ramon Sibiuda*. Barcelona: Institut d'Estudis Catalans, 1997.

Descartes, René. *Discourse on Method and Related Writings*. Translated by Desmond M. Clarke. New York: Penguin Books, 2003.

Dihle, Albrecht. "Die Theologia tripertita bei Augustin." In *Geschichte—Tradition—Reflexion: Festschrift für Martin Hengel zum 70. Geburtstag*, edited by Hubert Cancik, 183–202. Tübingen: Mohr Siebeck, 1996.

Dive, Bernard. *John Henry Newman and the Imagination*. London: Bloomsbury T&T Clark, 2018.

Donaldson, James, and Alexander Roberts, eds. *The Apostolic Fathers with Justin Martyr and Irenaeus*. Vol. 1 of *Ante-Nicene Christian Library: Translations of the Writings of the Fathers down to A.D. 325*. Edinburgh: T&T Clark, 1867.

Dulles, Avery. *A History of Apologetics*. 2nd ed. San Francisco: Ignatius, 2005.

———. "Reason, Philosophy, and the Grounding of Faith: A Reflection on 'Fides et Ratio.'" *International Philosophical Quarterly* 40, no. 4 (2000): 479–90.

Dumsday, Travis. "Ramified Natural Theology in the Context of Interdenominational Debate." *Philosophia Christi* 15, no. 2 (2013): 329–36.

Eagleton, Terry. *The Ideology of the Aesthetic*. Oxford: Blackwell, 1990.

———. *Reason, Faith, and Revolution: Reflections on the God Debate*. New Haven: Yale University Press, 2009.

Ebrahim, Azadegan. "Divine Hiddenness and Human Sin: The Noetic Effect of Sin." *Journal of Reformed Theology* 7, no. 1 (2013): 69–90.

Edwards, Jonathan. *Works*. 26 vols. New Haven: Yale University Press, 1977–2009.

Ellis, Fiona. *God, Nature, and Value*. Oxford: Oxford University Press, 2014.

Feingold, Lawrence. *The Natural Desire to See God according to St. Thomas and His Interpreters*. Rome: Apollinare studi, 2001.

Fergusson, David. "Types of Natural Theology." In *The Evolution of Rationality: Interdisciplinary Essays in Honor of J. Wentzel van Huyssteen*, edited by F. Le Ron Schults, 380–93. Grand Rapids: Eerdmans, 2007.

Fletcher, Patrick J. "Newman and Natural Theology." *Newman Studies Journal* 5, no. 2 (2008): 26–42.

Flórez, Jorge Alejandro. "Peirce's Theory of the Origin of Abduction in Aristotle." *Transactions of the Charles S. Peirce Society* 50, no. 2 (2014): 265–80.

Forbes, Robert J. *Short History of the Art of Distillation from the Beginnings up to the Death of Cellier Blumenthal.* 1948. Reprint, Leiden: Brill, 1970.

Ford, David F. *Christian Wisdom: Desiring God and Learning in Love.* Cambridge: Cambridge University Press, 2007.

Forsyth, P.T. *The Holy Father and the Living Christ.* London: Hodder & Stoughton, 1897.

———. *The Person and Place of Jesus Christ.* London: Independent Press, 1909.

———. *The Principle of Authority.* London: Hodder & Stoughton, 1912.

———. "Revelation and the Person of Christ." In *Faith and Criticism: Essays by Congregationalists,* 95–144. London: Sampson Low Marston, 1893.

Frei, Hans. "Eberhard Busch's Biography of Karl Barth." In *Karl Barth in Re-View,* edited by H. Martin Rumscheidt, 95–116. Pittsburgh: Pickwick, 1981.

———. *Types of Christian Theology.* New Haven: Yale University Press, 1992.

Führer, Marks L. "Albertus Magnus' Theory of Divine Illumination." In *Albertus Magnus: Zum Gedenken nach 800 Jahren: Neue Zugänge, Aspekte und Perspektiven,* edited by Walter Senner, 141–56. Berlin: de Gruyter, 2001.

Funkenstein, Amos. *Theology and the Scientific Imagination: From the Middle Ages to the Seventeenth Century.* Princeton: Princeton University Press, 1986.

Fyfe, Aileen. "Publishing and the Classics: Paley's Natural Theology and the Nineteenth-Century Scientific Canon." *Studies in the History and Philosophy of Science* 33 (2002): 433–55.

———. "The Reception of William Paley's *Natural Theology* in the University of Cambridge." *British Journal for the History of Science* 30 (1997): 321–35.

Gadamer, Hans-Georg. "What Is Truth?" Translated by Brice R. Wachterhauser. In *Hermeneutics and Truth,* edited by Brice R. Wachterhauser, 33–46. Evanston, IL: Northwestern University Press, 1994.

Gale, Richard M. *On the Nature and Existence of God.* Cambridge: Cambridge University Press, 1991.

Gales, Evan. "Naturalism and Physicalism." In *The Cambridge Companion to Atheism,* edited by Michael Martin, 118–34. Cambridge: Cambridge University Press, 2006.

Gärtner, Bertil. *The Areopagus Speech and Natural Revelation.* Uppsala: Almqvist & Wiksells, 1955.

Geivett, R. Douglas. "The Evidential Value of Religious Experience." In *The Rationality of Theism,* edited by Paul Copan and Paul K. Moser, 175–203. London: Routledge, 2003.

Gellman, Jerome. "Religious Experience." In *The Routledge Handbook of Contemporary Philosophy of Religion*, edited by Graham Oppy, 155–66. New York: Routledge, 2015.

Gerber, Judith. "Beyond Dualism: The Social Construction of Nature and the Natural and Social Construction of Human Beings." *Progress in Human Geography* 21, no. 1 (1997): 1–17.

Gill, Theodore A. "Barth and Mozart." *Theology Today* 43 (1986): 403–11.

Gillespie, Neal. *Charles Darwin and the Problem of Creation*. Chicago: University of Chicago Press, 1979.

Grabill, Stephen John. *Rediscovering the Natural Law in Reformed Theological Ethics*. Grand Rapids: Eerdmans, 2006.

Greenham, Paul. "Clarifying Divine Discourse in Early Modern Science: Divinity, Physico-Theology, and Divine Metaphysics in Isaac Newton's Chymistry." *The Seventeenth Century* 32, no. 2 (2017): 191–215.

Gregory, Brad S. *The Unintended Reformation: How a Religious Revolution Secularized Society*. 2012. Reprint, Cambridge, MA: Belknap, Harvard University Press, 2015.

Gregory I, Pope. *Epistola 76: Letter to Abbot Mellitus*. In vol. 77 of *Patrologia Latina*, edited by J.-P. Migne, 1215–16. https://sourcebooks.fordham.edu/source/601gregory1-lettertomellitus.asp.

Gunton, Colin E. *The Promise of Trinitarian Theology*. Edinburgh: T&T Clark, 1991.

———. "The Trinity, Natural Theology, and a Theology of Nature." In *The Trinity in a Pluralistic Age*, edited by Kevin Vanhoozer, 88–103. Grand Rapids: Eerdmans, 1997.

Guy, Alain. "La *Theologia naturalis* en son temps: Structure, portée, origines." In *Montaigne, Apologie de Raimond Sebond: De la theologia à la théologie*, edited by Claude Blum, 13–47. Paris: Honoré Champion, 1990.

Habermas, Gary R. *The Risen Jesus and Future Hope*. Lanham, MD: Rowman & Littlefield, 2003.

Habert, Mireille. *Montaigne traducteur de la Théologie naturelle: Plaisantes et sainctes imaginations*. Paris: Classiques Garnier, 2010.

Haines, David. *Natural Theology: A Biblical and Historical Introduction and Defense*. Oxford: Davenport, 2021.

Haldane, John. "Philosophy, the Restless Heart, and the Meaning of Theism." *Ratio* 19, no. 4 (2006): 421–40.

Harrison, Peter. "Physico-Theology and the Mixed Sciences: The Role of Theology in Early Modern Natural Philosophy." In *The Science of Nature in the Seventeenth Century*, edited by Peter Anstey and John Schuster, 165–83. Dordrecht: Springer, 2005.

———. "Supernatural Belief in a Secular Age." Lecture presented at the Bampton Lectures, University of Oxford, England, February 12, 2019. YouTube video, 1:02:19. https://youtu.be/paTZeJjH43Y.

———. *The Territories of Science and Religion*. Chicago: University of Chicago Press, 2015.

Harrison, Peter, and Jon H. Roberts, eds. *Science without God? Rethinking the History of Scientific Naturalism*. New York: Oxford University Press, 2019.

Hartshorne, Charles. *A Natural Theology for Our Time*. La Salle, IL: Open Court, 1973.

Hauerwas, Stanley. "The Demands of a Truthful Story: Ethics and the Pastoral Task." *Chicago Studies* 21 (1982): 59–71.

———. *With the Grain of the Universe: The Church's Witness and Natural Theology*. London: SCM, 2001.

Helm, Paul. "John Calvin, the *Sensus Divinitatis* and the Noetic Effects of Sin." *International Journal of Philosophy of Religion* 43 (1998): 87–107.

Holder, Rodney D. *Ramified Natural Theology in Science and Religion: Moving Forward from Natural Theology*. London: Routledge, 2020.

Hospers, John. *An Introduction to Philosophical Analysis*. New York: Pearson, 1996.

Howard-Snyder, Daniel, and Adam Green. "Hiddenness of God." In *The Stanford Encyclopedia of Philosophy* (Fall 2022 Edition), edited by Edward N. Zalta and Uri Nodelman. https://plato.stanford.edu/archives/fall2022/entries/divine-hiddenness/.

Howell, Kenneth J. *God's Two Books: Copernican Cosmology and Biblical Interpretation in Early Modern Science*. Notre Dame, IN: University of Notre Dame Press, 2002.

Hoyle, Fred. "The Universe: Past and Present Reflections." *Annual Review of Astronomy and Astrophysics* 20 (1982): 1–35.

Hubbard, Moyer. *New Creation in Paul's Letters and Thought*. Cambridge: Cambridge University Press, 2002.

Huebner, Sabine R., and Christian Laes, eds. *The Single Life in the Roman and Later Roman World*. Cambridge: Cambridge University Press, 2019.

Hughes, John. "Proofs and Arguments." In *Imaginative Apologetics: Theology, Philosophy and the Catholic Tradition*, edited by Andrew Davison, 3–11. London: SCM, 2011.

Hume, David. *Dialogues concerning Natural Religion*. London: Penguin Books, 1990.

Hunsinger, George. *Evangelical, Catholic, and Reformed: Doctrinal Essays on Barth and Related Themes*. Grand Rapids: Eerdmans, 2015.

———. *How to Read Karl Barth: The Shape of His Theology*. New York: Oxford University Press, 1991.

Husbands, Mark. "Calvin on the Revelation of God in Creation and Scripture: Modern Reception and Contemporary Possibilities." In *Calvin's Theology and Its Reception*, edited by J. Todd Billings and I. John Hesselink, 25–48. Louisville: Westminster John Knox, 2012.

Iliffe, Rob. *Priest of Nature: The Religious Worlds of Isaac Newton*. Oxford: Oxford University Press, 2017.

Irlenborn, Bernd. "Konsonanz von Theologie und Naturwissenschaft? Fundamental-theologische Bemerkungen zum interdisziplinären Ansatz von John Polkinghorne." *Trierer Theologische Zeitung* 113 (2004): 98–117.

Jager, Colin. "Mansfield Park and the End of Natural Theology." *Modern Language Quarterly* 63 (2002): 31–63.

Jaki, Stanley L. *Science and Creation*. Lanham, MD: University Press of America, 1990.

James, William. *Varieties of Religious Experience*. New York: Modern Library, 1902.

———. *The Will to Believe*. New York: Dover, 1956.

Jantzen, Grace M. *Becoming Divine: Towards a Feminist Philosophy of Religion*. Manchester: Manchester University Press, 1998.

———. *Power, Gender and Christian Mysticism*. Cambridge: Cambridge University Press, 1995.

Johnson, Keith L. *Karl Barth and the* Analogia Entis. London: T&T Clark, 2010.

———. "Natural Revelation in Creation and Covenant." In *Thomas Aquinas and Karl Barth: An Unofficial Catholic-Protestant Dialogue*, edited by Bruce L. McCormack and Thomas Joseph White, 129–56. Grand Rapids: Eerdmans, 2013.

Jones, Steven E. *Roberto Busa, S. J., and the Emergence of Humanities Computing: The Priest and the Punched Cards*. New York: Routledge, 2018.

Joyce, George Hayward. *Principles of Natural Theology*. London: Longmans, Green, 1922.

Jüngel, Eberhard. *God as Mystery of the World: On the Foundation of the Theology of the Crucified One in the Dispute between Theism and Atheism*. Translated by Darrell L. Guder. Grand Rapids: Eerdmans, 1983.

Kass, Leon R. *The Hungry Soul: Eating and the Perfecting of Our Nature*. New ed. Chicago: University of Chicago Press, 1999.

Kerr, Fergus. *After Aquinas: Versions of Thomism*. Oxford: Blackwell, 2002.

———. "Cartesianism according to Karl Barth." *New Blackfriars* 77 (1996): 358–68.

———. *Immortal Longings: Versions of Transcending Humanity*. London: SPCK, 1997.

Kilby, Karen. "Philosophy." In *The Cambridge Companion to the Summa Theologiae*, edited by Philip McCosker and Denys Turner, 62–73. Cambridge: Cambridge University Press, 2016.

Kim, Yung Han. "The Identity of Reformed Theology and Its Ecumenicity in the Twenty-First Century." In *Reformed Theology: Identity and Ecumenicity*, edited by Wallace M. Alston and Michael Welker, 1–19. Grand Rapids: Eerdmans, 2003.

Klauber, Martin. "Jean-Alphonse Turrettini (1671–1737) on Natural Theology: The Triumph of Reason over Revelation at the Academy of Geneva." *Scottish Journal of Theology* 47 (1994): 301–25.

Kock, Christoph. *Natürliche Theologie: Ein evangelischer Streitbegriff.* Neukirchen-Vluyn: Neukirchener Verlag, 2001.

Kretzmann, Norman. *The Metaphysics of Theism: Aquinas's Natural Theology in Summa contra Gentiles I.* Oxford: Clarendon, 1997.

Kwan, Kai-Man. "The Argument from Religious Experience." In *Contemporary Arguments in Natural Theology: God and Rational Belief,* edited by Colin Ruloff and Peter Horban, 251–70. London: Bloomsbury Academic, 2021.

Lane, Belden C. "Jonathan Edwards on Beauty, Desire, and the Sensory World." *Theological Studies* 65, no. 1 (2004): 44–68.

Lash, Nicholas. *Easter in Ordinary: Reflections on Human Experience and the Knowledge of God.* London: SCM, 1988.

———. *His Presence in the World: A Study in Eucharistic Worship and Theology.* London: Sheed & Ward, 1968.

———. *Holiness, Speech and Silence: Reflections on the Question of God.* Aldershot, UK: Ashgate, 2004.

———. *A Matter of Hope: A Theologian's Reflections on the Thought of Karl Marx.* London: Darton, Longman & Todd, 1981.

———. *Theology on the Way to Emmaus.* London: SCM, 1986.

Léchot, Pierre-Olivier. "Calvin et la connaissance naturelle de Dieu: Une relecture." *Études théologiques et religieuses* 93, no. 2 (2018): 271–99.

Lefebure, Leo D. "The Wisdom Tradition in Recent Christian Theology." *Journal of Religion* 76, no. 2 (1996): 338–48.

Lewis, C. S. *The Great Divorce.* New York: Macmillan, 1946.

———. *Mere Christianity.* London: HarperCollins, 2001.

———. *That Hideous Strength.* London: HarperCollins, 2005.

Licona, Michael R. *The Resurrection of Jesus: A New Historiographical Approach.* Downers Grove, IL: InterVarsity, 2010.

Lightbody, Brian. *Philosophical Genealogy: An Epistemological Reconstruction of Nietzsche and Foucault's Genealogical Method.* New York: Peter Lang, 2010.

Linzey, Andrew. *Animal Theology.* Urbana: University of Illinois Press, 1995.

Loke, Andrew. *The Teleological and Kalam Cosmological Arguments Revisited.* New York: Palgrave Macmillan, 2021.

Lonergan, Bernard J. F. "The General Character of the Natural Theology of *Insight.*" In *Philosophical and Theological Papers, 1965–1980,* edited by Robert C. Croken and Robert M. Doran, 3–9. Vol. 17 of *The Collected Works of Bernard Lonergan.* Toronto: University of Toronto Press, 2004.

———. *Insight: A Study of Human Understanding.* Edited by Frederick E. Crowe and Robert M. Doran. 5th ed. Vol. 3 of *The Collected Works of Bernard Lonergan.* Toronto: University of Toronto Press, 1988.

Long, D. Stephen. *Saving Karl Barth: Hans Urs von Balthasar's Preoccupation*. Minneapolis: Fortress, 2014.

Long, Tony. "May 13, 1637: Cardinal Richelieu Makes His Point." *Wired*, May 13, 2011. https://www.wired.com/2011/05/0513cardinal-richelieu-invents-table-knife/.

Lossky, Vladimir. *Orthodox Theology: An Introduction*. Translated by Ian Kesarcodi-Watson and Ihita Kesarcodi-Watson. Crestwood, NY: St. Vladimir's Seminary Press, 1978.

Lycan, William. *On Evidence in Philosophy*. Oxford: Oxford University Press, 2019.

MacIntyre, Alasdair. *Difficulties in Christian Belief*. London: SCM, 1959.

———. *Ethics and Politics*. Vol. 2 of *Selected Essays*. Cambridge: Cambridge University Press, 2006.

———. *Whose Justice? Which Rationality?* London: Duckworth, 1988.

Mackie, J. L. *The Miracle of Theism*. Oxford: Clarendon, 1982.

MacSwain, Robert, and Michael Ward, eds. *The Cambridge Companion to C. S. Lewis*. Cambridge: Cambridge University Press, 2010.

Malcolm, Norman. "Is It a Religious Belief That 'God Exists'?" In *Faith and the Philosophers*, edited by John Hick, 103–11. London: Macmillan, 1966.

Mallinson, Jeffrey. *Faith, Reason, and Revelation in Theodore Beza, 1519–1605*. Oxford: Oxford University Press, 2003.

Mandelbrote, Scott. "The Uses of Natural Theology in Seventeenth-Century England." *Science in Context* 20 (2007): 451–80.

Martin, C. B. "Religious Experience: A Religious Way of Knowing." In *Readings in the Philosophy of Religion*, edited by Kelly James Clark, 119–24. 2nd ed. New York: Broadview, 2008.

Mawson, T. J. *Belief in God: An Introduction to the Philosophy of Religion*. Oxford: Clarendon, 2005.

McCabe, Herbert. *Faith within Reason*. Edited by Brian Davies. New York: Continuum, 2007.

———. *The Good Life: Ethics and the Pursuit of Happiness*. New York: Continuum, 2005.

———. *Law, Language, Love*. New York: Continuum, 2003.

McCormack, Bruce L. "Karl Barth's Version of an 'Analogy of Being': A Dialectical No and Yes to Roman Catholicism." In *The Analogy of Being: Invention of the Antichrist or the Wisdom of God?*, edited by Thomas Joseph White, 88–144. Grand Rapids: Eerdmans, 2011.

McDowell, John C. "The Ascent of Theological Reading: Iconoclasm and the Divine Event of Making Readers." In *Ears That Hear: Explorations in Theological Interpretation of Scripture*, edited by Joel Green and Tim Meadowcroft, 94–113. Sheffield: Sheffield Phoenix, 2013.

————. "Being and Becoming in Gratuity: Barth after Maury." In *Election, Barth, and the French Connection: How Pierre Maury Gave a "Decisive Impetus" to Karl Barth's Doctrine of Election*, edited by Simon Hattrell, 235–56. 2nd ed. Eugene, OR: Pickwick, 2019.

————. "Much Ado about Nothing: Karl Barth's Being Unable to Do Nothing about Nothingness." *International Journal of Systematic Theology* 4, no. 3 (2002): 319–35.

————. "T. F. Torrance on Revelation." In *T&T Clark Handbook of Thomas F. Torrance*, edited by Paul Molnar and Myk Habets, 127–41. New York: Bloomsbury T&T Clark, 2020.

————. "Theology as Conversational Event: Karl Barth, the Ending of 'Dialogue' and the Beginning of 'Conversation.'" *Modern Theology* 19, no. 4 (2003): 483–509.

————. "The Unnaturalness of Natural Theology: The Witness of Rodney Holder's Barth." *Colloquium* 44, no. 2 (2012): 243–55.

McGrath, Alister E. "Arrows of Joy: Lewis's Argument from Desire." In *The Intellectual World of C. S. Lewis*, 105–28. Oxford: Wiley-Blackwell, 2013.

————. "Chance and Providence in the Thought of William Paley." In *Abraham's Dice: Chance and Providence in the Monotheistic Traditions*, edited by Karl Giberson, 240–59. Oxford: Oxford University Press, 2016.

————. *Emil Brunner: A Reappraisal.* Chichester: Wiley-Blackwell, 2014.

————. *A Fine-Tuned Universe: The Quest for God in Science and Theology.* Louisville: Westminster John Knox, 2009.

————. "A Manifesto for Intellectual Engagement: Reflections on Thomas F. Torrance's *Theological Science* (1969)." *Participatio: The Journal of the T. F. Torrance Theological Fellowship* 7 (2018): 1–16.

————. *Natural Philosophy: On Retrieving a Lost Disciplinary Imaginary.* Oxford: Oxford University Press, 2022.

————. "Natürliche Theologie: Ein Plädoyer für eine neue Definition und Bedeutungserweiterung." *Neue Zeitschrift für systematische Theologie und Religionsphilosophie* 59, no. 3 (2017): 297–310.

————. *The Open Secret: A New Vision for Natural Theology.* Oxford: Blackwell, 2008.

————. "Place, History, and Incarnation: On the Subjective Aspects of Christology." *Scottish Journal of Theology* 75, no. 2 (2022): 137–47.

————. "Reason, Experience, and Imagination: Lewis's Apologetic Method." In *The Intellectual World of C. S. Lewis*, 129–46. Oxford: Wiley-Blackwell, 2013.

————. *The Reenchantment of Nature: The Denial of Religion and the Ecological Crisis.* New York: Doubleday, 2002.

————. *Re-Imagining Nature: The Promise of a Christian Natural Theology.* Oxford: Wiley-Blackwell, 2016.

———. *The Science of God*. Grand Rapids: Eerdmans, 2004.

———. *A Scientific Theology*. 3 vols. Grand Rapids: Eerdmans, 2001–3.

———. *The Territories of Human Reason: Science and Theology in an Age of Multiple Rationalities*. Oxford: Oxford University Press, 2019.

———. "Theologie als Mathesis Universalis? Heinrich Scholz, Karl Barth, und der wissenschaftliche Status der christlichen Theologie." *Theologische Zeitschrift* 62 (2007): 44–57.

McGrew, Timothy, and Lydia McGrew. "The Argument from Miracles: A Cumulative Case for the Resurrection of Jesus of Nazareth." In *The Blackwell Companion to Natural Theology*, edited by William Lane Craig and J. P. Moreland, 593–662. Malden, MA: Wiley-Blackwell, 2009.

McLeish, Tom. *The Poetry and Music of Science: Comparing Creativity in Science and Art*. Oxford: Oxford University Press, 2019.

Mews, Constant J. "The World as Text: The Bible and the Book of Nature in Twelfth-Century Theology." In *Scripture and Pluralism: Reading the Bible in the Religiously Plural Worlds of the Middle Ages and Renaissance*, edited by Thomas J. Heffernan and Thomas E. Burman, 95–122. Leiden: Brill, 2005.

Midgley, Mary. *Science and Poetry*. London: Routledge, 2001.

Mongrain, Kevin. "The Eyes of Faith: Newman's Critique of Arguments from Design." *Newman Studies Journal* 6 (2009): 68–86.

Morley, Georgina. *John Macquarrie's Natural Theology: The Grace of Being*. Aldershot, UK: Ashgate, 2003.

Morse, Christopher. *Not Every Spirit: A Dogmatics of Christian Disbelief*. Harrisburg, PA: Trinity Press International, 1994.

Moser, Paul K. "Attributes of God: Goodness, Hiddenness, Everlastingness." In *Philosophy of Religion*, edited by Donald Borchert, 17–31. Macmillan Interdisciplinary Handbooks: Philosophy Series 8. New York: Macmillan, 2017.

———. "Biblical Theodicy of Righteous Fulfillment: Divine Promise and Proximity." *Irish Theological Quarterly* 88, no. 2 (2023): 1–16.

———. "Christian Philosophy and Christ Crucified: Fragmentary Theory in Scandalous Power." In *Christian Philosophy: Conceptions, Continuations, and Challenges*, edited by Aaron Simmons and Tom Perridge, 209–28. New York: Oxford University Press, 2019.

———. "Convictional Knowledge, Science, and the Spirit of Christ." In *Christ and the Created Order*, edited by Andrew Torrance and Tom McCall, 197–213. Grand Rapids: Zondervan Academic, 2018.

———. *The Divine Goodness of Jesus*. Cambridge: Cambridge University Press, 2021.

———. *Divine Guidance*. Cambridge: Cambridge University Press, 2022.

———. "Divine Hiddenness, *Agapē* Conviction, and Spiritual Discernment." In *Perceiving Things Divine: Towards a Constructive Account of Spiritual Perception*, edited by Paul Gavrilyuk and Fred Aquino, 177–92. Oxford: Oxford University Press, 2022.

———. "Divine Self-Disclosure in Filial Values: The Problem of Guided Goodness." *Modern Theology* 39, no. 1 (2023): 68–88.

———. "Doxastic Foundations: Theism." In *Theism and Atheism: Opposing Viewpoints in Philosophy*, edited by Joseph Koterski and Graham Oppy, 103–18. New York: Macmillan Reference, 2019.

———. "Experiential Dissonance and Divine Hiddenness." *Roczniki Filozoficzne* [Annals of philosophy] 69, no. 3 (2021): 29–42.

———. *The God Relationship: The Ethics for Inquiry about the Divine*. Cambridge: Cambridge University Press, 2017.

———. *Knowledge and Evidence*. Cambridge: Cambridge University Press, 1989.

———. "Paul the Apostle." In *The Oxford Handbook of the Epistemology of Theology*, edited by William Abraham and Fred Aquino, 327–39. Oxford: Oxford University Press, 2017.

———. *The Severity of God: Religion and Philosophy Reconceived*. Cambridge: Cambridge University Press, 2013.

———. "Theodicy, Christology, and Divine Hiding: Neutralizing the Problem of Evil." *Expository Times* 130 (2018): 1–10.

———. *Understanding Religious Experience*. Cambridge: Cambridge University Press, 2020.

Moser, Paul K., and Chad Meister. "Introduction: Religious Experience." In *The Cambridge Companion to Religious Experience*, edited by Paul K. Moser and Chad Meister, 1–22. Cambridge: Cambridge University Press, 2020.

Moser, Paul K., and Clinton Neptune. "Is Traditional Natural Theology Cognitively Presumptuous?" *European Journal for Philosophy of Religion* 9 (2017): 213–22.

Murphy, Francesca Aran. "Hans Urs von Balthasar: Beauty as a Gateway to Love." In *Theological Aesthetics after von Balthasar*, edited by Oleg V. Bychkov and James Fodor, 5–17. Burlington, VT: Ashgate, 2008.

Nagel, Thomas. *The Last Word*. Oxford: Oxford University Press, 2001.

Nash, Ronald H. *Faith and Reason*. Grand Rapids: Zondervan, 1988.

Newman, John Henry. *Lectures on Certain Difficulties Felt by Anglicans in Submitting to the Catholic Church*. 2nd ed. London: Burns & Lambert, 1850.

———. "Letter to William Robert Brownlow, April 13, 1870." In *The Letters and Diaries of John Henry Newman*. 29 vols. Oxford: Clarendon, 1973.

———. "Sermon XXIV: The Religion of the Day." In vol. 1 of *Parochial and Plain Sermons*, 198–207. New ed. London: Longmans, Green, 1891.

Nicholas of Cusa. *On Learned Ignorance*. In *Nicholas of Cusa: Selected Spiritual Writings*, translated by H. Lawrence Bond, 85–206. New York: Paulist Press, 1997.

————. *On Seeking God*. In *Nicholas of Cusa: Selected Spiritual Writings*, translated by H. Lawrence Bond, 215–31. New York: Paulist Press, 1997.

Niiniluoto, Ilkka. "Hintikka and Whewell on Aristotelian Induction." *Grazer Philosophische Studien* 49 (1994): 40–61.

Norris, Frederick W. *Faith Gives Fullness to Reasoning: The Five Theological Orations of Gregory of Nazianzen*. Leiden: Brill, 1991.

Oakes, Kenneth. "Revelation and Scripture." In *The Oxford Handbook of Karl Barth*, edited by Paul Dafydd Jones and Paul T. Nimmo, 246–62. Oxford: Oxford University Press, 2019.

Odom, Herbert H. "The Estrangement of Celestial Mechanics and Religion." *Journal of the History of Ideas* 27 (1966): 533–58.

O'Meara, Thomas F. *Mary in Protestant and Catholic Theology*. New York: Sheed & Ward, 1966.

Oppy, Graham. *Arguing about Gods*. Cambridge: Cambridge University Press, 2006.

————. *Ontological Arguments*. Cambridge: Cambridge University Press, 2018.

Ormerod, Neil. "In Defence of Natural Theology: Bringing God into the Public Realm." *Irish Theological Quarterly* 72, no. 3 (2007): 227–41.

Osler, Margaret J. *Divine Will and the Mechanical Philosophy*. New York: Cambridge University Press, 1994.

Ott, Ludwig. *Fundamentals of Catholic Dogma*. Edited by James Bastible. Translated by Patrick Lynch. 4th ed. Rockford, IL: Tan Books, 1960.

Padgett, Alan G. "*Theologia Naturalis*: Philosophy of Religion or Doctrine of Creation?" *Faith and Philosophy* 21 (2004): 493–502.

Paley, William. *Natural Theology*. Oxford: Oxford University Press, 2006.

Pelikan, Jaroslav. *Christianity and Classical Culture: The Metamorphosis of Natural Theology in the Christian Encounter with Hellenism*. New Haven: Yale University Press, 1993.

Peterfreund, Stuart. *Turning Points in Natural Theology from Bacon to Darwin: The Way of the Argument from Design*. New York: Palgrave Macmillan, 2012.

Phillips, D. Z. "God and Grammar: An Introductory Invitation." In *Whose God? Which Tradition? The Nature of Belief in God*, edited by D. Z. Phillips, 1–17. New York: Routledge, 2016.

————. *Religion without Explanation*. Oxford: Blackwell, 1976.

Pickering, David. "New Directions in Natural Theology." *Theology* 124, no. 5 (2021): 349–57.

Pinnock, Clark. "Karl Barth and Christian Apologetics." *Themelios* 2 (1977): 66–71.

Pinsent, Andrew, ed. *The History of Evil in the Medieval Age*. Vol. 2 of *The History of Evil*. New York: Routledge, 2018.

————. "Limbo and the Children of Faerie." *Faith and Philosophy* 33, no. 3 (2016): 293–310.

————. *The Second-Person Perspective in Aquinas's Ethics: Virtues and Gifts*. New York: Routledge, 2012.

Pius XII. "Apostolic Constitution, Munificentissimus Deus Defining the Dogma of the Assumption." *Acta Apostolicae Sedis* 42, no. 15 (1950): 753–73.

Placher, William C. *The Domestication of Transcendence: How Modern Thinking about God Went Wrong*. Louisville: Westminster John Knox, 1996.

————. *Unapologetic Theology: A Christian Voice in a Pluralistic Conversation*. Louisville: Westminster John Knox, 1989.

Plantinga, Alvin, and Nicholas Wolterstorff. *Faith and Rationality*. Notre Dame, IN: University of Notre Dame Press, 1984.

Plato. *Plato: Complete Works*. Indianapolis: Hackett, 1997.

Polkinghorne, John. "The New Natural Theology." *Studies in World Christianity* 1, no. 1 (1995): 41–50.

Popper, Karl R. *The Open Society and Its Enemies*. 2 vols. London: Routledge, 1945.

Porter, Jean. "A Tradition of Civility: The Natural Law as a Tradition of Moral Inquiry." *Scottish Journal of Theology* 56, no. 1 (2003): 27–48.

Price, H. H. "Faith and Belief." In *Faith and the Philosophers*, edited by John Hick, 3–25. London: Macmillan, 1966.

Pseudo-Dionysius. *The Divine Names*. In *Pseudo-Dionysius: The Complete Works*, translated by Colm Luibheid and Paul Rorem, 47–132. New York: Paulist Press, 1987.

Reichenbach, Bruce. "Cosmological Argument." In *The Stanford Encyclopedia of Philosophy*, edited by Edward N. Zalta and Uri Nodelman. Published July 13, 2004. Revised June 30, 2022. https://plato.stanford.edu/entries/cosmological-argument/.

Re Manning, Russell, John Hedley Brooke, and Fraser Watts, eds. *The Oxford Handbook of Natural Theology*. Oxford: Oxford University Press, 2013.

Ricoeur, Paul. "Religion, Atheism, and Faith." In *The Religious Significance of Atheism*, by Alasdair MacIntyre and Paul Ricoeur, 57–98. New York: Columbia University Press, 1969.

Robinson, Andrew. *God and the World of Signs: Trinity, Evolution, and the Metaphysical Semiotics of C. S. Peirce*. Leiden: Brill, 2010.

Robinson, Dominic. *Understanding the "Imago Dei": The Thought of Barth, von Balthasar and Moltmann*. London: Routledge, 2016.

Robinson, N. H. G. *Christ and Conscience*. London: Nisbet, 1956.

Rosenberg, Alex. *The Atheist's Guide to Reality*. New York: Norton, 2012.

Rushdie, Salman. *Is Nothing Sacred? The Herbert Read Memorial Lecture, 1990*. Cambridge: Granta, 1990.

Schillebeeckx, Edward. *Church: The Human Story of God*. Translated by John Bowden. New York: Crossroad, 1990.

Schreiner, Susan Elizabeth. *The Theater of His Glory: Nature and the Natural Order in the Thought of John Calvin*. Durham, NC: Labyrinth, 1991.

Schumacher, Lydia. "The Lost Legacy of Anselm's Argument: Rethinking the Purpose of Proofs for the Existence of God." *Modern Theology* 27, no. 1 (2011): 87–101.

Schwarz, Hans. *The God Who Is: The Christian God in a Pluralistic World*. Eugene, OR: Cascade Books, 2011.

Scruton, Roger. *I Drink Therefore I Am: A Philosopher's Guide to Wine*. New York: Bloomsbury Continuum, 2019.

Searle, John. "Chinese Room Argument." In *The MIT Encyclopedia of the Cognitive Sciences*, edited by Robert A. Wilson and Frank Keil, 115–16. Cambridge, MA: MIT Press, 1999.

Seipel, Peter. "In Defense of the Rationality of Traditions." *Canadian Journal of Philosophy* 45, no. 3 (2015): 257–77.

Sennett, James F., and Douglas Groothuis. "Introduction." In *In Defense of Natural Theology*, edited by James F. Sennett and Douglas Groothuis, 9–18. Downers Grove, IL: InterVarsity, 2005.

Siniscalchi, Glenn B. "Contemporary Trends in Atheist Criticism of Thomistic Natural Theology." *Heythrop Journal* 59, no. 4 (2018): 689–706.

Slattery, William J. *Heroism and Genius: How Catholic Priests Helped Build—and Can Help Rebuild—Western Civilization*. San Francisco: Ignatius, 2016.

Smith, James K. A. *Imagining the Kingdom: How Worship Works*. Grand Rapids: Baker Academic, 2013.

Sosa, Ernest. "Natural Theology and Naturalist Atheology: Plantinga's Evolutionary Argument against Naturalism." In *Alvin Plantinga*, edited by Deane-Peter Baker, 93–106. Cambridge: Cambridge University Press, 2007.

Spaemann, Robert. *Persons: The Difference between "Someone" and "Something."* Oxford: Oxford University Press, 2006.

Stump, Eleonore. *Atonement*. New York: Oxford University Press, 2018.

———. *The Image of God: The Problem of Evil and the Problem of Mourning*. Oxford: Oxford University Press, 2022.

Sudduth, Michael. *The Reformed Objection to Natural Theology*. Farnham: Ashgate, 2009.

Sweet, William. "Paley, Whately, and 'Enlightenment Evidentialism.'" *International Journal for Philosophy of Religion* 45 (1999): 143–66.

Swinburne, Richard. *The Coherence of Theism*. Rev. ed. Oxford: Clarendon, 1993.

———. *The Existence of God*. 2nd ed. Oxford: Clarendon, 2004.

———. "Natural Theology, Its 'Dwindling Probabilities' and 'Lack of Rapport.'" *Faith and Philosophy* 21 (2004): 533–46.

———. "Philosophical Theism." In *Philosophy of Religion in the 21st Century*, edited by D. Z. Phillips and Timothy Tessin, 3–20. Basingstoke: Palgrave, 2001.

———. *Was Jesus God?* Oxford: Oxford University Press, 2014.

Taliaferro, Charles. "Burning Down the House? D. Z. Phillips on the Metaphysics of Theism." *Philosophia Christi* 9, no. 2 (2007): 261–69.

———. *Cascade Companion to Evil*. Eugene, OR: Cascade Books, 2020.

———.*Consciousness and the Mind of God*. Cambridge: Cambridge University Press, 1994.

———. *Dialogues about God*. Washington, DC: Rowman & Littlefield, 2009.

———. *The Golden Cord: A Short Book on the Sacred and the Secular*. Notre Dame, IN: University of Notre Dame Press, 2012.

———. *Love, Love, Love, and Other Essays*. Cambridge: Cowley, 2006.

———. "Personal." In *Philosophy of Religion: A Guide to the Subject*, edited by Brian Davies, 95–105. London: Cassell, 1998.

———. "Philosophical Critiques of Natural Theology." In *The Oxford Handbook of Natural Theology*, edited by Re Manning, Brooke, and Watts, 385–94. Oxford: Oxford University Press, 2013.

———. "The Possibility of God: The Coherence of Theism." In *The Rationality of Theism*, edited by Paul Copan and Paul K. Moser, 239–58. London: Routledge, 2003.

———. "The Project of Natural Theology." In *The Blackwell Companion to Natural Theology*, edited by William Lane Craig and J. P. Moreland, 1–23. Malden, MA: Wiley-Blackwell, 2009.

———. "Sensibilia and Possibilia." *Philosophia Christi* 3, no. 2 (2001): 403–20.

———. "Three Elements of Creation Care from an Anglican Perspective." *Toronto Journal of Theology* 382 (2022): 228–33.

Taliaferro, Charles, and Jil Evans. *The Image in Mind: Theism, Naturalism, and the Imagination*. London: Continuum, 2012.

Taliaferro, Charles, and Jil Evans. *Is God Invisible? An Essay on Aesthetics and Religion*. Cambridge: Cambridge University Press, 2021.

Taliaferro, Charles, and Chad Meister. *Contemporary Philosophical Theology*. London: Routledge, 2016.

Tallis, Raymond. *In Defence of Wonder and Other Philosophical Reflections*. Durham: Acumen, 2012.

Tastard, Terry. *Nightingale's Nuns and the Crimean War*. London: Bloomsbury Academic, 2022.

Taylor, Charles. *Modern Social Imaginaries*. Durham, NC: Duke University Press, 2004.

Taylor, Richard. *Metaphysics*. Englewood Cliffs, NJ: Prentice-Hall, 1963.

te Velde, Rudi A. "Understanding the *Scientia* of Faith: Reason and Faith in Aquinas's *Summa Theologiae*." In *Contemplating Aquinas: On the Varieties of Interpretations*, edited by Fergus Kerr, 55–74. London: SCM, 2003.

Thielicke, Helmut. "The Resurrection of Christ." In *The Doctrine of God and of Christ*, translated by Geoffrey W. Bromiley, 423–52. Vol. 2 of *The Evangelical Faith*. Grand Rapids: Eerdmans, 1977.

———. "Rose Again from the Dead." In *I Believe*, translated by J. W. Doberstein and H. G. Anderson, 148–87. Philadelphia: Fortress, 1968.

Thiemann, Ronald F. *Constructing a Public Theology: The Church in a Pluralistic Culture*. Louisville: Westminster John Knox, 1991.

Thomas Aquinas. *See* Aquinas, Thomas

Topham, Jonathan R. "Biology in the Service of Natural Theology: Darwin, Paley, and the Bridgewater Treatises." In *Biology and Ideology: From Descartes to Dawkins*, edited by Denis R. Alexander and Ronald Numbers, 88–113. Chicago: University of Chicago Press, 2010.

Torrance, Thomas F. *The Ground and Grammar of Theology: Consonance between Theology and Science*. Edinburgh: T&T Clark, 1980.

———. "Introduction." In *The Incarnation: Ecumenical Studies in the Nicene-Constantinopolitan Creed*, edited by Thomas F. Torrance, xi–xxii. Edinburgh: Handsel, 1981.

———. *Space, Time and Incarnation*. London: Oxford University Press, 1969.

Turner, Denys. *Faith, Reason and the Existence of God*. Cambridge: Cambridge University Press, 2004.

———. *Thomas Aquinas: A Portrait*. New Haven: Yale University Press, 2013.

van Nuffelen, Peter. "Varro's Divine Antiquities: Roman Religion as an Image of Truth." *Classical Philology* 105, no. 2 (2010): 162–88.

Velecky, Lubor. *Aquinas's Five Arguments in the Summa Theologiae IaQQ2,3*. Kampen: Kok Pharos, 1994.

Vidal, Fernando. "Extraordinary Bodies and the Physicotheological Imagination." In *The Faces of Nature in Enlightenment Europe*, edited by Lorraine Daston and Gianna Pomata, 61–96. Berlin: Berliner Wissenschafts-Verlag, 2003.

Vidal, Fernando, and Bernard Kleeberg. "Knowledge, Belief, and the Impulse to Natural Theology." *Science in Context* 20 (2007): 381–400.

Viladesau, Richard. "Natural Theology and Aesthetics: An Approach to the Existence of God from the Beautiful?" *Philosophy & Theology* 3 (1988): 145–60.

von Balthasar, Hans Urs. *The Theology of Karl Barth: Exposition and Interpretation*. San Francisco: Ignatius, 1992.

Vos, Arvin. *Aquinas, Calvin, and Contemporary Protestant Thought: A Critique of Protestant Views on the Thought of Thomas Aquinas*. Washington, DC: Christian University Press, 1985.

Wallace, Dewey D. *Shapers of English Calvinism, 1660–1714: Variety, Persistence, and Transformation*. Oxford: Oxford University Press, 2011.

Watson, Francis B. "The Bible." In *The Cambridge Companion to Karl Barth*, edited by John Webster, 57–71. Cambridge: Cambridge University Press, 2000.

———. *Text and Truth: Redefining Biblical Theology*. Edinburgh: T&T Clark, 1997.

Webb, C. C. J. *Studies in the History of Natural Theology*. Oxford: Clarendon, 1915.

Webster, John. *Holy Scripture: A Dogmatic Sketch*. Cambridge: Cambridge University Press, 2003.

Welker, Michael. *Creation and Reality*. Translated by John F. Hoffmeyer. Minneapolis: Fortress, 1999.

Westfall, Richard S. "The Scientific Revolution of the Seventeenth Century: A New World View." In *The Concept of Nature*, edited by John Torrance, 63–93. Oxford: Oxford University Press, 1992.

Whitehead, Alfred North, and Bertrand Russell. *Principia Mathematica*. 2nd ed. 3 vols. Cambridge: Cambridge University Press, 1925–27.

Wiebe, Phillip. *God and Other Spirits*. New York: Oxford University Press, 2004.

Wildman, Wesley J. "Comparative Natural Theology." *American Journal of Theology and Philosophy* 27, nos. 2–3 (2006): 173–90.

Williams, Rowan. *Christ: The Heart of Creation*. New York: Bloomsbury, 2018.

———. *The Edge of Words: God and the Habits of Language*. New York: Bloomsbury, 2014.

———. *On Christian Theology*. Oxford: Blackwell, 2000.

———. "Teaching the Truth." In *Living Tradition: Affirming Catholicism in the Anglican Church*, edited by Jeffrey John, 29–43. London: Darton, Longman & Todd, 1992.

Willis-Watkins, David, and Michael Welker, eds. *Toward the Future of Reformed Theology: Tasks, Topics, Traditions*. Grand Rapids: Eerdmans, 1999.

Wilson, Edward O. *Consilience: The Unity of Knowledge*. New York: Alfred Knopf, 1998.

Wirzba, Norman. "Christian *Theoria Physike*: On Learning to See Creation." *Modern Theology* 32, no. 2 (2016): 211–30.

Wittgenstein, Ludwig. *Culture and Value*. Edited by G. H. von Wright. Chicago: University of Chicago Press, 1984.

———. *On Certainty*. Oxford: Blackwell, 1974.

———. *Philosophical Investigations*. 4th ed. Oxford: Wiley-Blackwell, 2009.

Wright, N. T. *History and Eschatology*. Waco: Baylor University Press, 2019.

———. *The Resurrection of the Son of God*. Minneapolis: Fortress, 2003.

Zahl, Simeon. "On the Affective Salience of Doctrines." *Modern Theology* 31, no. 3 (2015): 428–44.

Zeitz, Lisa M. "Natural Theology, Rhetoric, and Revolution: John Ray's *Wisdom of God*, 1691–1704." *Eighteenth Century Life* 18 (1994): 120–33.

Index